Seen Through My Eyes

A Journey Through Camino Frances

Gordana Murgovska

Published by Gordana Murgovska
Copyright © Gordana Murgovska 2025

Murgovska, Gordana
Seen Through My Eyes
ISBN 978-0-6489446-5-2

A catalogue record for this work is available from the National Library of Australia

The Author of this book accepts all responsibility
for the contents and absolves any other person or
persons involved in its production from any
responsibility or liability where the contents are concerned.
Names of people have been changed to protect their privacy.
For privacy reasons, no names have been included on photos.

All rights reserved. No part of this publication
may be reproduced, stored in a retrieval system,
or transmitted, in any form, by any means,
electronic, mechanical, photocopying, recording
or otherwise, without prior permission from the author.

Typeset in Garamond 11 pt

Produced by **TB Books**
P.O. Box 8138
Seymour South Victoria 3660
Email: tbbooks@collings.id.au

Cover Design: Natalie Janinski

Gordana tells the story of her life with uncompromising honesty as she navigates the seemingly never-ending and dauntingly brutal journey that is Camino Francis, taking the reader along with her as she examines her life journey step by step. And what a life it has been! I am about the same age as Gordana, and I have no idea how she managed to walk miles and miles each day for over a month!

Gordana talks incredibly openly about her humble beginnings in Macedonia to her new life in Australia. Gordana's honesty, courage and intrepid spirit shine from every page as does her love of life and her fellow humans. Gordana shares her searingly honest, very inspiring and uplifting journey. I highly recommend it!

Kristen M.

I just finished reading your book, and I wanted to take a moment to share my thoughts—it's truly incredible! Your story of walking the Camino Francés is so raw, inspiring and deeply personal. I felt as though I was right there with you, step by step, through the physical struggles and the mental challenges.

What struck me the most was how beautifully you entwined your life's journey into the narrative. The reflections on your childhood in Macedonia were so vivid—your family's struggles, joys and the cultural backdrop were fascinating and heartfelt.

Your ability to balance the deeply personal with the universal themes of endurance, self-discovery and healing was masterful. It's a story that so many people will relate to, whether they've walked the Camino or are simply navigating their own life's challenges.

I can't wait to recommend your book to others—I know it will inspire so many.

Snezana K.

Contents

Dedication	7
Prologue - Decision	9
Chapter 1 - A New Beginning	14
Chapter 2 - The Commitment	20
Chapter 3 - Arrival in Saint-Jean-Pied-de-Port	25
Chapter 4	28
Chapter 5 - On the Way to Pamplona	36
Chapter 6 - New Challenges, New Inspirations	40
Chapter 7 - Confronting the Past	53
Chapter 8 - The Struggles of Growing Up	68
Chapter 9 - Guiding Lights	74
Chapter 10 - Echoes of the Past	79
Chapter 11 - Shifts and Reflections	89
Chapter 12 - Seeking for Acknowledgment and Recognition	105
Chapter 13 - Finding Balance	117
Chapter 14 - Love at First Sight	122
Chapter 15 - Unstoppable Transformation	127
Chapter 16 - The Night in Ledigos	137
Chapter 17 - A Plea for the Future	142
Chapter 18 - Unbreakable Bonds	153
Chapter 19 - A Stranger in the Dark	158
Chapter 20 - Unravelling Truths	164
Chapter 21 - Reflections and Realities	177
Chapter 22 - Miracles and Hope	197
Chapter 23 - Overcoming Challenges	206
Chapter 24 - A Heavy Heart	212
Chapter 25 - Unyielding Determination	215
Chapter 26 - On the Edge of Endurance	220
Chapter 27 - Mission Accomplished	223
Epilogue	226
Camino Frances Walk Photos	234

Dedication

To my loving daughters,

You are my greatest blessings—the light that guides my path, the joy in every moment, and the inspiration behind every word. May you always know how deeply you are loved and how boundless your potential is. Follow your heart, chase your dreams, and remember that the journey of life is infinite.

And to my dear partner,

Your unwavering support and love are the bedrock of my strength. Thank you for entering my life and walking this journey with me, hand in hand, heart to heart. Your love, encouragement, and dedication go beyond words. Without you, the Camino Walk—and this memoir—would not exist.

With all my love,

Gordana

Prologue

Decision

"All happy families are all alike - each unhappy family is unhappy in its way."

Leo Tolstoy

It had been a long time since I'd been here. Sitting in my hotel room, I realised Macedonia had not been my home for a long time and couldn't be again. The few friends and family I kept in touch with were good to see again on this trip, but in the end, it all left me feeling alone, lonely, miserable, and unhappy.

I didn't know what I hoped to achieve by returning to this place. I had some dental issues and used them as an excuse to travel alone to a place that felt familiar. It didn't save me money—once I factored in travel and accommodation, it was more expensive—but it gave me a reason to return to Macedonia. Perhaps there were other reasons, too. I craved solitude now that my marriage had finally ended, or at least seemed to be coming to an end. One thing that I was sure of was that this place held so many memories that contributed to how I felt at that moment. I couldn't think about anything apart from my current situation. I was confused and uncertain about the path ahead. After nearly thirty years of marriage, I was at a crossroads, unsure which direction to choose. Being there alone, without close family nearby, deepened my sadness.

Over a quarter of a century ago, my brother, parents, and sisters all moved to Australia. Now, only the locked, empty family house and memories remain to remind me of my roots. After my father passed, my mother couldn't bring herself to sell the house. I tried to push these thoughts aside, especially about my mum and her indecision. With everything happening in my life right now, I already have enough to handle.

My so-called holiday wasn't bad. I still had days I genuinely enjoyed. For a few days, I joined an Easter tour to Greece, where I met some wonderful people and indulged in experiences I couldn't afford back when I lived there years ago. It made me realise how much I love travelling, though preferably not alone. I also spent a day in Skopje, where I had once studied, lived for several years, and called home.

I grew up in Bitola, not far from the village I was born in, but my memories were more bad than good. Those memories just added to my anger, an anger that I was only now acknowledging, but one that was rooted here where my dysfunctional marriage had begun.

I had to make this trip to escape Australia, where my husband, Greg, seemed oblivious to our problems. Technically, we were separated, but no one would think so. We spent so much time together still. Neither of us had moved on. We were both scared, scared that it might be worse.

We raised two daughters together, Christina and Madeline, two loving, wonderful daughters who supported and loved us both and whom we both loved. Since they were born, they were the centre of our attention.

They are my whole world. They kept me busy, and I enjoyed every moment I spent with them. Now, both adults are trying to navigate their lives; I felt I needed to do the same.

As a couple, Greg and I did not have much in common. Our conversations were usually related to our daughters.

The famous Tolstoy's statement: 'Happy families are all alike— each unhappy family is unhappy in its way', couldn't be truer. We were not always unhappy, but we were never truly happy. I always felt something was missing or wasn't right. Following Leo Tolstoy's statement, we were sad in our unique way regarding the family's happiness.

Thinking about Greg stirred up a mix of sadness and anger. I felt sad because the marriage had failed despite all my efforts. My hope that things would improve between us had long faded. I'm not one to give up easily, but deep down, I knew it was over and I had to accept reality.

A mutual friend introduced us, and for reasons I still can't fully understand, everything moved so quickly. We barely took the time to get to know each other. Soon after meeting, we began living together, and just eight months later, we married. I was twenty-six, and he was twenty-eight. We married in this city nearly thirty years ago and moved to Australia four years later.

Our marriage was challenging from the very beginning. Before we met, Greg, who used to work as a software engineer in Bitola, decided to go back to Skopje, to the university, to work as a lecturer and to pursue his master's degree. I had just completed my first year teaching contract, filling in for a teacher on leave, and hadn't applied for a job the following year. So, I moved to Skopje to be with Greg. Less than a year after our wedding, his mother passed away from brain cancer. His father had also died from cancer when he was only twelve. I felt deeply for him and his loss. Even early on in our relationship, I could sense unaddressed trauma in his behaviour.

The year after our wedding, I started working as a primary school teacher in Bitola. Every weekend, one of us would travel to be together. It wasn't easy, and I learned something important during this time. I discovered where my place was in the relationship. I began to adapt to married life, tiptoeing around my husband, accepting things as they were, swallowing hurtful and inappropriate comments, and pretending everything was fine.

In Macedonia, marriages like ours were common. Like many girls, I had been raised to listen to and obey my husband. The common sentiment that things at the start of a marriage usually are not smooth, but later will get better, and everything will be fine gave me some hope.

I felt utterly alone, with no one to confide in or share the depth of my feelings. The only person I could open up to about my marriage, to some degree, was my dear friend, Tanja.

Tanja and I met at university, and our friendship became a lifelong bond. She was like family to me. She lived in Skopje, and Greg and I often spent time with her and her partner, Jovan. She believed I should leave Greg and offered her unwavering support. Yet, I held onto the hope that things would improve. From as far back as I can remember, my family taught me to work hard and persevere, and that commitment to hard work and saving my marriage remained deeply ingrained in me.

Moving to Australia renewed my hope, and Greg was excited about it, too. He had a few colleagues who had relocated to Sydney, and he stayed in touch with them. We applied for a Skilled Migrant Visa using his qualifications, and when it was approved, I was overwhelmed with gratitude. My optimism soared. I could hardly wait to arrive in Australia, the land of new beginnings. I was grateful and promised myself I'd stay with Greg forever and work tirelessly to mend any cracks in our relationship, not yet realising that a true partnership requires both people to meet halfway.

Moving to Australia and settling in Melbourne marked a fresh chapter in our lives. Like many migrants, we set out to build a successful life in this new country. After about a year, Greg found work as a software consultant while I began learning English and teaching Macedonian at a Saturday school. It took me nearly seven years—and several English courses and a Graduate Diploma in Secondary Education—before I returned to teaching at a secondary school. In the meantime, I worked in childcare centres and, for some time, as a receptionist.

After eight years of hoping to start a family, we were blessed with two beautiful daughters, born eighteen months apart. On the surface, everything seemed ideal. We had our children, a home, stable professional jobs, new cars we needed and investment properties. Life appeared perfect, yet beneath it all, the fractures in our relationship remained. Greg poured everything into his work, seemingly oblivious to the unhappiness that quietly affected me and our daughters. I pleaded with him to seek help. I spent countless hours in the library, searching for resources on unaddressed trauma and depression. But Greg refused to acknowledge the issues, and any suggestion of seeking help was met with resistance.

The unhappiness between us only grew until we eventually separated, though neither of us fully moved on. To everyone else, we were still a couple. We stayed in touch, showed up together at family events, paid bills jointly, and argued about almost everything. We kept up the facade, telling ourselves we were doing the best for our two daughters, who were young adults and had grown weary of the charade by then.

Our dysfunctional relationship had become so familiar it felt normal. You can't see how things appear from the outside when you're stuck inside. The idea of leaving felt frightening. We knew our misery, and the fear of the unknown kept us bound for years. Though Greg sometimes stayed home, our separation was real.

I'd felt alone for over a decade. I wondered how to escape this cycle and start fresh, but I was lost, uncertain where to begin. For years, I lived without healthy boundaries, burying my unhappiness as best I could, feeling that I'd done this for as long as I could remember. I didn't know any other way.

I've lost myself in this marriage. I don't know who I am anymore. Do I even know what I want? I wondered. *I have to find out.* The voice inside me grew stronger.

"It's time for a change. Enough is enough. I must decide!" I said aloud, sitting alone in my hotel room, surprised to hear my voice, filled with resolve.

I opened my laptop, pulled up my now ex-husband's email, and began to type:

> *I feel lonely, unhappy, and empty. If I could, I'd leave now and return to Australia. I can't live like this anymore. If you don't decide, then I will. Our marriage hasn't been real for a long time. It's over.*

Within minutes, he replied:

> *I can't believe you feel lonely. You're such a friendly, positive person. How could you possibly feel lonely? Enjoy your time in Macedonia; see your cousins and friends.*

I read his response, stunned. *How little he knows me. How little he understands himself or our marriage.* He had taken so much for granted—never truly listening, respecting my boundaries, if I had any, or acknowledging our emptiness. I'd always felt like I was carrying the weight of our relationship alone. It wasn't about blame; neither of us needed to be blamed. We were simply a mismatch that somehow found ourselves bound together.

This marriage had to end, no matter what the future held. The realisation struck me like lightning.

Chapter 1

A New Beginning

"No matter how hard the past is, you can always begin again."

Buddha

Peter and I have been together for nearly seven years. We first met in May 2018, and from that day on, we were rarely apart. In each other, we found a soulmate, a friend, and the perfect companion.

I'll never forget that first meeting. We had planned to meet at a restaurant near my work at six p.m. It was a Monday, and I felt drained after a long day. My last meeting wrapped up at four-thirty, so I decided to visit my mum in aged care nearby to pass the time. She was surprised to see me, commenting that I looked tired and should head home to rest. I didn't mention that I had a date; I wasn't sure how she'd react. She was the one who truly understood the turbulent times Greg and I had gone through, and to this day, she still asks about him.

I hadn't told her I'd joined a dating site. Since my father passed, I'd watched my mum navigate life alone, leaning on her children, and I often felt sadness for her. She came from a different generation. I didn't want to end up alone. While I'm independent, I've always believed in the power of a meaningful relationship. Life feels so much fuller with a compatible partner. It took a long time to convince myself to try a dating site, but I'm glad I did. My daughter, Christina, encouraged me to join about a year ago and even signed me up. At the time, I wasn't ready. I didn't even want to put up a photo where I could be recognised. Just the thought of a 'dating site' was unsettling. My daughter's words that I am an adult and I know why I am there did not help much.

After returning from the trip to Macedonia, I finally created a profile, with photos from my travels in Greece. I wanted a genuine connection based on honesty, trust, and respect—qualities I wasn't willing to compromise. I even told Greg that I'd signed up for a dating site. His reaction was indifferent as usual; he ignored it and paid no attention. I shared with a few close colleagues that I hoped to meet someone.

One of my collegues, Diana gave me an advice and it made me smile: "Don't talk about your problems or difficult life on a first date. Don't treat your date like a psychologist. Talk about things that are funny and happy."

And there I was, two weeks into the dating site, preparing to meet someone I had spoken to the night before. We'd talked for nearly three hours, and he wanted us to meet. I was interested in meeting him, too. His name was Peter. I liked his simple, friendly photo and his warm smile. I waited for him to mark me as a favourite—and he did. He was five years older than me and semi-retired. We had both completed the compatibility test on the site, and it showed we aligned on many levels. We were so compatible that I wondered if the tests were real or just auto generated!

I said goodbye to my mum and arrived right on time. Standing outside the restaurant was a tall, slim man dressed in light-coloured pants and a matching jumper. *It has to be him*, I thought—and I was right. We introduced ourselves and headed inside.

Once seated, Peter handed me a small pack of Ferrero Rocher chocolates. I was pleasantly surprised. I didn't know people brought chocolates to a first date! We shared them, adding a sweet start to the evening.

A young waiter approached us. "Good evening, Ms. I'm glad I can serve you tonight." He greeted me with a smile. I looked at him, puzzled. His face looked familiar, but I couldn't remember his name.

"Do you remember me? You taught me for two years, in Years 7 and 8. I moved to another school two years ago," he tried to jog my memory.

"You're Andriana's brother, aren't you?" I finally made the connection. His sister had just finished Year 12, and I had taught her for five years.

"Yes, I am," he said, pleased I had finally recognised him.

We chatted briefly. I told my former student I was glad he was doing well at school and work. He took our order and left. While meeting former students is usually pleasant, tonight wasn't the best time.

Turning to Peter, I joked, "I'm sorry I didn't introduce you to my former student."

Peter smiled. "Don't worry. All good."

We started talking about our lives, our jobs, and our families. Peter shared a bit about his first marriage, which had lasted twenty years, and it felt so like my own experiences that I found myself nodding along, seeing our common ground. After his divorce, he met his late wife, with whom he shared a happy, nearly twenty-year relationship and almost fifteen years of marriage until she passed away from a massive stroke. Peter spoke fondly of the memories they shared and the beautiful times together.

He had worked as an engineer in telecommunications for the army and later for various companies until he decided to retire early to spend more time with his wife while she was unwell. He now drove a school bus part-time for an independent school. We talked about our hobbies and interests, and the conversation flowed so easily that it felt like reconnecting with an old friend I hadn't seen in years.

In a short time, I saw in Peter a confident man, grounded and clear about what he wanted from life. I could relate to that. By this point in my life, I'd also had plenty of time to understand what I was looking for.

I realised everyone else had left the restaurant. It was almost ten p.m., and the restaurant was getting ready to close. We had been sitting and talking for nearly four hours, though it felt like only forty minutes. I was struck by Peter's honesty, good manners, and communicative nature. In other words, I saw Peter as a true gentleman.

"Peter, we must leave now. The restaurant is closing. I didn't realise it was so late," I said, glancing at the time.

Peter looked at me curiously and asked, "What do you think about us?"

I didn't expect this question. "I don't know," I said naively.

We had just met and spent four hours talking like old friends. I felt confused, but I also had a strong connection, as if we had known each other much longer. We paid the bill and walked out of the restaurant. Peter held my hand and accompanied me to my car. It was the beginning of our beautiful relationship. Our maturity, experience, honesty, trust, respect, and connection helped our relationship blossom.

Peter and I began seeing each other more and more frequently. We usually met after work for a coffee or a walk, sharing conversations about anything and everything.

I felt I could talk to Peter about anything. He told me he was a member of Audible and often listened to books and podcasts.

One day, he surprised me with a gift. When I opened it, I found *The Power of Now* by Eckhart Tolle—a book that would change my life. I ended up reading it at least three times. It made me realise how easy it is to sleepwalk through life. I can't recall how many copies I've bought to gift to friends and family. That book opened a new horizon for me. Inspired, I signed up for Audible and started listening, something I still do and thoroughly enjoy.

Not long after I met Peter, Greg called and said he wanted to come by. I mentioned that our daughters weren't home, but he insisted on visiting. Soon after he arrived, I told him about Peter. It was a quiet, sad moment. The only question he asked was whether our daughters had met Peter. I explained that it was still too soon for introductions. That was the last time Greg visited the home that was once our family home.

My daughters were eager to meet Peter. After some time, once I felt comfortable, I introduced him to Christina and Madeline. Although they had encouraged me to meet someone and begin a new chapter, I knew it could be challenging for children to see their parents with a new partner. Ideally, children benefit from having two parents together, watching a loving relationship, and focusing on their lives. But that wasn't the case for us.

We had a lovely dinner that night. Christina, her boyfriend, Jack, and Madeline chatted a lot with Peter. They were happy with my choice, and Peter was delighted. The evening went very well.

Peter has four adult sons, and he shares them with his first wife. He introduced me to some of them, and I started building a good relationship with them. I felt that having a good relationship with your partner's children is crucial. You will never replace their biological parent, but you become a significant person in their parent's lives. Welcoming and treating them like your own, strengthens your bond with your partner.

Peter and I have many things in common, one of which is our love of walking. We often take walks after work, in the evenings.

One day, while walking, Peter said, "I'd like to go with you to Santiago de Compostela in Spain one day and ask you to marry me there. We probably need to marry there. What do you think?"

I was surprised. Peter had mentioned marriage before, but I never seriously considered marrying again. I ignored the word 'marriage' and focused on the place's name.

"Santiago de Compostela?" I repeated. "I don't think I've heard of Santiago de Compostela before. Where is it?" I asked.

Peter explained that Santiago de Compostela is in the northwest of Spain, where the relics of St James are housed in the cathedral. He began talking about the Apostle St James and the Camino Frances, an eight hundred kilometre walk from St Jean-Pied-de-Port in France to Santiago de Compostela in Spain.

I hadn't heard about the Camino or the pilgrimage to Santiago de Compostela, but I understood the concept. In Macedonian, a pilgrim is called an 'adjija'. I was born in Macedonia (now the Republic of North Macedonia) and lived there for thirty years. I knew that in olden times, some people walked to Jerusalem, and after completing the pilgrimage, they added 'Hadji' to their surname, such as Hadji-Petrevski. Many Macedonian stories—oral, written, or video—featured this pilgrimage as a main theme. While watching these stories, I often thought about the people making this journey, imagining the vast distances they walked to Jerusalem. Still, I could never truly envision what it looked like.

After hearing Peter describe the pilgrimage, I said, "Peter, I don't think I can walk such a long distance. It is not for me."

We changed the topic and continued walking.

However, Peter didn't drop the idea. Occasionally, we talked about the Camino Frances and the walk from St Jean-Pied-de-Port to Santiago de Compostela. I could hear in his voice how much he wanted to walk this ancient pilgrimage route.

I tried to tell him again that I could never walk such a long distance, as I didn't believe it would be possible.

"Peter, I can't walk the Camino. I don't think I can do it. Even after walking ten kilometres, I feel exhausted. It wouldn't be possible for me to walk twenty-five to thirty kilometres daily. Also, I don't want to use my long service leave to walk across Spain."

Peter responded, "If you don't want to come, I will walk it myself."

In 2019, we went on holiday in Europe. We had a few countries on our list: Spain, France, England and Macedonia. After visiting Barcelona and Madrid, we flew to Toulouse, rented a car, and drove to southern France to see Peter's friends, Jane and Denis. They live in a small village called Quillon, nestled near the Pyrenees. We stayed for three days, and Jane and Denis were amazing hosts. One evening, we went outside to observe the surroundings. Peter was watching the mountains, and his face was shining.

"This is the place we will walk to one day. St Jean-Pied-de-Port is not far from here," Peter commented.

As I watched the mountains, I felt fear in my stomach. I would never be able to climb these mountains and cross over. On the other hand, I realised that Peter was extremely serious about the Camino Walk.

If Peter decides to walk, I want to be with him, I thought. The idea of walking the Camino entered my mind but was far from my heart. Still, I accepted it as a possibility.

When we returned from the holiday, Peter brought home a large, framed picture of the Camino Frances route and hung it on the wall. The sight of it even put me off the idea of walking. It was such a long road. How could people walk these distances every day, and what was the purpose of this walk? I couldn't understand what motivated them.

I noticed that the Camino Walk was frequently on Peter's mind. Many times, he would bring it up, and I would listen. He watched numerous documentaries and YouTube clips about Camino Frances, and I often joined him in watching them. Peter found inspiration in the movie, *The Way*. We watched it together, and I enjoyed the film and the atmosphere surrounding the Camino.

After watching the movie, I began to reconsider the idea. My life motto is: "If someone else can do it, it's achievable, and I can do it too." I started questioning why I was so apprehensive about walking the Camino. I already enjoyed walking, so the main difference would be doing a long walk daily. I wouldn't need to rush home, prepare for work the next day, or grade students' work. My sole focus would be on walking.

Chapter 2

The Commitment

"From this day forward, you'll never walk alone."

Unknown author

The beginning of 2020 shocked the entire world with the outbreak of COVID-19, which dashed many travel dreams, including our plans for the Camino. We only briefly mentioned the Camino during this time, and I felt a sense of relief. The Camino Walk was temporarily crossed off our bucket list. Who knew when travel would be possible again? We occasionally watched YouTube clips about the Camino Frances, but it felt like a distant possibility. If we were unable to walk it in the coming years, would we be too old to do it later? Little did I know I needed to be corrected.

Peter has a caravan and loves exploring the Australian countryside. We both enjoy nature, especially road trips and walking through scenic landscapes. Before the pandemic, we went caravanning often. Since we both work in schools, the holidays were perfect for road trips around Victoria and even further afield to other states, including the Northern Territory. We once drove to Alice Springs to visit Tristan, one of Peter's sons. These holidays were filled with walks, and I loved every moment spent outdoors.

Like Peter, I realised I have a deep love for nature. It reminded me of my childhood in the Macedonian countryside. These trips also helped us get to know each other better. In Peter, I found someone who had done much personal growth work; nothing seemed too difficult for him. Our relationship flowed effortlessly. I felt like I'd seen the missing piece to complete my life's mosaic. We often talked about ourselves, our personal growth, and the importance of working on oneself rather than trying to change the world. So much seemed to fall into place on many levels in this relationship.

During 2020, amidst the COVID-19 lockdown, when we could only move within a five-kilometre radius, Peter and I could still visit each other as companions.

In the morning, on 20th July, Peter called and said he was coming to see me. It was eight o'clock, and I was busy preparing for online teaching. Like many teachers during the pandemic, I learned much about software platforms and technology. It was still stressful, and I needed every minute to prepare for each class and ensure my laptop was functioning properly. The students were incredibly supportive, doing their best to assist with the technology we used in class, for which I was deeply grateful. Peter assured me he wouldn't keep me long.

It must be something important, I thought. By then, Peter and I had been together for over two years.

In the meantime, Christina and Jack had moved in together, leaving just Madeline and me. Over these two years, I had noticed many changes in myself. I had always been fiercely independent and had taught my daughters to be independent from a young age. However, having companionship and a loving, independent partner meant much. The feeling that I had discovered a new version of myself made me smile. We had accepted each other as we were. It felt destined and having Peter in my life was the right decision.

Less than thirty minutes later, Peter arrived at my place. The doorbell interrupted my thoughts. I opened the door, and he greeted me with his big smile, hug, and kiss. We climbed the stairs together, and when we reached the top, Peter paused, took a small box from his pocket, and knelt on one knee. Opening the box, he revealed a beautiful, sparkling ring in his hand.

"Will you marry me, my love?" he asked.

I was momentarily speechless. I couldn't believe I was experiencing such a moment at my age.

"Yes," I whispered.

He slid the ring onto my finger and hugged me tightly. It fitted perfectly.

It was a profoundly special and romantic moment, unlike my first marriage, which lacked a proper proposal and felt rushed, as if we were afraid of being single. Peter had ordered the ring from Germany, which arrived early that morning. He didn't want to wait. He wanted to propose on the same day he received it.

As I admired the ring on my finger, I couldn't help but reflect on how much Peter had hoped to propose to me in Santiago de Compostela. A voice deep within me stirred, louder than my earlier hesitation about walking the Camino. I felt a shift in that moment—a newfound resolve to make this journey.

I can do it, I thought. *I'll walk with Peter to Santiago de Compostela at the first opportunity. If millions of people walked over the centuries, I can walk, too.*

I was excited to wake up each summer morning to walk through nature. For the first ten years, I spent time in the countryside of a remote Macedonian village, where my love for the outdoors had taken root. Walking beside Peter through such beautiful landscapes felt like a dream waiting to unfold. My optimism brushed aside any thoughts of obstacles or challenges. All I could think was how wonderful it would be to be there. The saying that every journey begins with a single step and continues one step at a time. I couldn't be more optimistic.

Shortly after getting engaged, I shared my decision with Peter. He asked me several times if I was certain, and I was more than sure each time. I wanted to spend two months in Europe with him.

Before the end of 2021, I applied for long service leave but missed the deadline, which meant I had to reapply the following year.

In 2023, I finally secured School Term 3. Now, the Camino felt within reach. I chose not to focus on potential challenges like the long distances or other obstacles. Instead, I was filled with excitement. I imagined spending the Australian winter in Europe, dreaming of the long, sunlit summer days ahead and the journey we'd embark on— just walking, walking, and walking. At times, fleeting early childhood memories would surface and fade in my mind, adding a layer of nostalgia to the adventure that awaited.

Once my leave was confirmed, the preparations for the Camino began in earnest. Peter spent countless hours researching on the computer and watching YouTube clips of those who had walked the Camino, some multiple times. He meticulously ordered appropriate clothing, walking shoes, backpacks, waterproof raincoats, pants, and all the necessary gear. While watching a few YouTube clips and listening to others' experiences of reaching Santiago de Compostela, I sensed nothing could truly prepare me for this mystical journey. Each experience on the Camino was deeply personal and unique, much like the paths we tread in our lives.

We increased our walking regimen, covering longer distances and exploring different terrains—roads, trails, and hills. Although I had never been involved in competitive sports and only occasionally visited the gym, walking had always been my primary form of exercise since my youth. I typically preferred flat surfaces and wasn't particularly fond of hilly terrain. While I felt reasonably fit, I knew I needed to build more endurance to tackle mountains and cover substantial distances.

The booking process continued. We opted to pre-book private rooms, preferring more comfort and space than hostels or albergues, as they are called in Spain, which is typical along the Camino. Securing accommodations proved challenging, especially in Pamplona, where our arrival coincided with the main bull run. After some effort, we managed to secure a room on the outskirts of Pamplona, in the suburb or small town of Burlada—at $AU300 for one night—pricey, but a relief to have secured something. We also planned a four-night stay in Paris to recover from jet lag before starting our walk. Flying from Australia to Europe and beginning the Camino the next day seemed ill-advised without rest. We booked all accommodations to Santiago de Compostela. The thought of 'What if we can't walk?'— was a scenario I was eager to avoid at all costs. Little did I know then what lay ahead of us on this journey.

The first semester ended, and we gave ourselves a week to pack up since we already had everything we needed. The backpack was supposed to be ten per cent of our body weight. I hadn't practised walking with my bag at all. It already looked heavy, and I wondered how it would feel with two additional litres of water. I left a few items behind, but the scale still showed the bag was too heavy.

I was heading to Europe for nearly two months, carrying around seven kilograms. I had never travelled with so few items before. This time, I tried to bring only the essentials. I would need to carry this backpack through all my walks across Spain to Santiago de Compostela.

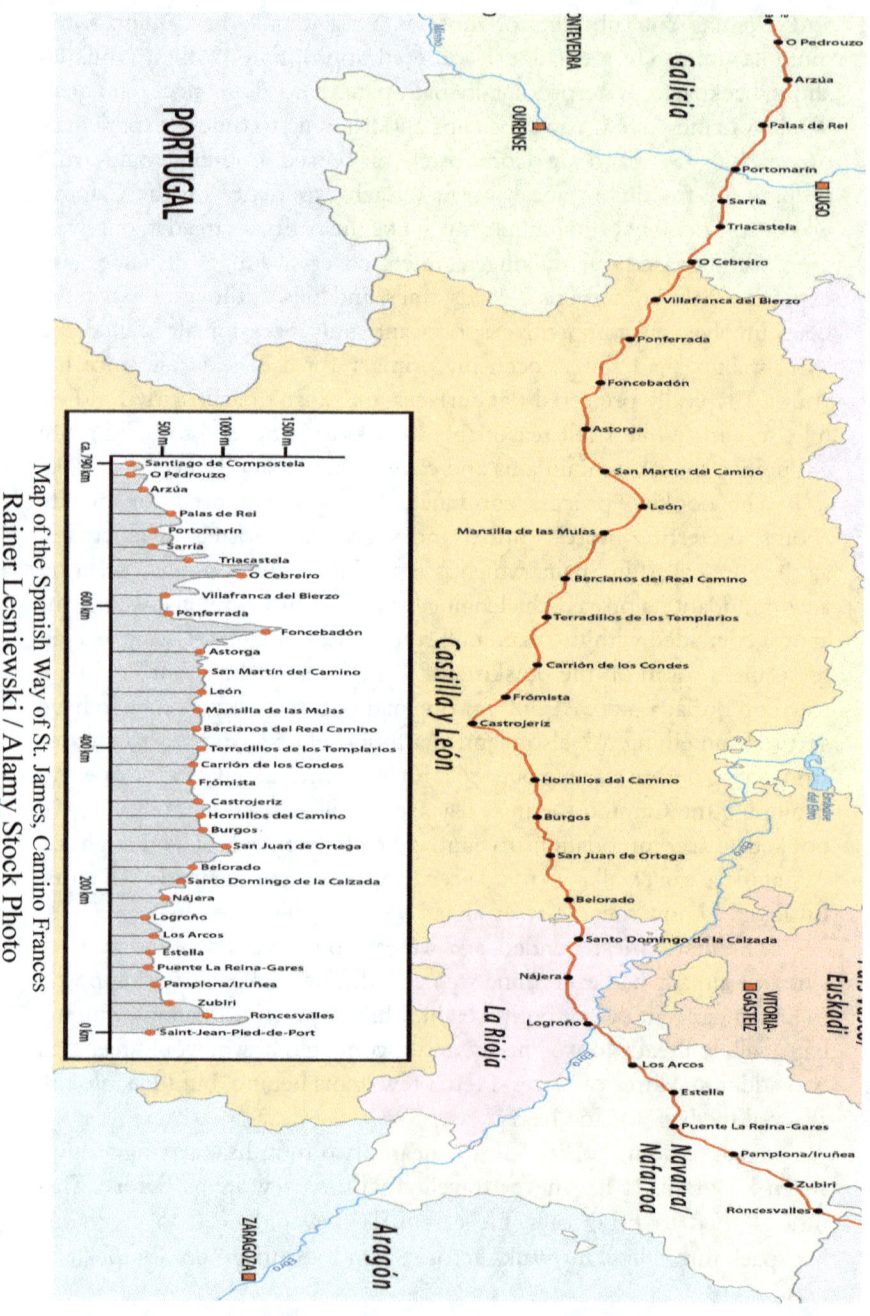
Map of the Spanish Way of St. James, Camino Frances
Rainer Lesniewski / Alamy Stock Photo

Chapter 3

Arrival in Saint-Jean-Pied-de-Port

The journey begins

We departed Melbourne on June 29th and checked into a hotel in Paris the following day. It was my second visit to Paris with Peter. I had also been there once before with Greg and our daughters. Having already seen the main attractions, we planned to explore the city on foot, covering approximately twenty kilometres daily. Walking around Paris allowed us to discover different facets of the city and its vast size. However, our minds were focused not on Parisian sights but on the impending long walk awaiting us.

On July 4th, we left Paris and headed to Bayonne. After a four-hour train journey, we arrived at the station and waited about an hour for our next train to Saint-Jean-Pied-de-Port, our destination, before starting the Camino. Many passengers boarding the train with us were fellow pilgrims, including Francesco from Italy, who planned to walk sections of the Camino.

Our excitement grew as we approached Saint-Jean-Pied-de-Port. Finally, after all our preparations, we had arrived. The train journey took us through the foothills of the Pyrenees, surrounded by lush greenery that seemed more like early spring than summer. After an hour and a half, we reached the town in the late afternoon. We took photos of the picturesque surroundings and went to the accommodation we had booked in advance. Climbing to the villa's third floor, we were greeted warmly by a young lady who was incredibly hospitable and helpful.

"We need to find two locations," Peter said. "The pilgrim office and the baggage transfer."

We consolidated all non-essential items into a single large bag, which we sent to Santiago de Compostela for retrieval upon our arrival more than a month later. Finding the luggage transfer service and the pilgrim office was easy, as they were conveniently close to our accommodation. We joined the queue at the pilgrim office along with other eager pilgrims. The office was bustling with activity, with only a few staff members to attend to everyone.

Eventually, our turn came, and we were invited to sit down. The staff provided us with pilgrim credentials, essentially passports for pilgrims, and proceeded to gather our details, including the purpose behind our Camino journey. As I pondered why I was embarking on this pilgrimage, I considered whether it was Peter's enthusiasm or something deeper. Perhaps it was more than that; I checked the box for religious reasons.

While I don't attend church weekly or adhere strictly to religious rituals, I consider myself deeply spiritual. I approached the Camino without specific expectations, uncertain what it might hold, or what to expect.

Peter and I had discussed St James the Apostle at length, whose relics reside in the cathedral of Santiago de Compostela. I was drawn to the historical route pilgrims had taken to this sacred place since the 12th century, honouring Spain's patron, St James. Curiosity also played a role; I've always been naturally curious, although the exact reasons remained unclear.

My upbringing was Orthodox, though, in a socialist country. Formal religious education was limited to what my family, particularly my grandmother, imparted. Nevertheless, religion held significant importance within our family. I vividly recall fasting regularly with my family during the first decade of my life, followed by attending church for communion or blessings, known as 'pricesta' in Macedonian. Sundays were special; I spent time with my grandmother at church, listening to the priest deliver the mass in old Slavic, where I could grasp some words.

Those moments in church were profoundly peaceful and etched forever in my memory.

After issuing our credentials and gathering our details, the pilgrim officer presented us with the Camino Frances map. He meticulously outlined the challenging sections of the route, emphasising that the initial two days involved crossing the Pyrenees, widely regarded as the most demanding part. Additionally, he highlighted other mountainous stretches in Spain that we would encounter along the way. He provided invaluable advice on greeting fellow pilgrims with either 'Buen Camino' or 'Hola', fostering camaraderie on the journey. He also handed us the scallop shell, a symbol we would affix to our backpacks. Later, we replaced it with one adorned with the cross of St James. Departing the office, we felt content and well-prepared for the pilgrimage ahead.

Chapter 4

"A journey of a thousand miles must begin with a single step".

Lao Tzu

It was the 5th of July 2023, the day beginning our long-planned journey. We rose before five to prepare and exchanged good luck wishes. Peter and I were so excited. We packed our backpacks, checked everything around and ensured that nothing was left behind.

We left the villa around six o'clock with our backpacks securely fastened and hiking poles in hand. At first, we looked for the yellow arrows and shells marking the route, but with so many pilgrims already on their way, it wasn't necessary—we followed the crowd. As we left St Jean-Pied-de-Port, we immediately began ascending the Pyrenees. It was our journey's shortest yet most challenging walk—only about eight to ten kilometres. We didn't want to rush or try to cross the Pyrenees in a single day. I think Peter was more concerned about me than himself. He didn't want the first day to be discouraging.

The atmosphere among the pilgrims was vibrant and eager, forming a cohesive Camino family united by the common goal of reaching Santiago de Compostela. Talking to other pilgrims almost started immediately. Most of us felt similar— excited, concerned or curious. We found out that not everyone planned to reach Santiago de Compostela. Some planned to stop along the way; some pilgrims aimed for shorter sections like Pamplona or Burgos.

I noticed that most pilgrims walked alone. Even those, like Peter and I, who came to walk together.

Peter and I started together. However, even when we walked together, the focus shifted to ourselves and our bodies. Each of us began to walk at our own pace, and from the outset, the path was steep and challenging.

From the first day, I noticed that this walk is not ordinary; it pushes you to be alone and focus completely on yourself. The steepness of the mountain path contributed to that. After only a kilometre walk, I was focused on my energy and on each step, pushing myself to keep putting one foot in front of the other.

The morning saw a surge of pilgrims starting their journey; pilgrims of different ages, nationalities and parts of the world. *Would every day be like this?* I wondered. We engaged with several fellow walkers on the first day, pausing often to capture photos of the breathtaking panoramas. The conversations were usually short. Each of us was focused on the walk, finishing one and continuing to the next steep section or dealing with the challenging path.

However, I soon found the climb taxing. I struggled to keep up with Peter, who had moved ahead. But it wasn't a problem at all. As I said, this walk somehow made one feel alone and focused. The weight of my pack compounded the difficulty. Unlike some pilgrims who opted for baggage transfers between accommodations, Peter and I chose to carry everything ourselves, aiming to embrace the true pilgrim experience.

As sweat covered my body, each steep incline gave way to another, demanding my full attention. The importance of proper walking shoes became evident, as did the necessity of remaining focused and present—any lapse could result in a misstep on the treacherous terrain.

Despite the physical exertion, the warm, sunny weather lifted my spirits, though my primary focus remained on placing one foot in front of the other. Amidst my challenges, I noticed a fellow pilgrim swiftly passing by, tears streaming down his face. He was crying loudly. His emotional state intrigued me. *What burden was he carrying?* I pressed on, intent on completing our first leg and reaching our initial destination.

Pilgrims dotted the edge of the path, taking a well-deserved break. Many aimed to cover twenty-five kilometres and stay in Roncesvalles, but I was relieved we had booked at Refuge Orison and looked forward to reaching our destination.

Finding Peter, we settled on the grass together and smiled. We were both very tired.

"Peter, I can't see the end of this stretch. It's tough." I sighed.

"Don't worry. We're almost there. Less than two kilometres to Orisson," Peter reassured me, his enthusiasm palpable.

We rested for a few minutes, taking a breath and observing the surroundings. It looked beautiful. However, my focus was on reaching our destination for that day. Peter and I agreed that splitting the walk over the Pyrenees in two days was a good idea.

Less than two kilometres later, my spirits lifted as we arrived at Refuge Orisson. The short distance had been gruelling, possibly the toughest part of the journey.

We encountered a few pilgrims who planned to spend the night there, including Cathy and Kelli, an aunt and niece from America heading towards Pamplona. Nestled in a serene pocket of the Pyrenees, Refuge Orisson offered an incredible view of the mountains. After settling into our room, we relaxed outside the bar, soaking in the breathtaking scenery. Joining Cathy, a retired schoolteacher and Kelli, a flight attendant, we engaged in lively conversation, discussing everything from education to politics in Australia and America. It was also a moment to unwind and appreciate nature's beauty.

When I went to buy coffee from the bar, a man on a motorbike approached the counter, asking in accented English if there was a free room. With a heavy French accent, the lady behind the counter curtly replied, "We are fully booked," adding, "No free, you have to pay." Her lack of a smile made me wonder if it was a language barrier or an attempt at humour. It amused me, and I returned to our group. Soon after, I noticed the man had settled at the next table, seemingly resolving the room issue.

That evening, all the pilgrims gathered for dinner at six-thirty. As we sat down, I observed one of the pilgrims rise and begin a prayer. It was the same German man who had inquired about a room earlier. Whether he was a priest or preacher remained unclear to me. Around twenty of us joined the meal, and his prayer set a solemn tone before we introduced ourselves—sharing our countries of origin and the motivations driving our pilgrimage. Hearing the diverse reasons of fellow pilgrims deepened my contemplation of my journey's purpose.

We enjoyed a hearty three-course dinner, engaging in lively conversation with our newfound companions. Among them were a couple from Israel planning a two-week walk and a mother with her fourteen-year-old daughter from Canada. She was a Spanish teacher with ties to the University of Santiago de Compostela, fulfilling her dream of walking the Camino. That evening, we revealed a surprising number of educators among us, including several from Iceland and various other countries, taking advantage of their summer holidays for this trek. Kelli and Cathy from the USA and others became our Camino companions over dinner and, these days, our Facebook friends.

Reflecting on the day's walk, we all savoured the camaraderie before retiring for much-needed rest and eagerly preparing for the next day.

It was the 6th of July, the second day of our Camino Walk. We collected our pre-paid breakfast and left Orisson around seven o'clock with most pilgrims with whom we had shared dinner the previous night. Our goal for the day was Roncesvalles, an ancient monastery nestled in Navarra, Spain. The weather was fresh and drizzling. We stopped and put our raincoats on. The terrain was changing slightly. The steepness of the path was more bearable compared to the previous day.

The rain had stopped, and the weather was perfect for walking. I felt grateful and thanked Peter for his encouragement to take on the Camino. It was a pleasant morning stroll. That day, we talked to a few people, including an American couple around our age. They had walked the Camino Francés in 2011 and had returned to do it again. They had also walked the Portuguese Camino but preferred the Camino Francés for its atmosphere and the number of people on the pilgrimage. Both were tall, slim, and looked very fit; I wasn't surprised they had walked several Caminos. This time, they opted not to carry their backpacks, transferring them from one stop to the next.

I loved how Peter would start conversations with other pilgrims, especially those from Ireland, England, or Germany. He connected with them naturally, even though his family has been Australian for over five generations. He would often dive into his heritage, discussing where his ancestors came from. A DNA test revealed that his roots are primarily in those three countries. His maternal grandfather, for instance, was born on a ship in the early twentieth century as his family migrated to Australia from Germany. Peter has a strong interest in his ancestry, believing it's helped him form a deep connection with his inner self. I remember when we visited Long Crendon, England, in 2019—the hometown of his paternal great-grandfather. While we were sitting in a coffee shop, Peter's face lit up; he felt like he had come home. Talking to the barista, he asked questions like his family had left just two years ago rather than two centuries ago. Watching Peter, I wondered how my children, grandchildren, and great-grandchildren might one day connect with their roots.

Crossing the border from France to Spain passed almost unnoticed as we continued our ascent up steep paths. The walk became more demanding with each mountain summit, yet my resolve grew stronger. My focus was entirely on the path ahead. Walking through the Pyrenees was simultaneously challenging and awe-inspiring. The breathtaking panoramic views made me feel as if I were scaling the world's top, gazing down at the clouds below.

My mind wandered back to my university days, where each passed exam felt like a monumental step forward. Standing atop these peaks and observing the clouds drifting in the valleys below echoed the sense of achievement I felt on graduation day—the culmination of years of effort and self-realisation. Although we were just at the beginning of our journey, I felt a similar mix of emotions. Peter and I took selfies and photos with an Irish couple we'd met. They were about our age and planned to walk as far as Pamplona to watch the main bull run.

Along the way, we spotted a food bus with a few pilgrims gathered around. We decided to stop, grab a bite, and chat with other pilgrims, including Aleks from Italy. Aleks was a young man in his twenties, planning to walk to Santiago de Compostela alone. He spoke about the challenges young people face today, and it was a pleasure talking with him. When I asked what had inspired him to walk the Camino, Aleks wasn't entirely sure. In some way, he hoped the Camino would help him find his path.

The three of us continued walking together until Aleks eventually said goodbye and continued on his own. We saw him several times on the way to Santiago de Compostela.

Peter and I settled into our own pace, lost in our thoughts or simply taking in the beauty around us. I reflected on how this pilgrimage is said to impact you in three stages: first, the body, then the mind, and finally, the soul. Already, I could feel the physical strain on my muscles—a reminder of the journey's demands. Despite the growing discomfort, I pressed on, aware that we still had thirty-two days ahead.

We arrived at the hilltop and spotted the monastery amidst the forested mountains. A surge of happiness washed over me. We were close, with only another five kilometres to go. We started walking down the hill, finally reaching Roncesvalles and headed to the hotel opposite the hostel. However, upon arrival, the receptionist couldn't find our reservation.

"We probably booked at the hostel. We couldn't find this accommodation on Booking.com," Peter said, disappointed. "Booking this place was difficult because everything was in Spanish, with limited English translations," Peter explained.

"No worries, darling. We'll be fine," I reassured him, trying to alleviate his concern about staying in the hostel.

We headed to the hostel, where so many pilgrims were waiting in line. It was clear our booking was indeed for the hostel. After depositing our shoes and hiking poles in a designated area, we climbed to our beds on the second floor. Across from us, a young girl in her twenties from Romania had already settled in, having walked over twenty-five kilometres from St Jean-Pied-de-Port to Roncesvalles, arriving before us. Such is the Camino—people cover distances at their own pace.

Both of us felt a bit let down. While the accommodation was clean and well-maintained, we longed for the comfort of a private room and a proper shower after a long day's walk. Peter took the initiative to return to the reception and secured a hotel room. Moving there turned out to be a much better choice. After freshening up and doing some laundry, we headed down to the restaurant for dinner, where we met up with the Irish couple we'd encountered earlier on the way to Roncesvalles. Like us, they were in their sixties and preferred the privacy of separate rooms to the communal hostel setup. After dinner, we went to bed as the rain started to fall, and I hoped for better weather the next day. Looking at the route map from Roncesvalles, I felt relieved that no more steep hills awaited us. Climbing had been especially challenging for me.

We rose early on July 7th, our third day of walking, with Lintzoain as our next destination. Most pilgrims we'd spoken with the previous day, including Cathy and Kelli, planned to continue to Zubiri. Due to a festive event in Pamplona, however, we couldn't find any accommodation there, so Lintzoain, a village just before Zubiri, became our alternative. The distance to Lintzoain was fifteen kilometres, and we knew the following day would be a long walk. We had booked our stay at Posada El Camino in Lintzoain nearly three months in advance.

The summer morning was refreshingly cool and ideal for walking. We left the hotel and stopped at a café for breakfast. Knowing it would be a shorter walk that day, I looked forward to an easier pace after the tough Pyrenees climbs of the past two days.

On the way, we spotted Cathy and Kelli outside a bar. We joined them for refreshments, and Cathy, excited about her birthday, invited us to celebrate with them in Pamplona the following evening. They'd booked accommodations in Zubiri, aiming to reach Pamplona the next day, just in time for Saturday night's festivities before the main bull run. Peter and I happily accepted the invitation, looking forward to Cathy's birthday celebration and an evening in Pamplona. For Cathy and Kelli, Pamplona would be their final stop on the Camino as they had other holiday plans.

Upon arrival at our accommodation, Carmen, a tall and friendly lady, opened the door and welcomed us warmly. She led us up to our room on the third floor. Using Google Translate to communicate, Carmen kindly offered us dinner and we accepted. Normally, meals weren't included in the accommodation, but we were too exhausted to venture out, especially as it was approaching four o'clock. We settled in, did our laundry, and tried to unwind. Suddenly, thunder rumbled, and heavy rain pounded outside. I felt relieved we had arrived before the storm hit. I thought about Kelli, Cathy, and the other pilgrims heading to Zubiri. We had heard that the descent there was challenging and rocky even in good weather, let alone during a storm with potential power outages.

I wondered about Carmen and how she would prepare dinner without electricity. Could she serve cold meals or use alternative cooking methods? At seven o'clock, Carmen called us downstairs. To our surprise, she had prepared a warm meal: pork medallions, soup, and mashed potatoes, all served by candlelight. I attempted to ask Carmen about her cooking method without electricity, but the language barrier made communication difficult. Despite this, Carmen's hospitality and effort to provide a warm meal in such conditions left a lasting impression on us.

We were the only pilgrims dining that evening. Carmen chuckled and gestured towards our spread. "Romantico! Romantico!" she exclaimed repeatedly. Indeed, it did feel romantic. The soup we enjoyed was simply delicious. I wished I could speak Spanish fluently to ask Carmen for the recipe, but communication proved challenging without Google Translate. After finishing our lovely dinner and a glass of red wine, we retired to our room.

My muscles were sore, and my mind turned to the next day's journey, which involved walking over thirty kilometres. Over the past few nights, I had noticed my body recovering despite the previous day's challenges. The following morning, I felt surprisingly well-rested. My entire focus was on my body—my feet, legs, and back—which would play crucial roles in our journey to Santiago de Compostela.

Chapter 5

On the Way to Pamplona

"Sometimes it takes only one act of kindness and caring to change a person's life"

Unknown author

It was the 8th of July. We left Lintzoain early in the morning. It was our fourth day of walking. Our routine of going to bed around eight or nine p.m. allowed us to rise at four a.m. We then spent about an hour getting ready: caring for our feet, covering any red spots with hiking wool, packing our bags, and double-checking that we hadn't forgotten anything. By six a.m., we were on the road, aware of the long walk ahead. Spain was still dark until seven a.m., so our head torches lit the way as we followed the Camino markers—the yellow arrows and shells. Our next stop was a B&B we had pre-booked in Burlada, a suburb on the outskirts of Pamplona.

We paused in several villages along the way, taking breaks for breakfast and lunch, often savouring Spanish omelettes or tortillas. After reaching Zubiri, the terrain eased a bit, but the earlier path had demanded physical endurance and intense mental focus. Each step required presence and concentration, especially on such a rugged and precarious trail—one of the most challenging I'd encountered, perhaps only matched by the path to Portomarín. In Australia, trails this dangerous would likely be closed, and I silently promised myself to revisit that memory later.

Peter and I supported each other, navigating sections with barely enough stable ground to place our hiking poles. Descending from the hills, we stepped carefully, mindful of every move. I couldn't help but think of Cathy, Kelli, and other pilgrims who had braved this route in harsh weather the day before. Reaching Zubiri was a relief.

We talked about Cathy's birthday and made plans to get ready, call a taxi, and head to Pamplona after we settled in. Peter expressed some concern about our accommodation for the night, noting he hadn't been able to locate it on the map. That day's trek exceeded thirty kilometres. After passing through Zubiri, the route eased up.

We paused in nearly every village we encountered, resting as needed and talking to a few pilgrims. By late afternoon, we neared the town of Burlada and crossed a bridge that seemed to mark its entrance. Following GPS guidance, Peter attempted to contact our accommodation but received no response.

Passing by an outdoor swimming pool filled with laughter and cheerful voices made me think, *If our accommodation is in one of these buildings we're passing, it would be great to put on our swimsuits and relax by the pool before we join Cathy and Kelli.* It was around five p.m.. The weather was scorching, and exhaustion had set in, leaving me drenched in sweat. Each step felt like a monumental effort, my body protesting with every movement. Ahead of me, Peter forged on, scanning street names and struggling with the GPS, which seemed confused by the unmarked roads.

We pressed on for another two to three kilometres without end. As we neared the town centre, I suddenly felt my legs give out beneath me. Unable to move, I leaned heavily on my hiking poles and, completely drained, stopped at an intersection.

I can't go on. I can't keep up with Peter, my voice echoed in my mind, surprisingly loud against the backdrop of bustling activity. The town was alive with people clad in white and red, chatting, laughing, and preparing for the main event—the grand bull run the next day, which was a Sunday.

A school bus halted at a nearby red light, filled with spirited fourteen- or fifteen-year-old students. Their boisterous laughter and animated chatter filled the air, adding to the festive atmosphere. Two girls near the back of the bus leaned out of the window and began speaking to me in Spanish. Despite their serious and concerned expressions, I couldn't comprehend their words.

"Thank you, girls. I'm sorry, I don't speak Spanish," I replied, grateful for their attempt to communicate.

Switching to English, the girls continued, trying to encourage me. "You need to keep moving, keep walking. You can do it! You must keep going!"

Their words were a boost of encouragement, urging me to push forward despite my fatigue and the daunting prospect of continuing the journey.

The traffic light turned green, and the school bus began to move. The girls leaned out of the window, hands waving, heads turned towards me, and their voices carried on the breeze:

"You can move! You can move! Keep walking! Move!"

Their genuine empathy touched me deeply. Tears welled up in my eyes as their encouragement resonated within me. At that moment, they understood my struggle and cared for a stranger they would likely never see again. In their faces, I saw echoes of my daughters and students—how they might react if they saw me in such a moment of difficulty. Seeing my reflection in a nearby shop window, I looked on the verge of collapse. Now I understood why those two beautiful souls, whom I would remember forever, had been so concerned. They had given me the courage I needed.

"I can move! I can keep walking, no matter how hard it seems. There's nothing wrong with me. The girls were right—I can do it," I reassured myself, summoning all my positivity and inner strength.

With Peter now ahead of me, I started moving again. Crossing the intersection, I focused on keeping him in sight. He paused and looked back, checking on me, which renewed my determination.

We walked another kilometre, entering the central part of town surrounded by buildings. A middle-aged man approached us as we circled, looking for signs of our accommodation. Despite not speaking English, he used gestures and body language to assist. He indicated that the address we sought wasn't in that immediate area but further ahead. With a kind smile, he invited us to follow him.

Grateful for his help, we walked on together. He couldn't pinpoint the exact location, but his willingness to assist buoyed our spirits. Eventually, we found the place, a building or apartment without a visible number. Thanking the man warmly, we discovered a coffee shop open for business. We settled in, ordered drinks, and checked the accommodation details once more—it was past six p.m., and the day's challenges were finally easing into a moment of respite.

The woman answered the call, but communication was difficult due to the language barrier. Peter quickly contacted the B&B office, explained the situation, and requested their assistance finding alternative accommodation. Within minutes, a woman and her ten-year-old daughter arrived to help. The young girl attempted to translate for us in English as we followed them to another building a few minutes away. It appeared to be a communal residence, but we only needed a shower and bed.

That evening, our plans to go to Pamplona and celebrate Cathy's birthday, our fellow pilgrim, were out of reach. We had walked a gruelling thirty-three or thirty-four kilometres that day, and were utterly exhausted. Peter emailed Cathy to let her know we wouldn't be able to join them. With no energy left to venture out for dinner, we settled for sharing an apple after showering and doing our laundry. It served as our modest meal before we collapsed into bed, grateful for the chance to rest.

Chapter 6

New Challenges, New Inspirations

"Challenges are what make life interesting and overcoming them is what makes life meaningful."

Joshua J. Marine

The next day, July 9th, we woke up around four o'clock and felt better than the previous day. I shared with Peter the story of the intersection and the girls on the bus, and we agreed to call a taxi if we faced a similar situation again. I knew the previous day's walk had been hard on him, but he never complained. He was my rock, taking care of nearly everything except choosing meals and doing laundry—those were my tasks, though he occasionally helped with the washing, too.

We inspected each other's feet each morning, carefully applying gauze and tape to any red spots or blisters. Before starting the Camino, I hadn't fully appreciated how essential foot care and proper footwear would be for walking such long distances daily. As the days passed, blisters developed around our feet, some growing large, almost like small balloons with toenails. Regular antiseptic treatments and protective covers made a big difference.

It was early morning when we left Burlada. We planned to stop for coffee and something to eat on the way. Sometimes, we had a second breakfast. Given the distance we covered daily, and the calories expended, it was common to have breakfast at eight-thirty a.m., brunch at eleven a.m., and lunch at two p.m. I cherished these breaks, not just for rest but also for the chance to converse with other pilgrims and locals.

Leaving Burlada, the Camino led us through the city of Pamplona. Despite the early hour, around six-thirty a.m., the town bustled as if it was midday. People were out walking or boarding buses heading toward the old part of town where the main bull run would commence at eight a.m.. We followed the Camino path, opting not to mingle with the crowds or watch the run. Cleaning crews were already tidying up the remnants of the previous night's festivities while some revellers, still drunk and jovial, lounged in the parks. I found the atmosphere vibrant and festive.

Two girls greeted us warmly and wished us "Buen Camino." They apologised for the mess and explained, "This isn't the usual Pamplona. The city looks completely different after the bull run festivities end." Their kindness touched us, and they admired our journey to Santiago de Compostela, sharing their aspirations to make the pilgrimage some day.

Along the way, we unexpectedly crossed paths with the Irish couple we'd dined in Roncesvalles. Their destination was Pamplona and seeing them amidst the bustling crowd was a pleasant surprise. We chatted before they headed toward Pamplona's old city while we followed the Camino signs.

As we traversed the city, we stopped at a bar on the outskirts for coffee, where glimpses of the bull run played on the TV. The scene looked intense and dangerous, and although we could have joined the spectators, I felt glad we'd opted to continue our walk, avoiding additional excitement. Peter and I mused about possibly returning to Pamplona one day for the festival, but our focus stayed firmly on our Camino journey.

Lost in conversation as we walked, we missed a turn and inadvertently continued in the wrong direction. I paused by a house drawn to a fruit tree in the yard that stirred memories of my childhood. For a fleeting moment, it brought me back to the dried fruits, rogushki', that my grandfather would buy every year before Christmas Eve. Reflecting on those fond memories, I saw Peter walking back toward me with a man who had kindly stopped to redirect us to the correct path. He shared that he'd walked the Camino Frances twice before. Grateful for his help, we thanked him and resumed our journey, more attentive to the yellow arrows and shells guiding us.

It was our fifth day on the Camino, with four more days until we reached Logroño. We'd already booked two nights of accommodation in Logroño, Burgos, León, and Astorga. We planned to complete the Camino Walk in thirty-four days, with four extra days for relaxation and sightseeing, assuming we wouldn't be too worn out by then.

By now, I was coming to terms with my physical pace. I couldn't match Peter's stride, and he often ended up one hundred or two hundred metres ahead. Walking long distances daily shifts your focus to simply moving forward; you find your rhythm and settle into it, often savouring the solitude. We'd stop and talk a bit when he paused to wait for me, sharing a few words, a hug, or a kiss before pressing on.

Seeing so many young people walking the Camino was inspiring, even if not all were heading for Santiago de Compostela. Connecting with other pilgrims, regardless of their destination, was always a highlight of the journey. I remembered talking to a couple from Isreal.

We met Orit and her husband in Orisson, the first night during the dinner time and we met a few more times later. They planned to walk for two weeks. Orit and I found out that we have read the same book, *The Choice*, by Edith Egar and discussed the book and the author.

The world is so small, I was thinking. These days I often think about Orit and her family, especially after the terrible things happening in their country at the moment.

Walking at my pace, I couldn't stop thinking about the past few days of walking. We traversed medieval towns and villages, admired ancient churches, passed through expansive fields, and conquered numerous hills. Our daily distances varied between twenty and thirte kilometres, with the weather generally cooperating, hovering between twenty-five and thirty degrees Celsius. We typically set out early in the morning to avoid the sweltering heat that would later follow. Walking beyond twenty-five or thirty kilometres proved challenging for me, as I began to feel pain throughout my body. Despite this, I tried not to complain, marvelling at Peter's unwavering resilience. His constant smiles and determination motivated me to press on, even though he could have reached our accommodations at least two hours earlier if he had walked alone as many other pilgrims did.

Nevertheless, the Camino isn't a race. Each pilgrim walks at their own pace. This path welcomes people from all corners of the globe without discrimination based on wealth or status. We are all equals—members of the Camino family. Conversations flowed freely among pilgrims; some even exchanged contact information to stay in touch. The camaraderie was palpable; gestures spoke volumes even when language barriers existed. I cannot emphasise enough how friendly and supportive the Spanish people were. It felt like a divine presence was guiding us through this country. The Camino mirrored life—a journey where we are identical and unique. We faced the same challenges along the route, yet each of us found a way to persevere.

Around four o'clock in the afternoon, we reached Estella Guja Solo in Puente la Reina. Stepping inside, we were warmly greeted by a young lady who promptly stamped our credentials, checked our passports, and escorted us to our room on the second floor. She mentioned that the atmosphere in the hostel had been very loud and lively the previous night due to many young visitors attending the bull run in Pamplona.

While Peter was checking in, I sank into an armchair. The lady observed and said, "You look exhausted."

Indeed, I was, and I replied, "More than exhausted," while the sweat dripped down my face and body.

Our host took my backpack and brought it to our room on the second floor. Peter and I walked into the room and collapsed on the bed in seconds. Within minutes, there was a knock on our door. Another lady offered us a massage. Initially declining, I quickly changed my mind upon Peter's encouragement. Though barely mobile, I stepped outside to find her, only to discover no more bookings were available for the night. I had missed my chance.

We left Los Arcos around seven a.m. after staying at Hostal Suetxe. The distances we'd covered over the past two days were manageable—about twenty to twenty-two kilometres daily. It was July 12, our eighth day of walking. We'd stayed at Pensión Buen Camino in Estella the night before, which I thoroughly enjoyed. So far, our accommodations had been comfortable and clean, except for the place in Burlada. The private rooms in hostels weren't much different from hotel rooms, and the prices were comparable.

On shorter walking days, we felt more relaxed. We didn't need to rush and often walked side by side, talking, especially in the morning. After two or three hours, the fatigue would set in, and we'd naturally fall into our paces, conversations quieting as the summer heat added to our weariness.

The day before, the path had taken us through forested areas, where we passed a woman sitting by the roadside playing the harmonica. Her music lifted the spirits of passing pilgrims, and I took a photo and a short video—she didn't seem to mind.

Along the way, we met a lovely young couple from Slovenia, Nina and Aljaž, who were engaged and planning to marry the following year. Though we once shared a country, our languages are quite different. Luckily, they both spoke fluent English, making conversation easy. We walked together for a while, and I admired their energy. They didn't plan to take extra rest days and were staying in hostels. I enjoyed talking to Nina, a trained teacher ready to start her career. Once again I was impressed by young people and their commitment to this challenging and mystical Camino Walk.

In various villages, we shared meals with a dozen pilgrims worldwide, bonding as though we were old friends. We ran into some pilgrims repeatedly; others, we never saw again—that's how the Camino flows. While the number of pilgrims was still high, it had dropped slightly since Pamplona.

I began to worry about my stamina, knowing there were so many days still to go until Santiago de Compostela, and exhaustion was setting in. I was grateful we'd booked two nights in Logroño. Peter and I hoped the extra rest would rejuvenate us.

Before reaching Logrono, we stopped in a town a few kilometres away to enjoy cold beer served with olives—a customary treat along the Camino route. Feeling refreshed, we noticed a local taxi number and decided to call one rather than trekking through the city. Within ten minutes, the taxi arrived and whisked us to our hotel. Only later did Peter realise he had left his hiking poles outside a bar where we had paused. He intended to buy new ones the next day. However, the replacement lacked the quality of his original.

Our hotel in Logrono was splendid, centrally located, and offered a large, comfortable room. We were delighted to have booked our two-night accommodation there and still had enough energy to explore the city. The weather remained pleasant as we strolled through the streets, enjoyed dinner, and retired early for a much-needed rest.

The following day, we visited the cathedral and a museum that particularly impressed me with its tribute to women in Spain. Exiting the museum, I was surprised to find the streets nearly empty in the afternoon—a familiar sight from my childhood in Macedonia, where shops closed after two p.m. for siesta. It was a nostalgic reminder of how things were then and how they are now in Spain.

Logrono marked our first prolonged rest after eight days of walking, and we eagerly anticipated the next stop—Burgos. We planned five more days of walking before reaching Burgos, where we would embark on the flat Meseta region for nine days. Many pilgrims avoid Camino Frances in July and August due to the sweltering heat, sparse shade, and long distances between villages. Armed with self-sticking umbrellas, we hoped they would provide some relief. While I tried not to dwell on the mental challenge ahead, focusing instead on adjusting to the physical demands of long-distance walking, we still had five days to prepare ourselves.

I was thoroughly impressed by the history, churches, and the melodic tolling of church bells each morning in the villages we passed through. The cathedral in Logrono left a lasting impression, as did the warmth and hospitality of the Spaniards we encountered and the diverse pilgrims we shared conversations with from around the world. Despite our challenges, I consistently felt blessed and privileged to be on the journey. I sensed deep in myself that I was exactly where I needed to be at that right moment, with profound reasons guiding me along that mystical path. It brought me immense happiness.

Later in the afternoon, we went shopping. I found a lovely summer dress, while Peter bought a new pair of hiking poles. The clothing shops reminded me of those back in Australia, where it seems everything nowadays comes from the same factory—it left quite an impression on me.

In the evening, we ventured out again. We wandered the city streets like the previous night, enjoying a delightful dinner with various tapas. The atmosphere was vibrant and lively, with everyone revelling in the evening. I spotted the lady playing the harmonica once more. It struck me as a delightful coincidence since we had seen her earlier in the forest days ago, prompting me to record her performance. She seemed to recognise me, too, adding to the sense of fate surrounding our journey.

After two restful nights in Logroño, we set out for Nájera in the province of Navarra on July 14. It was our ninth day of walking, not counting the rest day. Leaving Hotel Ciudad de Logroño behind, we started early, around five or six a.m., with our next stop planned at an apartment called Vino y Camino in Estella. Knowing we had over thirty kilometres to cover, we anticipated a long day ahead. The morning air was refreshing, and Peter and I took multiple breaks throughout the day as we passed through various roads, hills, and fields under the hot sun. Our first stop was a village where we enjoyed coffee and breakfast, talking about the countryside lifestyle of the places we passed. The Spanish villages looked well-maintained, the roads clean, and there were few cars and almost no petrol stations. Even so, we focused on the map, checking the day's remaining distance.

"Looks like we have a long walk today," I said, glancing at the map. "I'm glad we rested in Logroño. This afternoon, it'll be over thirty degrees."

Peter smiled reassuringly. "Don't worry, my love. We're together, we have already booked, and we'll get there when we arrive. We can rest as much as we need."

"I admire the pilgrims walking alone. I couldn't do this walk without you," I replied, grateful for his presence. Peter asked if my blisters bothered me. Although they'd formed despite using hiking wool, I assured him I'd manage.

We continued our walk, meeting mostly new faces along the way. Many of our Camino friends who hadn't taken an extra rest day were already ahead of us. We briefly chatted with a father walking with his two sons, who had started in Logroño and travelled from southern Spain. The intense heat made us focus more on maintaining our pace than socializing, leaving little energy for conversation or deep exchanges.

I was surprised at how little Peter and I talked during the walk. Most of the time we were exhausted, letting the silence settle around us as we pressed on, each of us deep in our thoughts.

By evening, our destination required a few extra kilometres off the main route, adding to our exhaustion after nearly thirty kilometres. Reaching the outskirts of Estella, I could barely move. Sensing my struggle, Peter paused to wait for me.

"Peter, we need to call a taxi again," I admitted, stopping at the roadside. "I feel just like I did in Burlada. My body's had enough."

Self-doubt crept in. *How did I think I could walk eight hundred kilometres?* I wondered, overwhelmed. We weren't even a third of the way through, and I was already feeling broken. Being sixty-one, I started to question my age's impact, especially next to Peter, who, at sixty-six, seemed unfazed—a testament to his fitness after twenty years in the Australian Army. But I kept those thoughts to myself.

Peter looked at me with concern. "Alright, my love. I'll try calling a taxi. Let's hope someone speaks English, otherwise explaining where we are at the moment will be tricky."

We emerged from the dusty paths cutting through the fields, and I couldn't help but be frustrated. *I'm a language teacher. Why didn't I prepare better, learn some Spanish—at least enough to get by and call a taxi?* I scolded myself inwardly.

Peter dialled the taxi number he found online, but as expected, the person on the other end spoke no English. He struggled to explain our location using gestures and the few signs around us. Eventually, the call ended abruptly, leaving us to continue walking without any other choice. We had about an hour's walk ahead of us, roughly four kilometres, but I felt like I was no longer in control of my body. Each day brought its challenges, but today seemed particularly tough.

I pushed aside my self-pity and negative thoughts. Life had thrown many emotional challenges my way, and I had long learned not to wallow in self-pity. But this physical challenge was new to me. The hills and long distances tested me, but I knew I had to push through. I came here to walk—to reach Santiago de Compostela and pay homage to St James on foot—or to accompany Peter. Yet, I struggled to grasp the significance of my journey. It didn't feel like walking; it felt like crawling. We estimated it would take two hours, not one, to reach our destination, and my prediction was correct. We arrived around five-thirty p.m.

Using the PIN, the host had sent to Peter's email, we unlocked the front door and climbed to the third-floor attic apartment. Even climbing those stairs after over a thirty-four kilometre walk felt like another challenge. Inside was a bottle of red wine and two glasses left by our host. After a shower and a glass of wine, we were too exhausted to venture out for dinner. When you're that tired, hunger seems to vanish—a revelation to me. My body and muscles had adapted to the long walks, and aside from the usual leg and back pain, I felt no other discomfort. I didn't feel hungry, even though we skipped dinner. I saw no reason to worry about the next day; I woke up feeling fine in the morning.

We woke up around four-thirty a.m., as usual. I stepped onto the terrace to collect the clothes we had washed the night before. My gaze fell upon the massive wall surrounding that part of the city—a reminder of the Roman Empire's enduring influence on this region of Spain.

I turned to Peter and said, "One day, we should return to Spain as tourists and explore the history of these ancient places." He agreed wholeheartedly. Before starting the Camino, I had imagined we'd have time for sightseeing. It was all we could do to get through each day and gather enough strength to continue the next.

It was the 15th July. We continued our journey through Najera before arriving in Santo Domingo de la Calzada, in the province of La Rioja. We had booked a room at the Parador de Santo Domingo, a former pilgrims' hospital transformed into a splendid hotel.

The walk remained challenging, but I found joy in the journey. I particularly relished our stops in villages and bars, savouring freshly squeezed orange juice, tortillas, and picadillo—a classic Spanish sandwich—and conversing with fellow pilgrims.

Along the way to Santo Domingo de la Calzada, we met Brian and Sue, a couple from New South Wales, Australia, accompanied by Mary, another Australian pilgrim from Victoria, who lived in Melbourne, like us. While we encountered Brian and Sue occasionally, Mary walked with us more frequently. We shared delightful chats and enjoyed several dinners together. Mary had previously walked parts of the Camino Frances with her son and embarked on the entire route this time, starting a day before us from Saint-Jean-Pied-de-Port.

We arrived at the Parador de Santo Domingo in the early afternoon, staying there for the night despite its high price. While we were waiting in front of the reception to check in, Peter and I were talking about the number of pilgims over the centuries who were admitted to this place, once called hospital, or who ended their lives there.

Peter lightened the mood with a joke when he asked the receptionist, "Are there any ghosts here?"

The receptionist replied without a smile, "I do not know. We haven't seen any so far."

After settling into our room, we followed our Camino routine: showering, washing up, and resting. Since we arrived early, we had the afternoon free. It was a shorter walking day, less than twenty kilometres. With many restaurants closed for siesta, we bought food from the nearest supermarket and enjoyed a pleasant dinner with Vino Tinto in our hotel room. We dined in our room a few times and found it quite enjoyable.

Dinners in pilgrim's restaurants typically consisted of a three-course meal with water, wine, or a soft drink as an option. I savoured almost every Spanish dish, especially mixed salads. In Logrono, we indulged in various tapas, which I loved.

After leaving Santo Domingo de la Calzada the following day, we stayed at Hotel La Huella Del Camino in Belorado. On the way we stopped and talked to a few of our Camino friends. Many familiar faces from the Camino greeted us there. The hotel host was warm and hospitable.

After unwinding, we had a delightful dinner in the hotel's backyard garden. I couldn't recall his name, but the host spoke some English, engaging Peter in a conversation about their shared love for music. He proudly displayed his collection of records and shared their significance. He, also told us that he was born and grew up in Madrid, but decided to come to the place his mum originated from and settled there. I liked how locals connect with pilgrims and shared their stories.

Looking ahead, we had two more days of walking before reaching Burgos. I looked forward to relaxing for two nights without the rush of early mornings. Observing other pilgrims, most retired to their rooms after dinner, and like them, we usually turned in before nine and left the albergue before seven in the morning.

* * *

After leaving San Juan de Ortega, we planned to walk more than twenty-five kilometres and reach Burgos. I was eager for the rest awaiting us with a two-night stay. Along the route to Burgos, we encountered Mary, who excitedly shared her plans to reunite with her brother and sister-in-law, who were visiting from Europe to spend a couple of days in Burgos with her.

As we approached Burgos, the city came into view from a distance, though we still had over ten km left to cover. We took a few photos together with Mary and continued our journey. I began to feel fatigued, uncertain if I'd have the energy to explore Burgos. The date was July 18th, and we planned to reach Santiago de Compostela by August 11th after walking for thirteen days and preparing for another twenty-one days of walking with breaks in Burgos, Leon, and Astorga.

Looking forward to walking through the Meseta, I appreciated its flat terrain, knowing there would be some hills but no mountains. I also anticipated the long stretches between villages, sometimes needing to walk fourteen km to reach the first village for breakfast. Our early starts meant we rarely ate breakfast where we stayed overnight, as breakfast typically began at seven o'clock. Something about walking through Meseta was exciting. Then, I did not know that Meseta Walk would produce this book.

Mary shared the weather forecast for the coming week, predicting an average temperature of twenty-five degrees Celsius during our Meseta crossing in July.

"We're lucky to have such mild weather," Mary remarked enthusiastically.

Reflecting on this leg of our journey, I thought, *Perhaps the Camino has been fixing my body in the first part and will now fix my mind.*

Peter walked ahead of me as usual, sometimes far enough to be barely visible. We both enjoyed walking by ourselves, like most of the pilgrims. Behind me, I heard people speaking Serbian, a language like Macedonian, which struck a chord of familiarity. Compared to Slovenian, Serbian is very similar to Macedonian. I can understand and speak fluently. I greeted them in Serbian and learned they were part of an alpinist association from Novi Sad, a city in northern Serbia. Zarko, who shared he was half-Macedonian, felt particularly familiar, as his father hailed from the same area I did. Their camaraderie and shared heritage made me feel connected, almost like family, reflecting on how language and culture bind people. I exchanged phone numbers with some of them. We walked together for a short time and moved on.

We met again at a bar later, where I enjoyed chatting and taking photos with Sonja, Gordana, Jadranka, and others from their group. These encounters reminded me of my roots and identity. On our way to Santiago, we encountered this group a few more times, cherishing each other's company before parting ways as the Camino often dictates.

We arrived in Burgos after three p.m. and picked up the key from the hotel, not far from the apartment we had booked. Our apartment was on the square, directly opposite the magnificent Santa Maria Cathedral. The area was bustling with many restaurants and cafes, and despite our fatigue, we were eager to explore. The weather was splendid, adding to the charm of Burgos. I instantly liked Burgos and the atmosphere in the central square.

We decided to visit the Cathedral first, and it was truly impressive. Later that afternoon, we enjoyed pizza and strolled around the city. What struck me the most was seeing people of various ages pushing wheelchairs with their loved ones. This compassionate sight was something I hadn't observed often in Melbourne or Macedonia, where I spent the first thirty years of my life. Once again, I was moved by the Spaniards and their care for disadvantaged individuals.

My thoughts drifted to my ninety-year-old mother, who resides in aged care. I used to visit her weekly, though her memory has faded these days. I wondered if she understood how long I would be away. She is the last surviving member of her and my father's family. In her younger days, she often visited doctors, as she often felt unwell. I'm grateful she's still with us, like a wing of our family. Over the last twenty to thirty years, I've witnessed her transformation from a confused and insecure person to someone trying to find her true self and stepping out of her comfort zone.

That evening, visiting Santa Maria Cathedral was a highlight. The architecture, spanning from the thirteenth to the sixteenth century, made me ponder the skills and dedication of those who built it, leaving a legacy for generations.

The following day, we had breakfast at a nearby restaurant and stopped at the chemist to buy supplies for our blisters. We also picked up hair dye; I wasn't fond of the grey hair showing beneath my dark brown locks. It wasn't an issue since I've always dyed my hair. Peter needed a haircut, but the closest salon didn't have an appointment. On our way back, we bumped into Mary, her brother and his wife. After a brief chat, we returned to our apartment.

Reflecting on Mary and her brother's closeness, I couldn't help but wish for a similar bond with my brother. Unfortunately, he has distanced himself from the family for many years. Despite efforts to reconnect, it hasn't been successful. I've learned to let go and focus on relationships where there is mutual effort and appreciation. It's a choice we all make, and I'm grateful to have stopped playing the role of family gatekeeper.

Chapter 7

Confronting the Past

"Love your children for who they are, not who you want them to be."

Unknown author

On July 20th, we departed from Burgos. Our day started as usual, around five o'clock in the morning. After checking out of our apartment, we returned the key to the nearby hotel. It was almost six-thirty a.m.. Finding the Camino route was straightforward from the Cathedral, marked by yellow arrows and scallop shells. We paused for photos before Santa Maria Cathedral and continued through Burgos towards our next stop, Isar. This village wasn't directly on the Camino route, so we planned to cover about twenty-seven kilometres to reach it, as we couldn't find suitable lodging in Hornillos del Camino, which lay along our path.

It took us nearly two hours to navigate out of Burgos, a predictable delay in larger cities like this, where the number of pilgrims dwindled noticeably. We observed that many pilgrims only walked sections of the Camino, often aiming for major cities as their destination.

As mentioned before, like many other pilgrims walking with a companion, Peter and I began and ended each day's journey together. Yet, for most of the long daily walks, we each walked alone, often keeping a hundred metres or more between us. We'd pause and rest together, sharing reflections, checking the map, and gauging distances before setting off again, immersed in our thoughts and the beauty of the surroundings. Somehow, the Camino seemed to encourage solitude. It was as if the path itself nudged us to walk alone. I sensed that we all cherished this time apart, much like in life, as we each followed our paths and connected to our inner selves.

Leaving Burgos behind, we entered the Meseta, a vast and open landscape unfolding before us. The early morning sun emerged as a small red ball in the sky behind us as we headed westward. The atmosphere was serene, with a quietness that resonated deeply with me. Walking through this expansive flat terrain felt oddly familiar, stirring emotions I hadn't encountered before. It was like I was transported back in time, a time that I was very familiar with. At the start I couldn't recall the familiarity, but the emotions were taking me back to a distant but familiar space and time, perhaps to my childhood in Macedonia.

I felt a strange connection as memories and sensations flooded my mind. It looked like once upon a time, I had been here. Everything seemed so familiar. I recalled a young girl, around seven or eight years old, lying in a sunflower field, gazing at the endless sky and dreaming of the future. The image came and went, fleeting yet profound. Even the taste of the local apples I found, called 'Petrovki', evoked memories from my past. These apples ripened early in July, coinciding with the feast of St Peter, celebrated by Orthodox Christians.

I felt an inexplicable nostalgia as I stood there, my heart pounding and sweat on my brow despite the cool morning. It was unlike my visits to Macedonia as an adult, where I had felt like a tourist, detached from the place I once called home. This time, the connection was visceral, pulling at my heartstrings.

Looking back towards a village perched on a small hill with its church visible in the distance, I couldn't shake the feeling of familiarity. It resembled Puturus, my birthplace, with its sprawling meadows and fields tended by local families. Mesete reminded me so much of Pelagonia. Puturus, a small village on the hill and down the valley, lay Pelagonia, smaller than the Meseta but equally picturesque with its sunflowers, cornfields, vineyards and dry endless space.

I began to feel an intense, unfamiliar sensation. Tears streamed down my face as I was overwhelmed by a deep longing to comfort that lonely girl from my memories. I wanted to reach out, to hold her close and assure her that she wasn't alone and that her life had meaning. The connection I felt to this image of the girl in my mind was powerful and profound.

I started to feel overwhelmed by my emotions. *Why am I feeling like this? Why do images of the young girl keep appearing and disappearing?* I wondered, realising I was thousands of kilometres from Macedonia—a place not even on our travel plans.

My last visit had been in 2019, and revisiting those memories wasn't something I typically dwelt on. I'd gone there with Peter; I loved showing him where I came from. We even visited Puturus, spending a week in Macedonia. But during that trip, waves of anger and negative emotions surfaced, catching me off guard. Sometimes, my feelings were so intense that even Peter struggled to understand them. In this deeply moving moment on the Camino, I just wanted to stay present—to fully immerse myself in the landscape's beauty and the journey ahead.

In the distance, I saw Peter, his pace a bit quicker than mine. I wiped away my tears, determined to focus on the path and not let my emotions consume me. I wondered if he was experiencing anything similar or if he was absorbed in his walk. This pilgrimage meant embracing each moment, step by step, leaving the past behind as we made our way toward Santiago de Compostela.

I began to sense pressure building in my head. No matter how hard I tried to push them away, my thoughts persisted, emanating from my heart and settling in my mind. The image of the young girl surrounded me, urging me to confront my past. Out of nowhere, I felt utterly alone in the vast openness of Meseta, with the little girl beckoning me to turn back and face what I had avoided for so long. The emotions were overpowering, coursing through my body, unsettling my stomach and bones. No, I wasn't losing my mind. I was grappling with something profound within me, something that demanded acknowledgment and resolution.

My thoughts took me to a few months ago, when I completed a diploma in counselling, with aspirations to work in the field once my teaching career concluded. Throughout my studies, I had engaged in self-reflection, exploring fragments of my life. Yet, amidst the busyness, some memories had remained suppressed, tucked away in a corner I had deliberately avoided opening. It felt like I had become a hoarder of memories, unwilling to confront the messiness within. Some memories surfaced intermittently, stirring sadness, anger, or curiosity.

Why had I resisted confronting my past? As my eldest sister often reminded me, it wasn't horrific, "There is always worse." The fear of what lay beneath had kept me in unease for much of my life. My sister's words rang true; it wasn't unbearable, but the chaos within hindered me from finding my true path. Each of my siblings, all four of us, struggled in our ways to navigate life's challenges. Some of us still do.

The moment had arrived amid the Meseta. I could no longer evade it. I had the time and space to confront my past. The image of the young girl, appearing and disappearing before me, handed me the key to unlock the room where my past lay waiting. The familiarity of this place, reminiscent of my birthplace, allowed my thoughts to wander freely through my mind and heart. It was as if a floodgate had been thrust open wide, and I could not stem the tide. I strolled along the dusty path, feeling as small and vulnerable as a child. It felt as though I was walking through the landscape of my early years, a time that left deep imprints on my soul.

This journey took me back to a small, remote village where I spent the first decade of my life. Nestled in the southern part of what is now the Republic of North Macedonia. The place was part of Yugoslavia during my childhood—a socialist state forged in the aftermath of World War II. The turbulence in Macedonia's history left its mark on its people, including my family. Wars, poverty, and lack of education left traces that passed down through generations.

In the quiet recesses of my mind, I could vividly see my parents, paternal grandparents, two older sisters, and younger brother. I could glimpse myself as I was during those formative years. Like many children in similar circumstances, I lacked exposure to many things. I knew far less than the average child my age, as resources to expand my knowledge or feed my curiosity were scarce or non-existent. We didn't even have a television at home; the only one in our village belonged to our teacher. Thinking of my primary school teacher still sends a shiver down my spine; he was strict and formidable.

We seldom turned on the radio we owned because we lived with my grandparents. If any relative, even a distant one, passed away, particularly from my grandmother's side, we observed mourning rituals that included refraining from any form of entertainment, including the radio. When I was seven, one of my father's sisters passed away, and that was the end of radio in our household. Books were also scarce; we relied on old textbooks from my older siblings.

The thoughts and memories rising to the surface were vivid as if everything were happening now, not more than fifty years ago.

Education wasn't a priority in our family. My father used to say, "If you study hard, you'll get a good job. If not, you'll work hard like me."

As I reflected on my education, a familiar anger surged. I felt it as intensely as I had in the years since. Why hadn't our parents recognised the value of education? I felt like I was the only one fighting to navigate through school, grappling with a loneliness that echoed the isolation I'd often felt at home. The lack of support was painfully clear, and the anger remained, still simmering beneath the surface.

Our future and education were left entirely to our own devices. Our parents provided no guidance; they believed we should forge our own paths.

My father often remarked, "I do my best with what I know. What I don't do, I don't do because I don't know how." He was the hardest working person I knew, doing his utmost to provide for our family with the limited resources available. And he was right. He always strived to do what was right and to be a role model for us as children.

In our family, education was less about learning and more about reinforcing a strong work ethic. From a young age, I understood we never had enough money to get by. I tried to grow up quickly, eager to start working and helping. Looking back, it's no surprise that all four siblings developed strong work ethic and now overcompensate with money and material things, trying to make up for those years when even basic needs were hard to meet.

Since I can remember, my curiosity has been endless. As a young girl, I often lay on the grass in the vast meadow near our house, pondering the mysteries around me.

Who am I? How big is the sky, and where does space end? These questions frequently filled my mind.

I felt so small in that expansive open space—grateful for my family, yet somehow alone and lonely. I felt small and invisible, like I felt that moment in Meseta. I felt just like my body was in Meseta. I moved through a different world and time, one that was once so familiar to me. From as early as I can remember, I knew I would never have come into this world if my brother had been born before me. He was born the youngest and the only boy, two years after me. These words somehow kept me excluded, alone and lonely, probably because I had heard them many times.

These thoughts filled me with sadness. Often, I felt like I was just an extra, a background figure. I didn't pay much attention to it when I was younger—and even later in life—but I always sensed a lack of respect from my siblings. That feeling, I realise, has probably lingered to this day.

"This is the girl we didn't want when she was born," my mum would often say with a laugh when introducing me to people for the first time.

I didn't take it to heart. I knew my place in the family. It didn't mean I was treated differently or loved any less. But in my family, love wasn't something expressed openly or verbally. My coping became loving my family unconditionally, working hard to earn their love, making my parents proud, and showing I was worth noticing and appreciating. I expected nothing in return. I felt a deep need to make up for any disappointment they might have felt and to prove I was worthy of love. These thoughts shaped me from childhood through adulthood, even into my fifties. I took on the role of holding the family together. From an early age, family became a value that nothing else could replace.

My thoughts drifted to me as an adult and I reflected on my marriage. I had continued with the life I knew. I couldn't recall ever truly feeling loved by Greg. I don't think he ever saw me as a partner or appreciated me. If I felt neglected as a child, I felt trapped as an adult, constantly walking on eggshells to avoid angering anyone around me. I often wondered why I kept mirroring the life I knew, perhaps because I didn't know any other way.

Reflecting on my childhood and adulthood made me feel unsettled. The emotions were so intense that they pulled me back to these memories.

As I returned to the present, I felt a surge of anger.

"Stop feeling like a victim, Gordana. Stop it! Stop it!" I almost screamed. I looked around, relieved that no one was close enough to hear me. I could see pilgrims in the distance ahead and behind me. My body shook, and tears streamed down my face.

"What is wrong with me? I'm over sixty, and I still feel this way. Why am I crying like a child? Why am I dwelling on something from the past? Who cares if I wasn't loved sixty years ago? Who cares? Who cares if Greg did not love me? Everything is over," I questioned myself as I stopped at the edge of the road.

As anger stirred within me, I felt the warmth of the sun. Something soothing coursed through me. A gentle, soft voice inside encouraged me to accept my thoughts and anger. Wiping away my tears, I walked slowly, delving deeper into my past. I journeyed beyond my life, revisiting the stories I had heard countless times, like broken records.

I picked up my pace, trying to catch up with Peter. When I reached him, he was already resting and waiting for me.

"How do you feel, my love? You look tired," he said, gently wiping the sweat from my face.

"I am tired—more from thinking than from walking," I joked, attempting to lighten the mood.

"Don't think too much, and don't believe everything you think," he replied, encouraging me to let the thoughts drift by without holding onto them.

I admire Peter's approach to his thoughts. He meditates regularly, and even on the Camino, he makes time for it early in the morning or just before bed. He's learned to observe his thoughts without getting caught up in them. In contrast, I noticed how easily my thoughts still stirred up my emotions.

We continued walking together, and I shared with Peter how the taste of apples reminded me of my childhood. It led us to talk about our early years. Peter's parents moved to Melbourne from Buford, a small town in western Victoria, when he was just a year old. He was the eldest of six children, with three sisters and two brothers, all born in Melbourne. He and his sister, Josephine, two years his junior, often spent time with their maternal grandparents in Ararat, a larger town in western Victoria near Buford. Peter spoke fondly of his grandmother, who was gentle and kind, making him feel like a favourite grandson. He grew up in a home with two parents who loved each other. They had moved to Melbourne to build their own family life. His mother, a nurse, was devoted to her children. Both his parents have since passed away, but he cherishes the memories of them dearly.

I mentioned to Peter that the Meseta reminded me of the region where I spent my childhood, though I didn't bring up the intense feelings and anger stirring within me. We had talked about our upbringings before, and Peter had noticed how unsettled those memories sometimes made me. He often encouraged me to stay present and not dwell too much on the past. Despite being born on different continents and raised in completely different worlds, we shared common ground—we came from large families with many siblings and faced similar financial struggles.

I started telling Peter about my parents again. Although I'd shared some of these stories before, in that moment, I felt compelled to revisit them and bring those memories back to life. I wasn't sure why events that happened even before I was born felt so significant now. Maybe they gave me a fuller picture of who I am, grounding me in my background and helping me understand the path my life had taken. I focused on the stories themselves.

My parents married in 1954, coming from different villages. My mother, Todorka, was twenty-two, and my father, Bele, was nineteen. It was common then for men to marry women slightly older than themselves. My father was encouraged to marry young so there would be someone to tend the land while he completed his compulsory military service, which lasted two and a half years. For those in the villages, this was how life was—the land was everything, vital to survival and central to my family's existence.

Unlike Peter's mother, who embraced having a large family, my mother never wanted more than two children, regardless of gender. Shortly after her wedding, she became pregnant, and my sister, Petra, was born prematurely, surviving only a few days. Petra's name was rarely mentioned, almost as if she had never existed. Sometimes, I wonder if they would have mourned her more deeply had she been a boy, given the significance placed on gender, especially at that time. Who knows?

Sensing my mood shifting and the anxiety creeping in, Peter gently tried to steer the conversation in a different direction.

"I just don't understand why people worry so much about a child's gender," I said, almost rhetorically.

"My love," he replied softly, "your story sounds more like something from my great-grandparents' time. Don't dwell on the past and family traditions—stay here, in the present."

I tried to follow Peter's advice and stay in the present, but memories from the past surged up, coming straight from my heart. I felt compelled to step back, even a little, to look directly at the thoughts stirring my emotions.

I felt I was listening to my mother and what she went through. After my father went to the army and returned, my mother faced years of unwanted pregnancies and children. She had never wanted a large family. Growing up with three siblings, her own needs were often unmet. She likely wished for a different life for her children, or perhaps she didn't want more than two kids, but she never openly expressed her feelings about having more children.

After my two older sisters were born in 1958 and 1960, my mother didn't want any more children. However, living with her in-laws, under the authority of a mother-in-law who ran the household and always insisted on what she thought was best, my mother had little control. In a rural village without access to proper guidance or contraception and being illiterate, she endured by doing what she was told—just as many women of that time did.

And then she got pregnant with me. She was not pleased and made it clear she did not want any more children, regardless of gender. On the other hand, my grandmother, a wise and strong-willed woman who had my father under her thumb until she died, had different plans. She couldn't imagine the family without an heir. My parents had to have a boy. Even my other grandmother, another strong woman, got involved. She came one day and raised her voice, telling my paternal grandmother that her daughter was not a 'machine' for making children and shouldn't be forced to have more after this pregnancy. Did my paternal grandmother let this happen? No. She persisted until she got what she wanted: a son for the family.

Like my sisters, I was born at home in 1962. The village was twenty-five kilometres from the city, and most women gave birth at home then. My grandmother acted as the midwife, helping my mum deliver all of us. Everyone waited to see the baby's gender. My mom said she didn't care, but knowing my persistent grandmother, I didn't believe her. Her frequent introduction of me as 'the girl we didn't want' contradicted her claim.

My grandmother was devastated. She had somehow believed that God would grant her a grandson, but it didn't happen. She couldn't hide her tears and retreated to another room, crying uncontrollably. This religious woman, who rarely missed church and Sunday services, cried and asked God what she had done wrong to deserve this punishment. She even prayed for God to take me. "We do not need a girl. We need a boy. Please take her." I heard the story of my birth many times throughout my childhood and adulthood.

The weight of these memories became overwhelming, and the pain felt unbearable. I stopped at the path's edge and realized I was quietly sobbing, unable to hold back the tears. I was grateful that Peter was far enough ahead, giving me the solitude I needed. I had suppressed this pain throughout my childhood and even into adulthood. As a young girl, I remember listening to other girls talk about the joyful stories their parents told them and the happiness they felt from those moments. I never wanted any of my friends to know the difficult story surrounding my birth.

I watched Peter walking off in the distance. There weren't many other pilgrims around, and I felt alone—a feeling I welcomed. I was processing something deeply personal, something stirring from within.

I thought, *Probably Peter is right! These thoughts have nothing to do with reality and belong to the previous century.* However, I was raised by a person who belonged to the previous generation. I couldn't stop going back more than half a century and digging into the past. The mixed feelings of anger, sadness and anxiety surged through my body. It felt like I could hear my grandmother's voice.

"I sinned. I made a big sin," my grandmother had said, looking at me sadly. "Because of you."

What did I do? Did I cause my aunt's death? the thought struck me.

I looked at her, feeling disappointed and sad. We both knew about the sin my grandmother was referring to. I loved her and didn't want her to be unhappy. I felt guilty.

I was around eight or nine years old, and we were still mourning my aunt, my dad's sister, who had died from cancer. She was thirty-nine and left four children behind.

I hugged my grandmother, and my tiny heart cried inside me.

"I will never disappoint anyone. I will always love my family. I should be grateful to be alive," I promised myself. Silently, I begged God to forgive my grandmother. Looking back, I realised this was time when the 'people-pleaser' in me was born. I learned to make myself invisible, avoiding any chance of upsetting those around me.

As I walked, the memories unfolded. The drama did not stop with my birth. It had just begun. After I was born, my mother became very sick and spent most of her time visiting doctors and hospitals. They were unable to find what was wrong with her. Did she feel guilty for giving girls instead of boys to the family? Was she worried that she had to have another child? Or what if the next child was a girl again? Probably all of these and much more. My grandfather took care of us children, during that time, and I loved him wholeheartedly, while my father and grandmother rushed my mum from one doctor to another.

In the meantime, my mother got pregnant again. She did not like the child she was carrying, as she often stated with guilt in her voice. This guilt persisted, and she and my brother never built a bond as mother and son, no matter how hard my mum tried. She wanted to have an abortion and get rid of the baby. My father was gentle and respectful toward my mum.

My grandmother, who had cried for a grandson, stood by my mother and ensured the baby was born. One of the doctors told my mum that he believed she was carrying a boy. Did the doctor know my mother was carrying a boy, or did he say it to make her feel better? Who knows? Finally, my brother was born. You can guess who the happiest person was. My grandmother got what she wanted.

She thanked God for listening to her prayers. "I do not need anything more. I will refuse even if you want to give me the whole world. My grandson is my world." I remember these sentences because I often heard them repeated during my childhood.

I do not know how the stories about his coming into this world affected my brother. We never talked about the past, and we hardly see each other. We were never close as children, especially the two of us. As adults, we became completely distant.

My brother's birth filled my grandmother's heart with joy, and I'm sure my mother was happy, too. But she knew her place and who made the decisions in the family, a reality that left lasting marks on her. A gentle and quiet woman, my mother spent her life as a passive presence—often a pushover, sometimes passive-aggressive—seen but rarely heard. We, her children, never sought out her opinions (if she even voiced them). I saw her as a broken woman, unable to live independently, withdrawn into her world, with little interest in anything, including her children. She didn't form a close relationship with any of us.

As for my father, I don't believe she was close to him either. I never saw them fighting, talking, or laughing together, unlike my grandparents, who were very close and always had something to discuss. In our home, we turned to my grandmother or father for anything we needed. Asking my mother for help seemed pointless; she would send me to my grandmother or father.

Many times, I was angry at my mother for being like that. I wanted to see a strong woman in her, a strong mother able to make decisions, protect and discipline her children, or fight for her children. My grandmother had other children and grandchildren. From an early age, I felt that something was wrong, something that no one talked openly about, and that affected us all and had long-lasting consequences. Many years passed before I saw who my mother was and the role she played in our upbringing.

The village appeared before us, and I saw Peter waiting for me. I was relieved to return to reality and stop thinking about the past. He smiled and hugged me.

"How do you feel, my dream girl?" he asked, gently kissing my forehead.

Peter often uses this expression, calling me his "dream girl". Not long after we met, he told me that, as a young man, he had dreamed of meeting someone with a personality like mine. I could easily say the same about him. I never imagined it was possible to find a partner who truly accepted me as I am, someone who felt like both a companion and a match on so many levels.

"I'm fine, my darling. I like the weather. It looks perfect for walking. I'm sorry for being such a slow walker."

Peter smiled as usual. "Don't worry. Take your time and enjoy the walk."

We continued walking, and my thoughts drifted to Peter. As the eldest child, he had always needed to forge his path. At fourteen, he joined a cadet program, and his career in the army suited him well. He married young, balancing work and studies, and earned most of his qualifications while working. Even before his wedding, he sensed they weren't a good match, but, as he said, "I didn't like leaving her before the altar."

Peter's stories resonated with my own. Like him, I worked my way through university, supporting myself along the way, and my marriage experience had similarities. However, I don't think I was as brave as he was for a long time. After his marriage ended, Peter turned inward, trying to understand himself better. Those years were tough, as he sometimes states, especially with two teenagers and younger children under ten. Eventually, he reached a point where he couldn't continue living that way and boldly decided to start fresh.

Thinking of Peter made me reflect on how easily someone like him could be lost or how sometimes even the best personalities don't always align. Relationships are complex, and finding the right partner feels like a matter of luck or destiny.

"You are such a lovely man, Peter. I am so happy to have you in my life," I said, smiling.

Peter smiled back. "I'm the lucky one, my sweetheart," he said, walking at his pace.

I felt a heaviness in my head as if the weight of my thoughts had become too much to bear. I was relieved to talk to a few pilgrims along the way, including our Camino friends from Serbia. I truly enjoyed our conversation, and their culture played a big part. I admired their strong sense of commitment to one another. Despite their varying ages—ranging from thirty to sixty—eleven of them stuck together, always waiting for each other and offering support. They told us they had booked an albergue in Hornillos, a village along the route. We, however, planned to walk a few kilometres further to Isar, a place slightly off the Camino route.

We passed through the village of Tardajos, but there was no place for breakfast. I couldn't believe we still hadn't had our morning meal after walking eight kilometres. It felt as if I had walked into a different time and place. My thoughts distracted me, making me forget to check the map or count the kilometres. We still had two more kilometres to the next village where we could rest, and I looked forward to that.

I let Peter walk ahead and sank back into my thoughts, picking up where they had left off. They flowed through my heart and mind like a river. I enjoyed being with my thoughts, alone, drifting as deep as my memories would take me.

My grandmother cared for us for most of our childhood while my parents and grandfather worked in the fields. The only 'treasure' our family possessed was land. When my grandparents married, they used the golden coins given as wedding presents to buy land. I hardly saw my parents. They left early in the morning at dawn and came back at dusk.

We lived in a small house in the central part of the village. My father and grandfather built it the year I was born. The house was simple, made of stones, with three small rooms and one large room meant to accommodate many people. This large room was called the guest room. The floor was dirt, and in the middle was a heater used for heating and cooking in the winter. A few metres from the house was a small one-room building called the bakery, with a built-in oven and a fireplace in another corner. We baked bread there and did all the significant cooking. All of us children were born in that small room, usually warm and cozy. The house was sold after we moved to the city, and it still exists, though no one lives there now.

We spent most of our time in one room, where my grandparents slept. All the children shared a big, uncomfortable wooden bed in another small room. My parents slept in another room that I hardly remember entering. Whenever we needed help, we called for our grandmother. As a young girl, I feared something would happen to her, our primary caregiver and attachment figure. I did not have that same feeling for my mother. I wasn't close to my parents at all. I don't think any of us children were. I felt like just a number, one of the children.

Was it like that because it was a different time? Having given the family a boy, my mother felt she had completed her duty and did not take much responsibility for raising her children. Did she have children against her wishes? Perhaps she thought, *You wanted children, and I accomplished my task. Now look after them.* Only my mother would know the answers to these questions. However, she never talked openly about anything. It seemed she hid and suppressed everything within herself and expressed it in words unrelated to reality.

These thoughts still leave me feeling unsettled. Growing up, we were taught to keep everything inside—to suppress our feelings and avoid speaking openly or honestly. Throughout my marriage, I often felt like my mother, repeating the patterns I had witnessed. But unlike her, I found joy in my children, work, and small moments of life. I tried to accept my situation, smile, and pretend happiness.

I built a strong bond with both of my daughters. My work with children brought immense satisfaction. I developed positive relationships with many of my students, often going above and beyond to help them reach their potential. I could easily recognise students who came from similar upbringings to mine. Sharing my experiences, I encouraged them to persevere in their education, especially those navigating the challenges of VCE. I never stopped emphasizing the importance of building a career and striving for independence.

When it came to my marriage, I spent a long time trying to fix it, but eventually, I gave up. There were nights when I silently cried in bed, masking my pain with a smile during the day. It was a relief when I finally broke that cycle and began seeing things as they were.

These days, I can see my mother always present in our upbringing, but with her mind absent. I often asked myself if my mother was always like that—living in her world, not taking responsibility, and doing whatever anyone asked, even us, her children. Was she unhappy? Why did she not connect with any of us? She never developed a bond with my brother. Later, she tried hard to show him that he was special, to show her love, but somehow it did not work. The two of them remained distant for many years. On the other hand, I saw, and still see, our distant, reserved, often indifferent mother as our rock, silently watching over us from a distance. As a child, this confused me deeply.

Chapter 8

The Struggles of Growing Up

"Strength and growth only come through continuous effort and struggle."

Napoleon Hill

It was still the 20th of July, and we knew that the distances between villages on the Meseta could sometimes stretch beyond ten kilometres. We had a kilometre to reach the next town called Rabe de las Calzadas, where we could finally rest and grab a bite. The weather was perfect for walking, and I didn't feel tired despite having already covered seven kilometres. Oddly, I hadn't noticed much of the scenery either. My mind was entirely absorbed in my thoughts. Along the way, we saw a few familiar pilgrims we'd met before and seeing them again felt like reuniting with old friends. Peter and I talked about the Meseta and compared it to places in Australia. We'd travelled a lot through the Australian countryside, but the landscape here differed entirely from anything we'd encountered along the Camino route.

"Peter, did we see any schools?" I asked. We had seen churches, cathedrals, and various buildings, but none that looked like a school.

"No, I didn't. You're right. The schools are probably not on the Camino route," Peter replied.

I asked Peter how he was feeling during the walk. He said he felt relaxed and was enjoying the journey through the Meseta. Walking through the flat terrain seemed to ease the strain on his body. He also mentioned how helpful the hiking poles were. "I don't think I'd be able to manage without them," I added. Evidence shows that hiking poles can reduce up to thirty per cent of the body's weight on the legs, making them invaluable for long distances.

"It's our thirteenth day walking and the first day through Meseta. Hopefully, the weather will hold. Whatever it is, it is," Peter said, checking the distance to the next destination on his phone.

We took our time and continued walking on our own. I drifted in my thoughts.

Somehow, my thoughts became my new companions. I liked my memories, regardless of the emotions and feelings they triggered. I began reflecting on the start of my school life. It felt like opening closed containers in my mind filled with drama or unaddressed past issues. Asking about schools in Spain made me think about my schooling.

It was September 1st, 1968, the first day of school in Macedonia. My two older sisters were getting ready. I wanted to go to school, too, but the teacher did not enrol me and left me to start the following year. I was six years and seven months old, and I felt more than ready. My begging and crying did not help. My mother tried convincing me that the teacher told her I was too young and had to wait another year. Later, during my school life, when I was the oldest student in the class, I realised I was right all along, but my parents and the teacher did not follow the school policy on the age for starting school. I always remember that day. I cried a lot and, with a broken heart, continued my boring childhood. Nowadays, I see my simple, often monotonous childhood as a time that helped me develop self-awareness early on.

As I stated before, education wasn't a priority in our family. Only my father and grandfather were literate. My grandfather, born in 1903, grew up when Macedonia was under the Turkish Empire, and education was not a concern, especially in remote villages. Daily life was consumed by survival, poverty, and struggle. Being involved in wars and trade made basic literacy and numeracy essential for men. My grandfather learned what he needed to get by.

My father was born in 1935 and completed four years of primary school during WWII. He initially studied in Serbian because from

1913 to 1944, Vardar Macedonia was part of the Serbian Kingdom. However, due to shifts in control during the war, his education and surname on school certificates changed from Murgovic (Serbian) to Murgov (Bulgarian). This instability significantly impacted people's lives, especially their education.

After WWII, when Macedonia became a republic within Yugoslavia, education stabilised somewhat. Children were taught in their mother tongue. In small villages like Puturus, schools offered Grades 1 to 4 education. After Grade 4, children had to walk to neighbouring towns to continue to Grade 8.

My father did well in school and continued to Grade 5 in another village, requiring a seven-kilometre walk each way. During the winter, he fell seriously ill with the flu. Worried, my grandmother forbade him from continuing his education.

As the only son and youngest child born after three sisters, my grandmother overprotected my father and believed he was born to look after his parents. True to her belief, my father prioritised his parents, loved and respected them, and remained a right-hand man for my grandmother. My grandmother made most of the decisions in our family, and my father dutifully followed her lead.

My mother is almost illiterate. She learned to read later in life but still struggles with it. She often says with regret, "In our village, there was a school very close to our house, but I found learning difficult. I disliked attending school, and my mother did not let me continue."

This situation was common at the time, especially where I came from. Many women were illiterate. None of my dad's sisters could read or write. Girls worked in the fields during spring, summer, and autumn, and in winter, they worked with wool, learning to make clothes, cook, weave, do housework, prepare for marriage, and care for children. Despite the school being next to her house, my mother only attended for less than two years.

My maternal grandmother was overprotective of my mother, who never seemed to grow up fully, either before or after marriage. My mother tried to instil this same attitude in us, affecting some of my siblings. As a child, I felt my mother wanted to raise us like she was. She protected us from taking risks and struggled to guide us. Looking back on that time makes me think how scary and insecure young children feel when there is no guidance and how this dysfunctionality can easily pass from one generation to the other.

I am grateful that I recognised my family's attitude toward education early on. I pursued my dreams, seeing education as my future from a young age. I don't believe my family's indifference to education affected me much. However, I felt robbed of my childhood. Deep in myself, I felt like an adult. I thought I was making decisions for myself when I wasn't ready.

Reflecting on my parents makes me think of the students I've taught over the years who were overprotected by their parents, preventing them from taking risks and overcoming challenges. Many of them struggled to engage in the learning process. As a teacher, I did my best to help. Seeing students make changes, progress, and break free from difficult family situations was gratifying. Unfortunately, some students remained trapped in the same cycle, finding it hard to escape. I often feel that some families repeat patterns until someone breaks the dysfunctionality and creates a new path.

When I was young, I often felt frustrated that my parents didn't prioritise education or pay more attention to us. This feeling lingered even into adulthood. However, looking back, I realise they were focused on meeting our basic needs, and it must have been hard to think about things they couldn't afford. Many parents raise their children the way their parents raised them, doing the best they can with the knowledge and skills they have. My parents were no exception. I recognized this pattern in myself as a parent. Parenting is where support and guidance are crucial—not just during the early years but throughout a child's development.

My thoughts returned to my younger self, the little girl with big dreams. Finally, on September 1, 1969, I started Grade 1. I don't think anyone was happier than me. I had found a place where I felt I belonged. It's no wonder I spent fifty-two years at school as a student and teacher and am still there, enjoying every moment.

It was a composite class encompassing Grades 1 through 4, totalling sixteen children. I knew most of the children, especially those in my grade. Our teacher's name was Tajan. I never knew his surname, as we addressed teachers as 'nastavnik' for males and 'nastavnicka' for females. Tajan was a tall man and extremely strict. I attended that school from Grade 1 to Grade 3, and I can't recall a day when someone wasn't punished, usually with physical force, mainly for not progressing academically. The classroom was consistently quiet, and my memory of Jagoda stands out most vividly. She was a year younger than me and left-handed. Jagoda, a left-handed girl, was constantly coerced to write with her right hand and physically reprimanded for not complying. Eventually, she started wetting herself and developed a stutter. It was heartbreaking to witness.

I was only struck once by Tajan. It was in Grade 1 when I forgot my homework book at home. He slapped me twice and shouted at me, instructing me to go back home and retrieve it. I left school crying uncontrollably. When I returned with the book, my grandmother vowed to speak with him. That afternoon, she confronted him as he passed our house on his way home. After that encounter, he never laid a hand on me again.

On another occasion, one of my siblings in Grade 3 was asked to solve a math problem on the green board but didn't know the answer. The teacher became enraged, grabbed her by the hair, and repeatedly banged her head against the board. She cried, and I cried too, feeling helpless. I wished he had hit me instead of her. That moment remains etched in my memory as one of profound pain, more so than when he struck me. Even now, recalling it brings tears to my eyes. I've always been grateful and indebted to my grandmother for protecting me and standing up for me during those difficult times.

Teachers wielded immense authority and power in those days. Parents lacked the confidence to challenge or stand up for their children against educators. They often respected the teacher's judgments and considered their disciplinary actions appropriate. Many children hesitated to report physical abuse at school to their parents, fearing blame or further punishment. There was a joking saying that physical punishment came from heaven. At times, misbehaving children at home were threatened by their parents with notification to the teacher for punishment. Some parents even permitted teachers to discipline their children if they didn't heed instructions physically. Most children felt they were left to fend for themselves. Some parents kept that attitude even when I worked as a teacher in Macedonia. Instead of taking responsibility and building a positive relationship with the children, they gave the teachers that responsibility.

Despite my deep love for my family—parents, grandparents, and siblings—I believed that I was alone and only I could protect myself. This feeling persisted throughout my life. From a young age, like many girls, I dreamed of having a loving husband and children whom I could cherish wholeheartedly and always support. I pledged to study diligently, educate myself and be there for my children. Even as a child, I believed children deserved protection, a voice, and understanding. While I often felt my parents didn't fully assume responsibility or engage fully in our upbringing, my father frequently reminded me that they did their best with what they knew.

The school was in an open area surrounded by fields at the village's edge. It was a modest building with one classroom and two small rooms. In contrast to my home's dirt floor, the school had a wooden floor, requiring us to remove our shoes before entering the classroom. Through its windows, we could see the vast fields reminiscent of Maseta.

I enjoyed going to school, though I often feared making mistakes that might anger my teacher. I strove to do my best, finding cursive writing particularly challenging. In Grade 2, the teacher began assigning me reading books, marking the start of my journey into literature and identification with book heroes. During Grades 2 and 3, the teacher occasionally brought his two to three-year-old daughter, Valentina, to school. He entrusted me with the responsibility to read to her and look after her in another room. I felt privileged and happy to spend time with Valentina in this special role.

Chapter 9

Guiding Lights

"Experience is the teacher of all things."

Julius Ceasar

We arrived in the village of Rabe de las Calzadas and found a cozy bar where we could rest. I ordered a freshly squeezed orange juice while Peter enjoyed a cold beer with olives and nuts. This break was what we'd been looking forward to. At the next table, an elderly mother sat with her son, helping her with her meal. He spoke some English, and we enjoyed chatting with them. I was again moved by the warmth and care Spaniards show for their elderly loved ones.

This scene brought back memories of my father and grandmother, and a pang of sadness surfaced as I thought of my mother. I don't think my brother and she shared many moments like the one I witnessed. I saw her struggles firsthand during the fifteen years she lived near me. She never judged, blamed or criticized us, accepting her children as we were. I don't think she expected anything from anyone, yet I always sensed that my brother held a special place in her heart.

My paternal grandmother would never have allowed that kind of separation. She knew how to keep her children and family close. All her children respected her as a thoughtful, intelligent and wise woman who knew what she wanted. But that didn't mean her choices always reflected what was best for everyone. Though illiterate and having never attended school, she possessed a wealth of knowledge gained from life and experience. If any of us—my brother or we girls—felt close to someone, it would have been her.

As Peter scrolled through his mobile phone, my thoughts drifted back to my grandmother, who passed away in 1985 when I was twenty-three. Her name was Sana—a name I've rarely heard elsewhere. She was born in 1901 in Bonche, near Puturus, where she married. Her birth certificate recorded only the year, without a specific date. She lost her father at a young age under unusual circumstances. While walking through the hills, he drank from a spring and swallowed something—perhaps a small snake or lizard—that left him in agony for two days before he passed, leaving behind his wife and five children—three daughters and two sons.

When my grandmother was about ten or eleven, she and her younger sister visited an uncle nearby, intending to stay for a few days. But the Balkan War broke out, making it too dangerous to return home, and they ended up staying with their uncle for three years. My grandmother remained deeply grateful to her uncle's wife, who treated them like her own children.

As a teenager, she survived the deadly virus. Towards the end of World War I and afterwards, the Spanish flu spread among the soldiers and population of Macedonia. Her village was severely affected, and she lost her eldest brother. My grandmother would often recount with sadness, "He was just married. Before he died, he asked his wife to dress up as a bride, and soon after seeing her, he died." Her stories were filled with sorrow over the losses she experienced.

Her youngest sister also died after two weeks. My grandmother often told me I reminded her of that sister, who passed away at around ten years old. She mentioned her sister many times, especially when giving me something. She survived the flu with her mother, older brother, and younger sister.

"During that time, some families disappeared entirely; everyone died, and it was hard to find people to bury them," she would say. Her stories reminded me of COVID-19.

Her life was marked by survival, much like many people in Macedonia at that time. From a young age, she experienced loss and grief. She lived through the period when Macedonia was under the Turkish Empire, the Balkan Wars, World War I, and World War II. During WWII, Vardar Macedonia became a republic within the Yugoslavian Federation. Though she didn't understand politics much, she often said she experienced freedom. She used to say, "You were born in heaven. You do not know what it means—life without freedom."

She married my grandfather, the eldest son among two other brothers, through a matchmaker known in Macedonian as 'so svodnik'. She was in her early twenties and saw him only once before the wedding. They had three daughters and one son, with my father being the youngest. She never used contraception and never had an abortion. She lived with presence and wisdom. I never heard her raise her voice or express enormous anger. She was a good listener, and her word was always final. She did not tolerate disrespect from anyone. If she wasn't the 'head', she was undoubtedly the 'neck' of our family. My grandparents lived in harmony with much respect and died six months apart in their eighties, just as they wanted. My grandfather passed away first, and six months later, my grandmother followed. They had a beautiful life together.

We left the bar, and I stopped questioning why these memories were resurfacing. The stories, told repeatedly over the years, were deeply ingrained in my mind. I accepted them as a normal part of my thoughts, letting whatever came to mind unfold without fear, judgment, or anger.

Does this endless open space trigger my thoughts? Do the vast fields, the sky, and the quiet surroundings try to bring me back to my roots? Who knows? I wondered. I felt the presence of my family and those who had played significant roles in my life. It was as if they were with me or close by. I wasn't sure what was happening. As the pilgrims passed, we greeted each other with "Buen Camino" or "Hola," each lost in their thoughts or enjoying the present and the magnificent landscape around us.

We came upon a small church. A nun came out and placed two blessed Virgin Mary Miraculous Medals on strings around our necks. We greeted her back and decided to step inside. Another nun was there. We used some coins to light the electric candles and gave our credentials/passports to get stamped. The nuns were so kind and welcoming.

"Wear them to Santiago de Compostela. They will protect you, my children," said one of them.

I felt tears in my eyes. They hugged us, and we hugged them back. It felt like embracing someone very close to me. Their faces were so gentle and kind, full of love, ready to give this love to any stranger passing through on this mystical journey. We kept our promise and wore those medals all the way. Moments like this would stay with us forever.

We walked another several kilometres, approaching the next village, Hornillos. I felt that most of the pilgrims we met that day stayed in albergues in Hornillos. When booking accommodation, we couldn't find a hostel offering a private room. I told Peter I wished to stay there and end the walk for that day. I knew the town where we had booked accommodation, Isar, was more than four kilometres from the Camino route. We saw our Serbian friends entering their albergue in Hornillos and exchanging smiles.

"Darling, I wish we could stay here. I don't feel like walking another four kilometres," I admitted to Peter.

"It would be nice if we were lucky enough to find a private room," he replied thoughtfully. "If you like, we can have lunch here, and I'll call the accommodation in Isar."

I nodded in agreement, and we found a bench outside a small food shop. After buying sandwiches, we sat down to eat. As we lingered, Peter checked his emails.

"It's almost two p.m.," he noted, looking up with a hint of excitement. "We can be picked up from here—we don't need to walk the rest of the way. And tomorrow, they'll bring us back here to the route. I need to call the accommodation now!"

I was overjoyed. We would have time to relax and do our washing earlier than usual. Reducing our walk by four to five kilometres made a big difference. After Peter called the provided phone number, someone arrived within ten minutes, picked us up, and drove us to the nearest village, Isar. A few other women were in the van, but I wasn't sure if they were pilgrims or guests at the so called hotel. Although the location seemed remote, the accommodation was lovely—a spacious, beautiful room on the second floor. We accepted the offer to have dinner in the restaurant. I didn't feel drained that day, having walked around twenty-two kilometres. My thoughts must have distracted me from the distance. We relaxed and did our washing, as we did every evening. Most of the time, the clothes dried or nearly dried by the next day.

At seven o'clock, we went down for dinner. To our surprise, Mary appeared. We hadn't known that she was staying in Isar. We hugged her, delighted to see her. Mary introduced us to another pilgrim, Virginia, a seventy-six-year-old American woman. I was impressed by Virginia and her spirit. She was a former yoga teacher walking sections of the Camino. It was lovely to have dinner and chat with Mary and Virginia; both were inspirational ladies.

The dinner was delicious—a three-course meal and a glass of vino. I don't think I've had so much vino in my life. Peter and I usually don't drink or only drink socially, but in Spain, having a glass of vino was quite acceptable. It reminded me of my family and our relationship with alcohol, especially vino. We always had a big barrel of vino at home, mainly to offer to guests. None of us children were interested in alcohol. I enjoyed a glass of vino here and there in Spain.

Besides the pilgrims, locals were in the bar, socialising and chatting. I thought about the villages we had passed. They all looked well-maintained and self-sufficient. The people seemed relaxed. I reflected on all the pilgrims walking and the locals supporting them. The mutual support likely helped the pilgrimage and the towns coexist harmoniously.

We talked with Mary and Virginia about the next day. We had booked to leave the accommodation at six-thirty. Mary said she would have breakfast and leave at seven.

We planned to follow our routine, usually having our first breakfast or coffee between eight-thirty and nine, after a two-hour walk. Walking through the Meseta would be different, as the distances between the towns are longer. We wished Mary and Virginia a good night and went to bed.

Chapter 10

Echoes of the Past

"No photos – just memories."

It was the 21st of July. We got ready in the morning and went downstairs at six-thirty a.m. A lady we saw for the first time drove us back to Hornillos, where we had been picked up the previous day. It was a short drive, less than ten minutes. We didn't see Mary and Virginia that morning; they planned to start walking later. Most pilgrims began hiking around seven a.m.

Our next destination was Castrojeriz, approhimatelly a twenty one-kilometre walk ahead of us, and the weather was expected to be hot. I knew we would have to walk another few kilometres as the accommodation we booked was on the other side of the village. The thought of the distance was daunting. The last ten kilometres were always the most challenging. After such a long distance, everything hurt. I kept positive, thinking, *Everything will be all right. I'll have plenty of time to think and reflect.*

Peter and I planned to take short breaks and cover most of the distance before lunch, before the midday heat. We also decided to use our self-stick-umbrellas for shade. They can be easily fixed to our pack bags and was very convenient as allowed to use our hiking poles. When Peter ordered them, I wasn't entirely convinced we needed umbrellas. But now, I was glad he had insisted on getting one for each of us.

As usual, we passed through Hornillos and began walking together before gradually settling into our own pace and retreating into our thoughts. Once I found myself alone, I was again lost in my reflections. I enjoyed the morning sun and the scenery. The villages in Spain continued to impress me. Perhaps because of their location on the Camino route, they were self-sufficient enough to support pilgrims.

My thoughts drifted back to the village where I was born and spent the first ten years of my childhood. I marvelled at how we had survived. It was more than fifty years ago. My memories were so vivid that it felt like I was reliving those days, experiencing my family's struggle for survival.

Life in the village was incredibly challenging. I wondered how we and our ancestors had managed to survive for centuries. We lived in the nineteenth century rather than the twentieth.

One of the most basic needs, water, was a constant struggle. When I was young, there were probably twenty families, or around two hundred to two hundred and fifty people living in the village. Dirt and dust were everywhere.

The town was on a hill, and a narrow, steep path led to the primitive tap where drinking water was available. This single water tap served the entire village and was a five to ten-minute walk from our house. The water came from the mountains and was used without chlorine or filtration.

Like other families, we had clay pots, 'stomni' and 'bardinja' in Macedonian, to keep the water cool and fresh. In summer, many women, girls and children waited hours to fill their clay pots as the water flow slowed. Sometimes, I wanted to ensure we wouldn't be left without water. When temperatures dropped below freezing in winter, we worried the tap would freeze and leave us without water. Fortunately, it never happened. The universe seemed to help us, and the generations before us, survive. We always had fresh water to drink.

One memory that stayed with me was the day I went to fill the clay jars at the village tap. The water was scarce, and I waited long for the jars to fill. As it got dark, I became increasingly aware of the cemetery on the other side of the tap. Once the jars were filled, I started running down the hill. Close to home, I fell and broke the jars. No one was angry about what happened, but I couldn't forgive myself. I cried and felt guilty.

A few families managed to dig wells in their yards. We also had a well, but the area was arid, and often, there wasn't enough water. The water from the well was primarily used for our animals' drinking. We had all sorts of domestic animals: sheep, bulls, cows, horses, farm dogs, cats, chickens and turkeys.

About a half-hour walk from the village was a small creek we called a river. Once or twice a year, my mum and the other village women would wash the big clothes—blankets, coats and rugs, or 'pokrivi', 'diftici' and 'chergi', as we called them in Macedonian. At that time, everything was made from wool at home.

The struggle for water was endless. For centuries, my ancestors and all the villagers depended on the village tap and the creek.

While walking, buried in thoughts, I was greeted by a pilgrim, Kevin from Michigan, with "Buen Camino". We started talking, and Kevin mentioned that he was walking Camino with his wife, Joan, who was walking ahead of him at that moment. We talked about the walk and the challenges we were overcoming. Like us, they stayed in the hostels in private rooms, booking day by day. I asked Kevin what made him walk the Camino. Kevin had wanted to walk the Camino for years, and it took him almost four years to convince Joan to join him. Joan worked as a teacher, and the summer holiday was perfect for the journey. They had tried convincing their daughter, who just finished high school, to walk with them, but she wasn't interested. Later, I met Joan, and she was lovely. Peter and I encountered the couple a few more times along the way.

After walking more than ten kilometres, we arrived in the village of Hontanas. We found a bar and managed to sit inside. Many of the pilgrims we had met before on their way to Castrojeriz were there, and it was nice to see them again. Most of them walked faster than I did, but I didn't mind. Some of them were still lingering in the bar. These stops had become my favourite part of the journey. However, I noticed that my tiredness kept me from talking, even to Peter. We sat silently, each lost in our thoughts about the long walk ahead. Despite our plan for short breaks, our rest stretched to over an hour. We listened to our bodies, knowing we'd already covered more than ten kilometres. It was always difficult to get back into motion after such a long rest, but it was all part of the journey.

After a good rest and a refreshing coffee and breakfast to recharge, we continued our walk. As we left Hontanas, I talked to Peter about our next rest stop. Peter also seemed tired. I could feel the hot sweat covering my body. Just thinking about the kilometres ahead made me feel even more exhausted. But Peter's positive energy somehow lifted my spirits, encouraging me to stay focused and take it one step at a time.

After some period walking together, I found myself alone. Somehow, I liked being alone with my thoughts. I started to feel peaceful and again thought about my grandmother, who played a significant role in me and my siblings' lives. I don't believe I ever truly dedicated time to reflect on her. I didn't think much about her after she died or see her in my dreams. However, I learned much from her actions, more than her words. Some things were seemingly irrelevant, like properly cutting chicken meat pieces.

My grandmother often talked about her family and moments when she fought for what was right. One significant moment was when my father was born. At that time, the godfather strictly gave the child a name. However, my grandmother had a name she liked and wanted to call her son by the name she chose, which was very progressive and unacceptable then. Mothers were not even allowed to attend the church during the child's baptism when the godfather announced the child's name for the first time. She enlisted her sister-in-law's help to tell the godfather the name she wanted for her son. My father received the name Bele, an ancient and unusual name. I have never met anyone with that name, and I do not blame my grandmother for wanting to change it. Someone in the family a long time ago had that name. The sister-in-law tried to convince the godfather, but he was adamant about his choice.

When my grandmother discovered the name given to her son, she decided to call him Kire instead of Bele. She told everyone the name she chose and instructed her daughters not to reveal the godfather's name. Everyone called my father Kire for a few months, and everything seemed fine until my grandmother had a very spooky dream one night. In her dream, which felt like reality, she saw a tall woman dressed in black with a jar walking toward her and asking how she was. My grandmother proudly replied that she was happy and feeding her son, Kire. The woman told her to call the boy by his real name, warning that she would take the baby otherwise. My grandmother woke up petrified, fearing something terrible would happen to my father. The next morning, she told everyone to call my father Bele, the name the godfather gave him. She accepted the name and never complained or blamed anyone.

I recognised a part of my grandmother in myself. While fiercely persistent in my youth, I learned the value of acceptance—embracing what cannot be changed over time. I likely learned this lesson most profoundly from my mother. She was the only person I knew who accepted life and maintained a deep connection to her inner self.
As my thoughts flowed, they made the walk easier and served as a welcome distraction. Returning to the present moment felt refreshing. I suddenly realised I had covered several more kilometres without noticing.

In the distance, I spotted Peter adjusting his umbrella, trying to get it just right. He was waiting for me. As I caught up, I noticed the landscape had changed. We were now walking through rolling hills with almost no trees or shade.

Peter offered to help fix my umbrella, but I assured him I could manage without it. We walked side by side, exchanging only a few words. Fatigue had settled over us, making the conversation feel like an effort. With so many kilometres ahead and few opportunities to rest, we focused on putting one foot in front of the other.

Memories resurfaced as I walked, returning to when my father left to work in Germany. It was a period of change, as our lifestyle and financial situation shifted slightly.

The year I started school, my father and two other men from the village went to work in Germany. I missed him deeply, although I didn't see much of him before he left. I remember him working tirelessly in the fields or going to the city markets to sell and buy goods. It was only during dinner that I got to see him. I wasn't close to my father, but I greatly respected and trusted him. We all missed him greatly. I still recall the hard work my mother and grandfather put in. We had no machines or tractors to aid farming; everything was done by hand. To this day, I marvel at how my family and many others survived. They worked relentlessly from early morning until late night, except on Sundays or religious holidays.

Walking alongside the sunflower fields and vineyards of the Meseta, I felt transported back to my childhood, wandering through fields and dusty paths to bring lunch to my mum and grandpa. It felt like the whole village was out working and harvesting. My grandmother was always at home, cooking and caring for us. As I walked, waves of emotion washed over me, stirred by the striking similarities to those cherished memories.

I wish I had at least one photo of me from that time. I have no photos of myself before fourth grade because we couldn't afford school photos, or we could probably, but it wasn't prioritised. While my father was in Germany, a photographer took a family photo of us, one just with my mother and brother. The purpose was to send the pictures to my father, but we lost our only photo during a move, and I miss them terribly. They were the only photos from my childhood. The priority back then was having bread on the table. From a young age, I understood that we didn't have money and never asked for anything. Even if I had, I wouldn't have gotten it.

Reflecting on that time made me think about what we prioritise in life. If they had prioritised us, the children, they might have found the money, especially if my grandmother had, since she had the final say. If my mother had considered what was important for her children, we might have those photos now. It seemed like I was judging my family, and my anger stemmed from not prioritising us, the children.

As I walked, I noticed something—anger would occasionally rise within me, snapping me back to reality. The heat was unbearable. I stopped and struggled to open my umbrella. Nearby, under the shade of a tree, I spotted the girl we had met earlier from Belgium, sitting on her sleeping bag. We exchanged a few words. She mentioned she planned to sleep there as it was too hot to walk without shade.

Just then, Peter appeared, coming back to help me adjust the umbrella.

"I can't believe you've been walking without it," he said, securing it to my pack.

"I didn't realise how hot it was," I replied, attempting to lighten the mood. In truth, I probably hadn't noticed at all—I'd been so lost in my thoughts.

The walk felt like a strange blending of time, as though I was shifting between past and present. "There aren't many places to rest or trees for shade," I added.

Peter nodded. "The next stop is the Hospital de San Anton. We still have a lot to walk, so don't forget to drink water and stay hydrated."

Looking around, I noticed how empty the trail felt. Most other pilgrims had already passed this stretch, walking faster, likely rushing to secure a bed at the next albergue. Many hadn't pre-booked their accommodations and faced the pressure of arriving early or walking another ten kilometres to the next village.

I felt relieved knowing we had pre-booked all our stays. It lifted a weight off my shoulders. Not having to hurry or worry about where we would sleep each night was a small but significant comfort in this long, arduous journey.

Peter and I walked together for a while before I naturally fell into my own pace, finding myself alone once again, drifting into the past. It felt like the child within me longed for solitude, pulling me back to memories of my family—the family that once meant everything to me. My thoughts began to swirl around the happy moments we had shared, vivid and comforting, like a warm embrace from the past.

My family was happy, or at least they appeared to be. They didn't know anything better, and I was pleased, too. I remember laughter and storytelling around the table in the evenings, especially before my father left. I loved listening to my father talk about his experiences at the market or elsewhere. We often had guests, neighbours or other people over. My family was extremely welcoming and caring. After my dad left, things changed. Fewer people came by, and we eagerly awaited his letters.

As children, we rarely went anywhere. We only visited my maternal grandparents once a year for their celebration of 'St Nikola.' In Macedonia, it's traditional for every place to have a patron saint celebrated annually. Our village's patron saint was St Dimitri, celebrated on November 8th.

My maternal grandparents lived in another village, about an hour away. My maternal grandfather died before I started school, so I barely remember him. My grandmother lived with my uncle, my mom's eldest brother, and his family. We usually had a sleepover there. My father always taught us how to behave, especially not asking for food before dinner. I was shy and listened to my father, promising to show my best behaviour. I had to, as it was almost the only time we went somewhere, and I didn't want to ruin the opportunity. These visits to my maternal grandmother's house were etched in my memory as the only place we regularly visited once a year. Occasionally, though rarely, we visited my aunt's home, my dad's sister, but I have no clear memory of those visits.

Not asking for food was something that influenced my relationship with food. Being unable to eat in front of others was a challenge that followed me from childhood into adulthood. I was painfully shy about eating in public, convinced all eyes were on me. This insecurity became especially evident when I went to university in Skopje. My boyfriend at the time, Miki—who played a significant role in my life—quickly noticed my avoidance of the student canteen.

When he asked, I admitted that eating in front of so many people made me so anxious that my throat would close up. Miki, ever understanding, tried to encourage me gently.

One day the canteen was packed with students, and he brought us lunch.

"Please, don't force me. I can eat in the room, just not here," I pleaded.

With a kind smile, Miki replied, "I'm not forcing you. Please, try. No one is watching you; they're all focused on their meals." Then, with a playful glint, he added, "Do you know how I *could* get their attention?"

"How?" I asked, intrigued despite myself.

"I'll stand up and start singing," he said with a grin. "If you don't mind, I'll do it now."

We both burst out laughing. I admired Miki's confidence—and so many other things about him. At that moment, he didn't just make me laugh; he helped ease my fear. Little by little, with moments like these, I began to feel comfortable eating in public. Miki had a way of turning my world upside down in the best possible way. The saying that everything happens for a reason, especially when meeting people, couldn't be truer. Meeting Miki brought a new sense of direction to my life.

My thoughts returned to my young me. As a child, I rarely visited the nearest city. The medical clinic was in a village five kilometres away, and we only went there when we were sick. Usually, during the winter, we got the flu, and the doctor often prescribed injections, which terrified me. On the other hand, being sick meant I received attention and felt loved.

The nearest city, Bitola, was twenty-five kilometres from our village. I remember visiting the town once before starting school. My mother and I walked to the next village, where the bus stopped, and we went to the market. I was so happy and excited.

Holding my mum's hand, I saw beautiful plastic strawberries with elastic bands for ponytails. I instantly fell in love and begged my mum to buy them. She said, "Later when we come back." I didn't trust that we would return and that she would buy them for me. At least, I wanted to touch them and feel them in my hands. I went closer to the table with many things for sale. I picked up the plastic strawberries and didn't notice I had let go of my mum's hand. I started looking for her, but she was nowhere to be seen. Scared, I left the strawberries on the table and began crying, calling for my mum. It was market day, and there were many people around. Strangers approached me, tried to calm me down, and advised me to stay and wait for my mum to return. They were right. Shortly after, my mum appeared. I don't know who was more scared, she or me. Happy to be reunited with my mum. I forgot about the strawberries. This moment stayed with me forever.

These thoughts brought me back to the challenges surrounding my family and other people from the village. Going to the city was hard for many people, especially in winter. The closest bus stop was five kilometres away. Winters were very cold, with snow from November until April. Sometimes, there was so much snow that the buses couldn't run.

I remember, one year, the night before Christmas Eve. My parents had gone to the city early in the morning to buy things for Christmas. We waited and waited until late that night for them to come back. We were so worried. I was terrified that something had happened to them. There was so much snow outside. Finally, they arrived after midnight, carrying all the items in their hands and walking twenty-five kilometres from the city to the village. The bus hadn't run because the roads were unsafe. They bought me red rubber boots. Deep down, I didn't want anything; I was just happy they were home, and nothing terrible had happened to them. It happened the year before my dad went to work in Germany. These moments still make me cry. I loved both my parents with all my heart. They struggled so much. How can I be angry and judge them? But sometimes, I do.

Lost in these thoughts, I approached Peter, resting beneath one of the few trees along the way. The umbrella had been a relief, but the heat was still unbearable. We checked the map—just two more kilometres to the Hospital de San Anton. Our water supply was running low. We were both eager to reach the place, knowing we could rest there for as long as needed.

Chapter 11

Shifts and Reflections

"Problems must be confronted, not hidden."

After a small rest on the side of the road, we began walking slowly, feeling the weight of our fifteenth day on the Camino. As we walked, we reflected on the early days of the journey and the photos we had taken of the surroundings. Peter admitted he had almost stopped taking pictures, feeling too tired to do so.

I realised I had also taken only a few photos in the past few days. My focus had shifted from capturing the beauty of the Camino to delving into my introspections. I found comfort in being alone with my thoughts. It helped distract me from the long distances we had to cover. Yet, as much as I valued this solitude, reflecting on my past often left me feeling a deep sadness and unease.

I tried to convince myself to stay present and focus on the walk. I hadn't come to Spain to dwell on my past but to complete the Camino and reach Santiago de Compostela. Still, something about this journey kept bringing my past to the surface. I felt this in every cell of my body: a strong desire to recall all my pleasant and unpleasant memories. My heart and mind opened, and memories flowed. They came as full stories, not just fragments. It felt as if I was walking through my own body and self.

As we continued walking toward the Hospital de San Anton, my thoughts drifted to my father and a deep sadness settled over me. I wished I'd had more time with him, to know him as I later came to know my mother. But that chance never came.

My father worked in Germany for nearly two years—a place I couldn't fully comprehend as a child. To me, Germany was just a distant country, one that held the promise of improving our lives. He returned home only once during that time, for Christmas, arriving with several suitcases filled with gifts for everyone—his sisters, brothers-in-law, nieces, and nephews included.

It struck me even then that my father seemed born to please everyone. Yet, in all his giving, I longed for more of his time, presence and stories.

Throughout my life, I've understood the pitfalls of pleasing others. When you raise a child to prioritise pleasing you, you risk creating a people-pleaser. My father exemplified this. He spent much of his time and energy pleasing his parents, sisters, and others, often at the expense of his own needs, his wife, and his children. I missed having a deeper connection with him, and I can't help but wonder how different things might have been if he had invested more time in us and my mother.

My grandmother often said she had a son so that he could care for her. This mindset created a ripple effect, and I still see traces of it in some of my siblings. The expectation that children should prioritise their extended family—even as adults—over their own immediate family created an imbalance that lingered.

As I've mentioned, my father was heavily influenced by his parents, especially my grandmother, who had the final say in everything. Whether it was a need we had or a decision to be made, everything had to go through her. Both my grandfather and my mother deferred to her judgment without question.

As children, we were excluded from decisions, particularly those related to money, which created a distance between us and our parents.

Were my parents close as partners? I don't think so. While they respected each other and rarely fought, I never saw them engage in deep conversations or work through issues together. I felt the problems in our family weren't addressed—they were buried and ignored. Everything seemed fine on the outside, but there was a lack of emotional connection beneath the surface.

The behaviour I learned at home was to avoid discussing problems or situations that made us unhappy. I often felt confused about what was acceptable and what wasn't. This confusion led me to invent small lies when asked about things because I wasn't sure if honesty was safe. It took me a long time to unlearn that habit and embrace truthfulness.

Looking back, we needed guidance aligned with our age and individual needs. Without it, we were left to navigate life with gaps in understanding, often carrying patterns that required years of unlearning.

My grandmother's teachings were centred around preserving virginity until marriage and avoiding pregnancy, warning that bringing shame to the family would mean we were no longer welcome at home and would have to find our way. In her way, she was trying to protect us, but this was the extent of my sexual education.

Her words instilled an underlying fear about the consequences of straying from these expectations. On the other hand, my mother took a more accepting approach, embracing life as it came. While this perspective offered some comfort, it also left me feeling that we lacked proper guidance. We each paid the price for that gap in understanding our ways.

I felt I was coming to the present, and these thoughts stirred up anger and anxiety in me because I saw these patterns still existing in my extended family. Control and fairness were something that followed me throughout my marriage. I suppressed so much until it all boiled over during a visit from Greg's sister more than fifteen years ago. I'm grateful that moment happened because I didn't want to be an extension of my mother and have someone from outside making decisions for me and my family. It marked the beginning of the end of my marriage, and I've never regretted it. I learned that problems must be confronted, not hidden. What's wrong can't be made right, and issues will surface sooner or later. When problems are brought to light, there are always solutions. Keeping things bottled up inside only makes them a part of you, and it's hard to rid yourself of them once they've taken root.

Reflecting on this has made me realise the profound importance of intentional guidance and conscious parenting. I believe in teaching children honesty and problem-solving skills early on rather than encouraging them to hide from their problems. Children can navigate challenges more effectively with the right support and the confidence to ask for help.

Parents or primary caregivers play a crucial role in shaping these abilities. Unfortunately, in my upbringing, I saw little of this. The lack of open communication and guidance left gaps I've had to fill over time.

I stopped by the side of the road, letting my thoughts wash over me, each one stirring a fresh wave of pain. It felt as though I had been robbed of my parents, and the little girl within me was crying. Tears mixed with sweat streamed down my face as I wept uncontrollably, lost in memories that blurred the boundaries between past and present.

At that moment, I was grateful to be walking alone, with Peter visible only in the distance.

My grandmother had tried to fill the void, teaching us and offering advice, but it often felt lacking in relevance.

Despite her efforts, I frequently sensed my mother's unhappiness, a passive-aggressive tension beneath her gentle exterior. She seemed to live in her own world—distant and alone—a feeling I often shared, and I suspect my siblings did too. I struggled to understand who my mother was.

It wasn't until later, after my father passed away and she came to live with my family briefly before moving closer to me, that I had the chance to spend meaningful time with her. That time made me wish I could have done the same with my father.

We don't truly appreciate the time we have with our parents while they're alive. Only when they're gone do we realise their true value, and by then, it's too late to share more moments or mend the past.

My mother was very close to her mother and often overprotected by her. When my grandmother visited us, which was rare, she would shield her daughter from us, her grandchildren. Instead of spending time with us, she taught us not to upset my mother. I saw in my mother a child who had never fully grown up—scared, insecure, lacking confidence. I never fully trusted my mother for as long as I can remember because she rarely kept her promises or made decisions. Often, if we asked her for something, she would ask us to talk to my grandmother. I felt both angry and sad at her passivity and sadness, wanting her to be more involved in our lives—to give advice, speak to us, hug us, and express her love. But for many years, this was just a hope.

It seemed to me that both my parents remained close to their parents and struggled to forge strong connections with us and with each other.

The people I respected most were my father and my grandmother, while my grandfather was the one I loved deeply.

My father took charge of disciplining us and making decisions, big or small, concerning our needs. I respected and loved him deeply, though I didn't feel close or confident asking him for things as a young child. Yet, I trusted him implicitly. If my father promised something, he always followed through.

From him, I learned a great deal. He was friendly and social, with many friends, but carried himself with dignity and wouldn't tolerate disrespect. I knew that if I misbehaved in front of others, he would disapprove with a look rather than words. Sometimes, I'd even go to bed early to avoid disappointing him. He never swore before us and was a true role model of hard work. I rarely saw him relax. The work ethic he and my mother instilled in us from a young age was profound. His opinion of me mattered immensely; I cherished listening to his stories. As an only son, my dad was raised by his parents to take responsibility, lead the family, and be confident in his dealings with people of all backgrounds. Despite only completing fourth grade, he was wise beyond his years.

After returning from Germany, my father secured a job at a construction company in Bitola, the nearest city, and would come home on Friday nights. He had taken up the job because some workers were on sick leave. Two months into his new job, my father returned home one day with sad news. He shared that a colleague who had been ill had passed away, leaving behind his wife and three children—two girls and a boy. I was deeply saddened by the news and couldn't sleep that night, thinking about the family and their loss. Little did I know then that, fifteen years later, I would meet and marry that boy who had lost his father.

I remember the day I introduced Greg, now my ex-husband to my parents. My father asked him about his family, and shortly after he started talking, my father's face changed.

"I never had the chance to meet your father, but I took his place at work while he was on sick leave. I remember hearing about his passing. He was a good worker, and everyone spoke fondly of him," my father said sadly.

It was such a coincidence. I noticed tears welling in Greg's eyes. Later, I learned more about what his family endured after the tragedy. His father, the family's breadwinner, left them not only in emotional despair but also in financial hardship—a trauma Greg never fully overcame.

A few months later, my father arrived with more news. As usual, important matters were not discussed openly in front of us children, but the hushed tones and excited whispers hinted at something positive. Eventually, they revealed the news that thrilled us all—my father had purchased a house in Bitola. It was thrilling to contemplate moving from our village to the city for a better life.

I turned ten. It was 1972 when many people from the village migrated to cities across Europe and even farther to America and Australia. My father's first cousin, who lived nearby, had moved to America with his family and had urged my father to join them, but he couldn't bear to leave his parents alone.

I imagined my life beyond the village—the new school, the friends I would make, and the adventures awaiting me. Life in the village had been simple and, at times, uneventful, but it was all I had ever known. Everything came directly from nature—our food, water and toys.

I fondly remember making dolls from corn. When autumn arrived, and the corn and sunflowers were ripe, I would husk the corn and create dresses for my corn dolls, even giving them hair tied up in ponytails. They were my favourite playthings, cherished companions in my little world. Inspired by these dolls, I dreamed of having dark burgundy hair, imagining it flowing like theirs.

Playing with corn and sunflowers, I gave them roles as friends, guests, or even children, nurturing an early sense of maternal instinct. From a young age, I dreamed of being a mother who would love her children unconditionally—a vision that has stayed with me throughout my life.

I believed that life in the city would surpass my wildest imagination, a world so different from the quiet simplicity of the village.

* * *

I paused and gazed across the vast expanse of the Meseta, which, in my mind, resembled a Macedonian meseta. It felt as though nothing had changed in half a century—everything looked the same except for the name of the country and the observer's age. The little girl who once walked the dusty roads, leaving her village behind, had grown into a middle-aged woman, now treading a similar path, searching for herself.

In the distance, I spotted Peter waiting for me, his face lighting up with a smile as I approached.

"We're almost there—less than a kilometre to the Hospital de San Anton," he said, his excitement clear.

"I hope the weather changes tomorrow," I replied, a note of hope in my voice.

"It will," Peter assured me with confidence. "Tomorrow's going to be cooler."

The weather was scorching hot, and as we walked together, I found myself engaging in conversations with passing pilgrims. My mind drifted back to my discussion with Kevin and the time it took him to persuade Joan to join him. Their story resonated with ours—mine and Peter's. Speaking to other pilgrims, I discovered that each had unique reasons for undertaking the Camino, or was still searching for their purpose, much like me. Deep within, I felt everyone on this path to Santiago de Compostela was called to be there, including me. Initially resistant to this 'invitation', I had thought it was impossible to embark on such a journey. Yet, the call persisted, and despite my doubts and protests to Peter, I knew I had to answer it.

The previous week, we had talked to Nina and Aljaž, a young couple from Slovenia. Nina felt a deep calling to walk the Camino, and Aljaž, devoted to her, chose to accompany her. Like so many others, we journeyed over eight hundred kilometres, sharing moments of joy and hardship along this extraordinary path. Each pilgrim's journey was as unique as the Camino itself.

Some, like Sara from Germany, walked to gain clarity about her life and decide which direction to take. Then there was Nick, also from Germany, a charming young fashion model who had started the walk alone, planning to meet his mother in Sarria and continue together. When asked why he was walking, he smiled and said, "I don't know—I just felt drawn to be here."

We arrived at the Hospital de San Anton ruins, steeped in history. Many pilgrims were still gathered there, lingering in the moment. Outside the remnants of what was once a hospital for pilgrims run by nuns, there was a small chapel where people wandered in and out. Curious, we stepped inside. Tables were set up with sweets and coffee, offered on a donation basis.

I spotted our Serbian friends and other familiar faces we had met earlier on the Camino. Beyond the ruins stretched endless fields of vibrant sunflowers. We couldn't resist taking a photo in front of them with Veronika and Sara, capturing the beauty and camaraderie of the moment.

Ever curious, Peter delved into the site's history, fascinated by how this once significant place for pilgrims had fallen into ruins. Though an albergue was nearby, most pilgrims we knew planned to stay in Castrojeriz instead.

I wandered around the ruins for a while, taking in their quiet dignity, before finding a bench to sit and reflect. I realised how tired I felt. Castrojeriz was three to four kilometres away from the Hospital de San Anton. We needed another two kilometres to the albergue we had booked. I didn't worry. We deserved a good rest. As Peter said, we did not need to rush.

I sat on the bench, relaxing and taking in the surroundings. My mind wandered back over the past two days, reflecting on the thoughts circling me. My mind remained consumed by memories of my past—childhood, adulthood, and the lingering anger I had carried toward my family for years.

Had I come to the Camino seeking answers to these unresolved emotions? Certainly not. Outwardly, my family seemed fine, like many others of that time. My elder sister often reminded us, *"Some families had it worse. They struggled just to put food on the table."* Another sister would say, *"We were looked after like flowers."*

I agreed with both statements, and how I saw my upbringing through my eyes—filtered by my experiences, shaped by my emotions and layered with my perspective.

I knew this to be true. Yet beneath the calm surface, each of us carried a storm within. A deep sense of neglect had been a constant source of anger for me throughout my life. My family's affection was understated, expressed through few words and minimal actions. I yearned to feel genuinely loved for much of my life, yet I didn't know how to love myself.

Did my siblings feel the same way? Perhaps. But, as I mentioned before, open discussion was never encouraged in our household. Feelings were left unspoken, buried beneath the surface, where they quietly festered.

My grandmother skillfully smoothed over any conflict, ensuring an outward appearance of harmony. It was no surprise that after her passing, everything seemed to unravel.

From a very young age, I sensed our family's instability. I quickly learned not to expect anything from anyone, realising I had to care for myself and not rely on my family for support. Looking back, I was right to prepare myself in that way.

Yet, despite it all, my love for my family never wavered. I cherished each member dearly without expecting or waiting for reciprocation. I could find forgiveness and understanding for each of them in my heart. As my father used to say, "I do as much as I know." Perhaps, I mused, they all did their best with what they knew.

Sitting on the bench in the cool shade, I allowed myself to drift into my thoughts. It was a rare moment of peace, free from the need to focus on each step or push my body forward. I let my mind wander.

Meanwhile, Peter busied himself with his camera, trying to capture every corner of the mystical place built along the pilgrimage route, its history and aura reflected in its crumbling beauty.

My thoughts drifted back to 1972 when I completed Grade 3, and my family left the village where our ancestors had lived for generations. It was a bittersweet moment, filled with sadness for what we were leaving behind and curiosity about the life ahead. We sold everything—our house and land—valued at just one thousand dinars, the currency of Yugoslavia at the time, to buy a home in the city costing eight thousand dinars. My family never directly discussed money with us, but I overheard their conversations with others. I doubt we had any savings from farming; the funds likely came entirely from my father's hard work in Germany.

This financial struggle wasn't unique to my family—it extended into my adulthood in Macedonia. Even when Greg, now my ex-husband,

and I decided to move to Australia, both of us university graduates with professional jobs, we had only twelve hundred dollars. We sold everything we owned—our car, furniture, and other possessions—to afford the move and buy plane tickets. For many Macedonians, life was challenging, and financial hardship often drove people to seek opportunities elsewhere.

The day of our move finally arrived. As we stepped off the bus and walked toward our new home, my heart raced with anticipation. The street buzzed with activity; cars were still a rarity then. Our new house was about ten minutes from the main bus station, and compared to our village home, it felt like a dream. It was a two-story house, far more beautiful than what we had left behind. The ground floor, which resembled a basement, had two rooms and a kitchen, while the second floor featured a large balcony and two additional rooms. The improvements were thanks to my father's hard work renovating it that summer.

When we entered the house for the first time, we were greeted by a constant stream of guests. Almost every evening, relatives, neighbours, and acquaintances would visit to welcome us or introduce themselves. I was surprised by how many people my family seemed to know in the city, most of whom were strangers to me—distant relatives, family friends, or my father's colleagues. My father's eldest sister, who lived nearby, came by almost every evening with her husband.

Pleasing others was deeply ingrained in our family dynamic, especially for my grandmother and father, who were naturally social and welcoming. Their warmth and hospitality attracted many visitors, but amidst the lively gatherings, I often sought refuge in a room with two old couches where we children slept. I shared a sofa with my eldest sister, four years older than me. If I felt close to anyone during this adjustment period, it was her. I tried to recall whether we argued or disagreed, but nothing significant came to mind.

Our neighbours were intensely curious about us. The houses in our neighbourhood were tightly packed, with barely any space between them. Conversations from the street or nearby homes were easily overheard. Our house had a small front yard that felt like a narrow passage, and no backyard. Nearly every second house on the street seemed to have children around our age, creating a lively atmosphere as they eagerly introduced themselves to the new family.

I was delighted to meet Ruzica, a girl slightly younger than me who would end up in the same Grade 4 class when school began. Although we shared a classroom for several years, we never became close friends—our personalities were too different.

After moving to the city, my father enrolled me in Grade 4 at Dr Trifun Panovski, a primary school from prep to Grade 8. I was eager to start but filled with nerves and excitement. I imagined making friends easily, but I didn't realise that being a 'village girl' in the city was frowned upon. Despite my anxieties, I reassured myself I would succeed. I vowed to work hard, complete my homework diligently and make my parents and teachers proud.

Starting school in the city, I quickly realised I would be among the oldest in my class each year because I had started school later. This fact bothered me deeply and lingered with me for years. I always felt like I was missing out on something, and, in hindsight, I believe my early maturity kept me from fully enjoying my childhood. I rarely played with other kids or formed close friendships. Instead, I found myself drawn to conversations with older girls, preferring their company over that of my peers.

City life was a stark contrast to village life. In the village, everyone seemed occupied with work and leisure time was rare. However, in the city, especially in the evenings of spring, summer, and autumn when the weather was warm and inviting, women often congregated outdoors. Many of them adhered to the traditional role of homemakers, not working outside the home. Streets would come alive with clusters of women sitting and relaxing, mainly gossiping. It was a vibrant scene. Older teenagers, dressed stylishly, would venture out, sparking much gossip and speculation among the women.

As a younger girl, not yet old enough to go out, I would join these gatherings and listen intently to the gossip about who was dating whom and other intriguing details of teenage social life.

My grandmother and mother were not inclined to socialise with others. It often left me feeling melancholic. While I wished they would join community gatherings, my mother, in particular, preferred solitude over socialising. She rose early each morning to begin her work at a public farming company, often labouring in the fields or knitting sweaters for us. During our village winters, she diligently wove blankets, called 'divtici' in Macedonian, for our future marriages—a gesture that, in hindsight, seemed futile since we eventually used proper duvets and blankets.

Reflecting on these memories, I prioritised the present over distant aspirations. I understood the immense importance of investing time in children, nurturing relationships and offering meaningful guidance, rather than becoming consumed by impractical pursuits. My mother, for instance, often spent hours creating things that were unusable or out of fashion instead of spending that time with us.

I see this same pattern repeated in many parents today—struggling to find even a moment to attend parent-teacher interviews, constantly busy with work to provide a 'better life' for their children. Yet, many fail to realise that the real treasure lies in the moments of quality time spent together.

As a teacher, I often emphasise to my students how invaluable it is to cherish those moments with their parents. Relationships and shared experiences are irreplaceable, forming the foundation of lasting connections and emotional growth.

My grandmother preferred visitors coming to our home for conversations rather than venturing out. Our household was constantly bustling, especially on market days—Tuesdays and Fridays. Following village customs, my grandmother would wake early to prepare generous meals like giant bean pots or casseroles for our guests. Living just a ten-minute walk from the market, the market days were particularly busy with guests coming over.

After school, I often assisted visitors by carrying their bags to the bus station near the market.

I felt embarrassed and insecure while helping my cousin's wife one day. I feared being seen with the bags, especially by classmates who might mock me as a 'village girl', or worse. As we passed the medical centre, a tall, stylish woman emerged, observing us closely. She suddenly took the bags from my hands, inquired about our destination, and accompanied us to the bus station. Her confident demeanour contrasted sharply with my discomfort. Without a word, she returned the bags, bid farewell and walked away gracefully. I was left wondering about her identity. Was she a doctor, a nurse or a patient? Her elegance and poise left a lasting impression on me, resembling heroines from the books I loved. That moment taught me a profound lesson about confidence, generosity and grace, qualities I aspired to embody after that. I liked to be like her!

I struggled with timidity and insecurity during my early years in the city. Although I excelled academically, deep down, I felt unworthy and tried to conceal my background.

It all began in Grade 4, where I was fortunate to have a kind and gentle teacher named Lenche Poprcova. She was a stark contrast to my village teachers.

However, in our music and art classes, we had specialist teachers. My music teacher asked me to introduce myself during my first music class. Standing up, I struggled to speak confidently and shared where I came from and the name of my previous school. The class erupted in laughter when the teacher expressed confusion and mocked my pronunciation, imitating me. It was a moment of profound embarrassment, and I wished to vanish. The only girl who didn't laugh, Jagoda, looked at me sympathetically and our friendship began. She invited me to her home several times, where I observed her mother managing the household, unlike my family dynamics, which I longed to see mirrored.

In Grade 5, another humiliating incident occurred. Following the music class incident, I avoided speaking in front of the class whenever possible. However, during an introduction session with our Macedonian teacher, she asked us to reveal what our fathers did for a living. This information was to be recorded alongside our names in the teacher's diary. As I reluctantly stood up, I quietly admitted that I didn't know my father's occupation. I was well aware he worked as a labourer in construction, but I didn't want to be judged by my classmates or the teacher. Little did I expect my response to evoke laughter and embarrassment.

"Gordana, you're in Grade 5 now. You should know what your father does for a living," the teacher asserted. Feeling ashamed, I promised to find out and report back the next day. My classmates stared at me, some snickering quietly. As I reflected on my father's sacrifices and hard work, a wave of guilt washed over me.

I need to study hard and become educated so that my children can be proud of me one day, I resolved inwardly, grappling with my ingratitude and remorse. *How can I be embarrassed of my father? He's the one who moved us from the village to the city. He's our pillar of strength.*

This moment triggered compulsive behaviours in me during my young adulthood. The fear of something terrible befalling my father or any family member led me to develop compulsive rituals that persisted for over a decade. I would touch objects, kiss doors, chairs, or windows and pray fervently to ward off misfortune. At times, overwhelmed by negative thoughts, I'd bury my head in my hands until the distressing thoughts subsided. I got rid of that behaviour while I studied at university, with support and help from my dear friend, roommate, and college student, Tanja.

The next day at school, I approached the teacher's desk and quietly disclosed my father's occupation, hoping to end the embarrassment and reclaim my dignity.

Thinking back to that time, I couldn't stop thinking about Greg and how the loss of his father had affected him. The thoughts led me to Greg and his struggles, and a wave of sadness washed over me. It was 1972, the same year when we moved to the city when he lost his father. The once-happy boy, born in Bitola, who loved spending time outdoors with friends, had withdrawn and turned into a boy who rarely left his room or interacted with anyone, even close friends and relatives.

Like many traditional women of that time, his mother had never worked outside the home; her life revolved around caring for the house and children. In Macedonia, there was no social support system to fall back on. In the middle of winter, the family was left not only grieving the loss of a beloved husband and father but also without any financial resources.

Greg's older sisters had just finished or were finishing high school, unable to contribute much to the family's dire situation. While the family received much sympathy from the community, this only eroded Greg's confidence further. Sympathy, however, did not equate to financial support, leaving the family to struggle on their own.

During the summer, Greg's mother, sent him and his siblings to Smilevo, a village in western Macedonia where his parents originated, to stay with their paternal grandmother and uncle. They remained there until his mother secured a farming job to support the family.

Greg immersed himself in books. He excelled in every subject, particularly math, and quickly gained recognition as an outstanding student. With the school's support, he competed in various math competitions across the former Yugoslavia, earning prizes, accolades, and the admiration of his peers.

His achievements earned him a scholarship to study at the University of Kiril and Metodij in Skopje, where he graduated as the top student in the university's history. His success made him a celebrated figure within his community. Greg began working as an engineer, before returning to academia to study and teach at the university.

Though the family's financial situation improved significantly, the trauma of Greg's early years lingered. Shy and insecure, he channelled all his energy into his work, often retreating to the solitude of his room, unable to fully escape the hardships of his past. The fear that something might happen to him, leaving the family vulnerable, became a constant shadow in our marriage, influencing his every decision.

I saw Peter talking to Kevin and Joan, who passed by the Hospital de San Anton. I joined them, and the four of us continued our journey. Joan said that she usually booked accommodation the previous day, and they were lucky to find something at the start of the village, opposite the church. They planned to visit the castle on the hill, not too far from the town. I wasn't sure if we could see the castle. We both felt very tired.

Joan and Kevin moved ahead while Peter and I continued slowly. After a short walk, we caught our first glimpse of Castrojeriz. The village, perched on a hill, featured a large church at its entrance and a castle crowning the top.

As we walked, I shared with Peter how my initial plans for sightseeing had faded. Before starting the Camino, I had envisioned leisurely exploring each place we stayed—wandering through quaint villages, each with its charming church at the centre. However, the reality of the journey soon set in. The daily distances, averaging twenty-five to thirty kilometres, were exhausting. When we arrived at our destination, even climbing the stairs to second or third-floor accommodations felt like a monumental effort, leaving little energy for sightseeing. Peter admitted he felt the same way.

With six more days ahead before reaching León, I eagerly looked forward to our planned two-night stay in the city, which promised a much-needed break.

Despite the physical challenges, I still cherished the moments we spent visiting magnificent cathedrals in Logroño and Burgos. The intricate gold leaf adorning the icons and the ornate details of the cathedral walls were awe-inspiring, a vivid reminder of Spain's deep history and cultural richness.

We arrived in Castrojeriz late that afternoon, checked in at the hostel Cien Leguas, completed our laundry, had dinner, and retired early to bed. The warm weather hastened the drying of our clothes. The host at the albergue informed us about the Garlic Festival starting at eight p.m. in the town centre, but we needed more time to rest. We would have loved to see the event but did not have the energy. Peter was very tired, too. The albergue was situated towards the outskirts of town, adding a few extra kilometres to our day's journey. After dinner, we went to bed.

That night, I had a poignant dream. In it, I found myself with my father, grandmother, and grandfather—a rare sight as I had never dreamt of them collectively. Unaware of their passing, I approached my grandfather, embraced him tightly, and kissed his forehead. They observed me silently, their expressions unreadable. The dream stirred me awake.

I felt disoriented; the dream had been so vivid and real. When I opened my eyes, I found only darkness around me.

"I love you," I whispered into the void. "Are you watching over me? Perhaps you always have and this is how I've come to understand it—how I've seen things through my eyes." I felt tears in my eyes.

My thoughts lingered on the dream. Their expressions had been unreadable, yet they focused entirely on me. Were they trying to tell me that if I had shared what troubled me, they would have helped? Who knows? Perhaps they would have.

Growing up, many parents in our time did not openly express love or address their children's emotional needs. I believed that if they could hear me, they would understand my sentiments, yet I kept my emotions to myself, thinking it was the right thing to do. Reflecting on how different it could have been if we had openly communicated our feelings and thoughts, I drifted back to sleep with these musings.

Chapter 12

Seeking for Acknowledgment and Recognition

"Do not worry when you are not recognised but strive to be worthy of recognition"

Abraham Linkoln

It was the 22nd of July. We got up around four-thirty a.m. We checked our feet, covered the blisters, checked the room and left the hostel, Cien Leguas, quietly through the back door, careful not to disturb the other pilgrims still asleep in the early morning. It was still dark. Our destination was Fromista, the next town where we had already booked our accommodation. It promised another twenty-five kilometre walk ahead of us. It was our sixteenth day walking, excluding two days' rest in Logrono and Burgos. The morning greeted us with warm weather, urging us to cover most of our journey during the early hours.

I often glanced back, captivated by the sunrise. There was something serene about watching the sun ascend behind us, casting a red glow across the sky like a small, radiant ball.

Despite the physical exertion and the increasing complexity of the walk, the beauty of our surroundings filled me with happiness and a sense of privilege. As we traversed through the landscape, I couldn't help but think of the countless pilgrims who had walked this path to Santiago de Compostela over the centuries, likely experiencing similar emotions.

Nature enveloped me, blending my existence with the plants and earth around me. I pondered whether the vastness and openness of the natural surroundings somehow stirred the thoughts and memories of my childhood and family that had recently surfaced. Perhaps there was a connection. The saying goes, 'You can take the child from the village, but you cannot take the village from the child'. I smiled to myself, feeling a kinship with that sentiment.

"What thoughts will come to mind today?" I mused aloud. "I've been retracing my childhood steps these past few days. I'm eager to revisit them."

No matter what memories or emotions surfaced, I resolved to embrace them all with openness and curiosity. Some memories might be painful, evoking judgment, tears, or anger, but I was eager to face and explore them freely. The landscape around me symbolised freedom, where I didn't rush to reach any destination but existed, absorbing the moment. I felt liberated and relaxed, as if the thoughts were akin to sweat, releasing pent-up energy from within me.

I shared my dream from the night before with Peter. I could sense something deeply spiritual about the dream.

"Darling, all the ancestors are here, surrounding us," he said gently. We stopped walking, and he pulled me into a hug. "You think so much about your family. I don't think about mine as much. I cherish the memories of my parents, but I don't get sentimental. My sisters do, though. Maybe women are just different," he added, trying to lighten my mood.

As we continued walking, my thoughts lingered on Peter. He grew up in Altona North, a western suburb of Melbourne. Being the eldest child, he took on responsibility early, finishing high school and stepping into work to make space for his younger siblings. He spent some time working in Newcastle, got married, and returned to Melbourne after his eldest son was born.

Peter managed to balance work, study and raising a young family without relying on his parents or expecting help from anyone. I deeply admired his independence and practical approach to life. He accepts life as it comes and keeps moving forward.

On the other hand, I felt like I was still untangling my past, striving to grow and heal. Something was urging me to go back to my thoughts.

My thoughts took me to the second half of primary school, from Grades 5 to 8. During my fifth grade, a new school named *Gorgi Sugarev* opened nearby and all students from two neighbouring schools in our area were supposed to transfer mid-year. I couldn't have been happier. It felt like a fresh start where I could make new friends and truly belong. While I had friends before, I hadn't felt particularly close to anyone. Those next three and a half years until I finished Year 8 were some of the most enjoyable of my school life.

The school was a marvel. Everything was new, clean, and sparkling. I felt incredibly fortunate to be studying in such a beautiful environment. I made a promise to myself to give it my all. Despite not knowing if I was particularly intelligent (aside from occasional praise from my uncle Lube, my mum's brother), I worked diligently. I developed a deep respect for many of my teachers, especially our Maths teacher, Ristana, whose lessons stayed with me forever. I was lucky to have her throughout those formative years.

Although I struggled with English initially, finding it extremely challenging without much support, little did I know then that I would one day become a language teacher. Reading became a passion. I joined the local library and devoured numerous books during primary school. Balancing time with friends, studying and indulging in my favourite books felt fulfilling.

However, Year 7 brought a difficult experience with bullying. The school's response to bullying was inadequate at the time. I tried to avoid the bullies and their hurtful comments. Especially they bulled those students who excelled academically, and at times when the teachers recognised their achievements.

During parent-teacher interviews, my mother always attended faithfully until Grade 8. It was the time that I started to feel closer to her. Despite her limited literacy, she always tried to be there for me. Sometimes, she misinterpreted the teachers' terms in Macedonia and asked me about them. As a teacher, this experience gave me empathy for students in similar situations, helping their parents navigate an unfamiliar educational system or the language barrier.

By the end of Grade 7, I had achieved the best results. Apart from English, where I struggled, I excelled in every subject. I got a book as a reward. I had earned books as a reward in previous years, but that year, I felt different. I had proven to myself, that with hard work, I could succeed.

I rushed home eagerly to share my achievements with my parents with a certificate and a book in my hands. When I proudly showed my father my certificate and book, expecting praise, he said, "Well done."

Those words hurt me deeply.

"Dad, all these years, I've only heard 'Well done!' I'm the only one in this house studying and doing well at school. It feels like no one notices anything I do."

My father was busy sawing a broom. Making brooms was his side job after work, and my grandfather sold them at the market, sometimes even from our home. He paused, setting the broom aside to look at me.

"What do you want me to do?" he asked.

"Dad, I don't expect anything material. I want to feel noticed and loved. I want you to be happy for me, like I'm happy with my achievements. Something feels off in my heart," I said, tears welling up.

He listened to me until I finished, then replied, "Listen and remember what I'm about to tell you. Everything you do in your life, good or bad, you do for yourself, not for anyone else. Doing well at school is good for you. It will lead to a better job one day. Your siblings may not like school, but they find their path. I can't single you out and give you awards. You're all the same to me."

I listened intently, realising he had given me something valuable—his time and attention—exactly what I had been seeking. His words have stayed with me ever since.

My father was right. Our actions ultimately serve us, but a little acknowledgment doesn't hurt. Thinking of him brought tears to my eyes, and I let them fall freely. When he passed away unexpectedly from a heart attack at the age of sixty-one, the same age I was at that moment, I felt he had so much more to teach and share with us, but time ran short.

When we moved to the city, my father was the sole breadwinner. Having never paid into a pension plan, my grandparents had no benefits. To help make ends meet, my grandfather, then over seventy, crafted the simpler parts of brooms, selling them at the market every Tuesday and Friday. Meanwhile, my father took on the bulk of the broom-making, travelling annually to Serbia and Croatia with other artisans to purchase materials. Depending on my schedule, I often accompanied him to the market before or after school to assist my grandfather and give him some much-needed free time.

I had a deep affection for my grandfather, Vangel. He was a reserved man who was incredibly diligent. My father inherited his strong work ethic from him, passing it down to all of us, his children. My grandfather held a special place in my heart. He was the type of person who would offer you change without being asked. He cherished my grandmother deeply, always attentive to her and eager to join in when she spoke. He would often surprise her with something she liked from the market. Seeing them together was heartwarming.

Once, I asked my grandmother if they ever had arguments or disagreements. She recounted one from their youth. "Yes," she said. "When we were young, I once angered him with something hurtful I said. He grabbed a large piece of wood and threatened, 'Now I will kill you!' He was so upset. I truly believed he might. I hid until he calmed down, and we didn't speak for days after that."

There was a day I went to the market to assist my grandfather. He wasn't feeling well and headed home early, leaving me in charge. I had some experience selling at the market and decided to push myself to sell all the brooms to make my father proud. And I succeeded. When my father arrived after finishing his work, I eagerly awaited his reaction. I proudly informed him that I had sold all the brooms.

"How did you manage that?" he asked.

I explained that I slightly lowered the price, which led to quick sales. My father didn't react with anger or excitement.

"Listen," he said, and I knew he was about to impart something important. "What's done is done, but don't change the price next time. It's not just about money; it's about something deeper. Look at all these people selling brooms." He pointed out a few familiar faces, relatives and villagers. "We work together. Every market day, we set the price in the morning and stick to it until the end. If we feel a change is necessary, we discuss and decide together. Without teamwork, this business wouldn't survive. I'll speak to them and explain what happened with the price today because they all need to know."

I had yet to realise this aspect of the business. I admired the way my father communicated and led. He was wise and understood the importance of teamwork. It was no wonder many sought his counsel and enjoyed his company.

I spotted Peter waiting for me, a familiar sight as he often paused to chat and rest when I caught up. It helped ground me from my wandering thoughts and brought me back to the present moment. As I approached him, he chuckled, pulling me gently from my reverie.

"How are you feeling, my love? Are you tired?" Peter asked, his voice filled with concern.

I chose not to share the inner whirlwind of my thoughts. "I'm fine, darling. How far is the next village? I'm starting to feel hungry," I said, shifting the focus.

"Not far," Peter replied with a reassuring smile. "We're almost there—just two more kilometres. I told you, through the Meseta, the distances between villages are often more than ten kilometres." Then, sensing more, he added, "Are you hungry?"

"Yes, I am," I admitted, "Also, I'd love a coffee."

Lost in my thoughts, I hadn't even noticed we'd already walked nearly eight kilometres.

I felt a wave of gratitude for having him by my side. With Peter, I felt like myself. We shared everything. Since we met, every moment together has been memorable and joyful. We accepted each other fully, not needing anything more. Though we were engaged, we referred to each other as husband and wife, content with our relationship. Maybe one day, we would marry, but we felt no rush.

We continued our walk together, the distant tolling of church bells accompanying us—a sound I cherished— echoing across the villages of northern Spain. As a child, I remember hearing those bells on Sundays, religious days, or when a death occurred. Though I couldn't recall the name of the village we stopped in, we enjoyed a pleasant breakfast there. Remembering the names of all the places we passed through seemed impossible; there were so many, both large and small.

After a good rest, we resumed our walk. The weather was pleasant, and our self-sticking umbrellas added comfort. We strolled through expansive fields, surrounded by vibrant greenery. I was amazed by the large-scale irrigation systems; unlike anything I had seen before. The places we passed and the agricultural practices in northern Spain fascinated me. It was clear they had made excellent use of the land.

We had another nine kilometres to go before our next rest stop, a place called Boadilla del Camino.

I welcomed the solitude, retreating into my past. It felt like I was walking through my own life, uncovering memories I hadn't even realized existed. Letting Peter set his own pace, I fell behind, wrapped in the embrace of my thoughts. I felt like I was simultaneously playing the lead role and watching it unfold in a movie.

My thoughts shifted from primary to high school. I completed primary school and entered high school, known as 'gimnazija' in Macedonian. Most students in this school aimed to pursue higher education at university, although I knew little about it. No one in my immediate family, including siblings and cousins, had attended university; most had only completed high school. Therefore, I didn't have familial expectations of attending university, but I set high expectations for myself after achieving excellent results in primary school.

My confidence from primary school didn't immediately translate into high school. The new environment was daunting, with large classes of thirty to thirty-five students. Despite my determination to succeed and make new friends, the reality was challenging. Teachers, whom we respectfully called 'professors', often maintained a distant demeanour that made me feel insecure and insignificant from the start.

One unforgettable moment occurred during Macedonian class while we were analysing a book. Eager to participate, I raised my hand to read my homework aloud. Upon finishing, the teacher asked which primary school I had attended. Her response was unexpectedly harsh and dismissive. She criticised my primary school's teaching standards and implied I couldn't possibly have learned proper analysis there. I was deeply embarrassed, my face burning with shame. Instead of constructive feedback, she disparaged my former teachers, particularly my beloved primary school teacher, Darinka.

At that moment, I recalled Darinka's impact on me. Although she might not have taught me formal book analysis, she nurtured my confidence, encouraged my creativity, and believed in my potential. Even though I didn't win the role, she nominated me as an eighth-grade class president. Despite occasional setbacks like this, Darinka's influence resonated positively with me.

I struggled to connect with this harsh high school teacher for four years and seldom volunteered in class. I left her class without clearly understanding what I had learned. Yet, Darinka's lessons in confidence and self-belief remained a guiding force, helping me navigate through challenges and setbacks.

Reflecting on this brings me to consider my role as a teacher today. I deeply cherish and respect my students and strive to ensure they feel valued and appreciated in my classroom. If ever I unintentionally hurt someone's feelings, I sincerely apologise, understanding that such memories can linger and resurface unexpectedly.

Another vivid memory from high school was the disparity in expectations for students from disadvantaged backgrounds like mine. I often felt overlooked both at home and at school. Teachers favour students from more affluent families or those with established academic success. These distinctions were palpable and pervasive in Bitola, a city of around 100,000 people.

My struggles extended beyond the classroom to my home life. During harsh winters, we had just one heated room where everyone gathered, including daily guests. Amidst the noise and distractions, I carved out corners to study, sometimes retreating upstairs to a cold room where our seldom-used heater barely provided warmth. Financial constraints were a constant worry, and to this day, I marvel at how I managed to complete high school under such circumstances.

A significant event unfolded at the beginning of my first year in high school. A classmate introduced me to a friend of her boyfriend's, a young man named Greg, known to his friends as Goche. He was four years my senior and recently graduated from high school at nineteen. Initially, I was still deciding about having a boyfriend, but I enjoyed Goche's company as we walked home from school together, chatting amidst the bustling streets of central Bitola.

It was October 1977 when Goche, who stood a towering one hundred and eighty-eight centimetres tall, began expressing his interest in me as more than a friend. Despite his polite and kind demeanour, I hesitated to commit to a relationship, feeling uncertain about my readiness for something more serious.

While strolling through town, acquaintances approached us one day and inquired about Goche's impending military service, mandatory for Yugoslav boys who hadn't pursued higher education.

Curious about his intentions, I questioned Goche's sudden interest in having a girlfriend, knowing he would soon leave for military duty. He confessed that while he liked me, he hadn't revealed his feelings earlier out of fear of rejection. He suggested writing letters to stay connected during his service and proposed that we might be ready to pursue a relationship upon his return.

I contemplated his proposal and found merit in his approach. It offered companionship without the pressures of a typical teenage romance, a relief from the societal expectations prevalent among high school girls at the time. Many felt compelled to have boyfriends, seeking validation and a sense of worth through external affection. Navigating these feelings was complex, as I hadn't yet grasped what genuine love entailed.

After he departed for military service, we began exchanging letters, but eventually, I struggled to find words to continue. Goche remained persistent, visiting during army leave, and our relationship persisted, although was somewhat forced. I grappled with guilt over my inability to reciprocate his feelings, convincing myself that perhaps my emotions would eventually evolve.

I entered my second year of high school, determined to improve my grades. No longer at the top of my class, like in primary school, I faced a decline in my results. There was little support available and home life remained unchanged. I began to worry, especially about my poor performance in Maths and English, fearing it would hinder my chances of attending university. Uncertain about my future path, I considered studying law or primary teaching at Bitola's local university. However, I was also intrigued by Pedagogy, a field I first encountered through Bojan, a young and well-dressed Pedagog at our school who worked with students facing behavioural challenges.

Dreaming of pursuing Pedagogy, I discovered the university offering this course was in Belgrade, Serbia, making it seem like an unattainable dream. To bolster my academics, I considered organising private lessons in Maths and English with other interested students, but financial constraints at home thwarted my plans. Frustration grew as I realised my family struggled with financial management despite outward appearances. My mother, who worked and kept her finances separate, could not control the household's money as my grandmother did with broom sales.

Reflecting on family dynamics, I recalled my grandmother's candid remarks about beauty and gender, which, despite their bluntness, often brought laughter. Determined to fund my private lessons, I devised a plan: daily pleas for money under the guise of hunger allowed me to amass coins from my grandmother and grandfather. Without parental inquiry into the source of the funds, I quietly saved for my lessons. Once, rushing to class with coins, I felt embarrassed handing them over to my Maths teacher, who chuckled and asked where I had acquired such a stash.

They were aware of my involvement in drama classes. As my friends laughed, so did I. Eventually, even the teacher joined in. Finally, I spoke up:

"No, these coins aren't from the theatre. I apologise for not having had time to exchange them. I wanted to arrive on time. It turns out that it was a good thing that I didn't. We wouldn't have had this good laugh otherwise."

It's funny how some uncomfortable situations can unexpectedly lead to laughter.

As we approached the village of Boadilla del Camino, I glanced at Peter. He looked exhausted, and I felt just as drained. My thoughts wandered to the terrain we had crossed. The Camino Walk defies explanation. It's a journey through every kind of landscape imaginable. We had walked through the countryside, rugged terrain, rocky paths, cities, fields, vineyards—almost everything. My legs felt like lead.

We decided it was time for a longer rest. From there, it would be about six more kilometres to Frómista. Entering the village, we found a cozy bar and sat down. It was nearly two o'clock. Over lunch, we tried to relax, speaking very little.

I found myself drawn to the map, checking the distances left to travel. Yet, it always seemed like we walked a few kilometres more than the map indicated.

After a long rest, it was hard to get moving again. The weight of my bag felt heavier with each step. Peter's bag was much heavier than mine, yet he never complained. We continued walking, making our way down the hill.

We crossed paths with Mary, our Camino companion, and Peter walked ahead with her while I lagged, feeling the strain in my legs and growing fatigue. Mary had found accommodation nearby, and we made plans to dine together. Arriving at the hotel lobby, we waited briefly until the receptionist returned to stamp our credentials and hand us the room key. The hotel, conveniently located opposite the town's central church, provided a welcome opportunity to rest and wash up.

Later, on our way to dinner, we ran into Veronika, our spirited friend from Canada. I admired Veronika's positivity and how she and her son always managed to socialise with fellow pilgrims despite their brisk pace. Veronika expressed concern about shin splints that threatened to hinder her walking, prompting an evening appointment with a doctor. I empathised with her plight, grateful that my blisters weren't causing me much trouble—yet uncertain of what lay ahead.

Our dinner with Mary at a local restaurant was delightful. We swapped stories about the Camino, discussed the distances we'd covered and shared anecdotes about our families. Mary, a few years older than me, a psychologist who decided to work as a high school teacher, came from a large, close-knit Catholic family. Hearing about her well-educated siblings who pursued their dreams and maintained strong bonds warmed my heart. It reminded me of the irreplaceable value of family—a gift given to us, cherished or squandered by our choices.

As we returned to the hotel, thoughts of family filled my mind. I admired families who could set aside differences and nurture positive relationships, especially among siblings. Building and maintaining these bonds requires effort. Parents play a crucial role in fostering friendships among their children from a young age, teaching them to respect and accept each other for who they are. It's vital to support them without judgment and refrain from assigning them parental roles.

Reflecting on family dynamics made me consider my relationship with my siblings and how I parent my daughters.

In our youth, it seemed we had a close and loving bond, yet looking back, I realised we were often tasked with parenting each other, leading to a somewhat chaotic childhood. My eldest sister, who is four years older than me, usually resembled our mother in her actions. As adults, our paths diverged, and we rarely crossed paths. This experience taught me valuable lessons.

As a parent now, I strive to encourage my daughters to embrace their individuality, pursue their paths and utilise their full potential. Rather than assuming parental roles towards each other, I want them to nurture a genuine sisterly bond. I support them whenever they need parental guidance, ensuring their relationship flourishes.

We arrived at the hotel close to ten, much later than our usual bedtime. After preparing for the next day, we settled in and drifted off to sleep.

Chapter 13

Finding Balance

"You cannot force love – It's there or it isn't"

Richelle Mead

We left Frómista a bit later than usual, around seven a.m., on the 23rd of July. Our goal for the day was Carrión de los Condes, a town about nineteen to twenty kilometres away. Along the route were several villages where we could stop to rest and refuel. We had already booked our stay at Hostal Santiago, which gave me peace of mind. I was glad this stretch of the journey offered more villages between Frómista and Carrión de los Condes, providing plenty of opportunities to pause and recharge.

Walking such long distances burned many calories, often between 3,000 and 4,000 per day, making it essential to refuel at bars and restaurants along the way. We stopped at every village with a bar or eatery, taking the opportunity to have coffee, use the facilities, and replenish our energy. The meals served were hearty and calorie rich. I especially enjoyed the freshly squeezed orange juice and long rolls filled with cheese and prosciutto. As we trekked toward Carrión de los Condes, near the Church of Santa María la Blanca, these kept us going.

Peter began talking about a church in a town called Villalcázar de Sirga. It was on our route, and we planned to stop if it was open to look inside. The Templars built the church in the twelfth century and their task was to protect pilgrims during medieval times. It made me think about the past pilgrims, and I looked forward to seeing the church.

I cherished the sunny, warm morning as we walked through fields and dusty roads, enveloped in peaceful stillness. The tranquillity felt timeless, though I also appreciated the vibrancy of city life. Striking a balance between nature and urban environments has always been important, especially after spending over five decades predominantly in cities. In Macedonia, I lived mostly in Bitola and Skopje, where I attended university. I stayed in Skopje for a few more years after meeting Greg, now my ex-husband. Later, we moved to Australia and settled in Melbourne.

My thoughts drifted back to Bitola and my teenage years. I thought of Goche and felt a pang of guilt for the way I had hurt him. I remembered pushing myself to keep seeing him, even when I was uncertain about my feelings. The saying, *'Love takes two people'* had never felt more true.

I recalled when Goche returned from the army toward the end of my second year of high school, just after I turned seventeen. I had stopped writing to him, unsure where our relationship stood. After his return, we spent most of our time with mutual friends and things seemed normal on the surface. But instead of growing closer to Goche, I felt more distant, anxious, and uncertain. There was no clear reason to end things, but my heart wasn't in it. I yearned for someone I could truly confide in, someone who could understand how I was feeling.

One day, when we were alone, Goche shared his desire to marry me after I finished high school. His words took me by surprise, making me realize my true feelings. I wasn't ready to get married right after high school, and I wasn't sure if I wanted to marry him at all. I felt guilty for not being able to return his feelings and for not having the clarity to end the relationship and let him find happiness with someone else. It wasn't about him; it was about my own uncertainty. I was indecisive, torn between wanting someone and struggling to express how I truly felt about Goche. I felt trapped in something that resembled a relationship, yet I felt alone.

The next time we went out together, I gathered my courage and told Goche I didn't think we should continue. I explained that I was confused about our relationship and needed time to figure things out. We went out several times after that conversation, but something unexpected changed my life forever.

* * *

After passing through a few villages, we arrived in Villalcázar de Sirga and immediately spotted the town centre's Santa María del Temple church. The large restaurant across from the church was filled with people, mostly pilgrims, making it hard to find a seat. Among the crowd, we recognized several familiar faces—Kevin and Joan from Michigan, the group of Serbian pilgrims, and Veronica with her son. I felt relieved to see Veronica there. I hoped she could walk better after her recent struggles. They were all sitting outside the bar. Before entering the church, we took photos with our Camino friends and shared a pleasant lunch. These moments on the Camino, when we gathered, shared our stories, and supported one another, are truly precious to me.

Veronica, a tall and lively art teacher from Toronto, Canada, was perhaps the most vibrant pilgrim I had met. But that day, she sat with tears welling in her eyes. Veronika explained that she and her son had taken a taxi to the bar, and she had forgotten her hiking poles in her hurry. "I can't walk without them," she said, trembling. The split shin on her foot was causing her immense pain.

Her mood shifted dramatically when the taxi driver returned, bringing her walking poles back. Overcome with gratitude, Veronica hugged the driver tightly and then turned to me with a smile, asking me to take a photo of them together. I felt deeply for Veronica, moved by her struggles and resilience and the selflessness of the female taxi driver.

After lunch, we walked inside the church. The atmosphere was deeply mystical. I marvelled at the grandeur of such an ancient church nestled in the small towns of Castile and Leon. After exploring the church, I noticed Mary sitting quietly, gazing at the ceiling. I joined her, feeling calm, and spirituality washed over me in that serene space.

After leaving the church, we continued our walk under the scorching sun, using our umbrellas for some much-needed shade. As we crossed the flat terrain, I struggled to adjust my umbrella. I was grateful for Peter's help in setting up our umbrellas, and I couldn't resist teasing him.

"Darling, I may be independent, but I don't know what I'd do without you," I said, genuinely appreciating everything he had done for us on this journey. It was true; I couldn't imagine undertaking this pilgrimage without him by my side.

Peter paused to show me how the self-stick umbrellas worked, making sure they were securely in place before we moved on. His gaze was full of love and understanding as he reassured me. "You'll be fine."

"No," I admitted, "I wouldn't. I wouldn't have walked the Camino without you."

Peter smiled softly. "I don't think I would have walked without you either."

Peter continued walking at his steady pace, and I found myself reflecting on our relationship. Since we first met, everything had felt right and harmonious. I hadn't had much experience with stable relationships before. I often felt alone in my previous marriage. I had thought I knew what strong love was. Still, those relationships were tumultuous, like my childhood—lacking clear communication, boundaries, or resolution of conflicts, just a cycle of placating and avoiding issues. In those times, I unwittingly mirrored the roles of my mother, unsure of my identity or what I truly wanted from a relationship.

My journey through love compelled me to confront myself more deeply, especially after my ex-husband and I separated. I committed to self-improvement by joining a gym and walking daily. I made time for myself and cherished the positive influences of friends, colleagues and some members of my family who embraced me for who I am and supported my growth. Some longstanding friends drifted away from my life, and I accepted this as part of my evolution. As changes unfolded, they touched every aspect of my life.

Throughout it all, my children remained my top priority and greatest support. I learned to stand independently, choosing relationships that aligned with my values and establishing healthy boundaries. I grew to love myself fully and didn't rely on anyone else to make me feel complete. Meeting Peter came when I was ready, clear about what I wanted, and unchanged in my desires since we met.

Yet, in my life, there were deep emotions and experiences I struggled to articulate until now, buried and hidden within me, causing pain, tears, and turmoil in my marriage. These were parts of myself I avoided touching or discussing for many years, compartmentalising them away. Now, on the Camino in Meseta, I felt compelled to explore those forbidden corners of my heart. I felt ready, prepared to face whatever emotions surfaced, even if it meant crying as I had years before. Despite my apprehension, I felt my heartbeat steady—I was no longer afraid.

Peter and I had begun discussing these buried aspects of my past, allowing bits and pieces to emerge in our conversations without judgment. This openness was the essence of our relationship's beauty.

I walked a few steps behind Peter, my mind drifting back many years. *Now I'm ready,* I thought, a blend of sadness and curiosity washing over me. *I will face every memory. I'll unpack it all.* It felt like opening an old book I had read before, but it brought up intense emotions this time.

Chapter 14

Love at First Sight

"What the day can bring, the year cannot."

My thoughts brought me to the day that changed my life and gave me another direction. It was a beautiful sunny morning on Sunday, June 17, 1979, just a week after I completed my second year of high school. My family was preparing to attend a wedding in Prilep, about forty kilometres from Bitola. I hadn't planned to go, and no one had asked if I wanted to. My parents, sister, and grandmother were all getting ready, along with my already-married eldest sister and her husband. Most of my grandmother's family from Prilep would be there, too. The wedding was for my Uncle Milan's stepson, whom he had accepted as his own after remarrying following his first wife's death.

    At the last moment, my grandmother decided she was too unwell to go. Seizing the opportunity, I asked if I could take her place. My father agreed, but they couldn't wait long for me to get ready. I promised to get ready in five minutes, and true to my word, I was. I was thrilled at the chance to go, especially since I'd never been to Prilep before. I didn't mind wearing a T-shirt from my Physical Education class and a skirt my cousin had sewn, mainly intended for lounging at home. I had plans to meet Goche at six p.m. that evening, though I was uncertain about continuing our relationship.

    When we arrived at the wedding venue, I felt underdressed compared to the other guests, but I brushed off the feeling, happy to be there. I found a seat opposite the entrance and watched as guests filtered in. That's when I saw him—a tall, dark-haired young man with a perfectly shaped face. He looked several years older than me and incredibly handsome. I couldn't recall ever seeing someone quite like him before. I couldn't help but stare until our eyes met, and then I quickly looked away, feeling embarrassed. When I dared to glance back, he was staring at me. I smiled nervously and turned my head.

Minutes passed, and he wasn't in sight when I looked again. Guilt crept over me; I had a boyfriend, yet I couldn't help but be captivated by this stranger. It was a realisation that I didn't truly love Goche.

I wondered who the young man was. *Perhaps he has already left*, I thought.

The wedding venue was on the second floor, with a large balcony near the entrance. After about an hour, I exited to the balcony for some fresh air. Leaning against the railing, lost in thought, I suddenly felt someone approach from behind.

"Hello," a voice said.

I turned and nearly lost my breath. It was *him*, standing so close. I was speechless.

"Hello," I managed to reply quietly, shaking his extended hand.

"I'm Miki," he introduced himself.

"I'm Gordana," I responded, noticing a smile on his face upon hearing my name. I wondered if I reminded him of someone else—perhaps a past or current girlfriend with the same name. I would find out the answer to that question two years later.

Miki continued to smile at me, dressed in a dark red T-shirt and cream-coloured pants that mirrored my attire. His presence swept me off my feet, and I couldn't help but smile back.

"Tell me about yourself," he said gently. "You don't seem like you're from around here. I don't think I've seen you before."

He held my gaze with warmth and curiosity, and in that moment, I felt a connection that would change everything.

I had never seen anyone quite like him before. His charming smile revealed his white teeth and warm, large brown eyes, making him incredibly attractive. Everything about him seemed perfect. I introduced myself in a few sentences and then asked him the same.

He explained that he was the groom's second cousin, with their mothers being first cousins. Miki was twenty-three years old, living in Prilep, and studying dentistry in Skopje, already in his third year at university.

I listened intently to everything Miki shared. *This young man is the man of my dreams*, I thought. He wasn't just handsome; he was intelligent and articulate.

A surge of excitement rushed through me like lightning. My heart raced, and I could feel the blood pulsing through my body. I shared my plan to continue studying in Skopje after high school with Miki.

"Now, here's an important question," he said. "Do you have a boyfriend?"

I hesitated, then turned my head away and softly replied, "No," before looking back at him with a smile.

He smiled in return and confidently stated, "The answer is 'yes.' Am I right?"

I spoke to Miki about Goche, our relationship, and my conflicted feelings. "After what happened today," I told Miki, "I know what to do about that relationship."

"What happened today?" Miki asked with a broad smile that made my face flush even more. I blushed like a young girl, realising my naivety and innocence at that moment.

I gazed at Miki and declared, "If someone has a boyfriend like me and falls in love with someone else, something is wrong, and that relationship should end. That relationship will end today."

"Tell me," Miki insisted gently, leaning closer to me, "who have you fallen in love with today?"

He was so close now. "I'll never tell you because you already know," I said, ignoring my head, overwhelmed by the rush of love and powerful emotions.

Miki hugged me tenderly. "Tell me," he whispered.

The feelings were overwhelming and tears welled up in my eyes. "You," I whispered back. Miki kissed my lips gently and held me close.

"I don't know what this is, but there's something very special and extraordinary about you," he said, looking deeply into my eyes.

A photographer passed by, and Miki called him to take our photo.

With his arm around my shoulders, he said, "I don't know if I'll see you again, but I hope you don't mind taking a photo with me."

I nodded eagerly, feeling like I was living a dream that I never wanted to end. The photographer captured us together, and Miki's hand rested gently on my shoulder. I didn't know if my actions were right or wrong; it felt incredibly romantic, and I savoured every moment.

Later, Miki found a piece of paper and a burnt match on the floor. He quickly jotted down my address, promising to send me the photo. We spent the rest of the day dancing together, holding hands and talking on the balcony, so absorbed that we even missed lunch and shared the last remaining plate.

Eventually, we said our goodbyes, not expecting to see each other again or to stay in touch.

On returning to the car, I remained silent, lost in my thoughts. At seventeen years old, I had never felt happier. I didn't inquire about Miki's relationship status. Perhaps he had a girlfriend, but I didn't want anything to spoil my newfound joy. The question lingered: Was this real love or just a fleeting illusion?

That evening, I mustered the courage to meet with Goche and tell him everything that had transpired. It was difficult; I didn't want to hurt him, but I knew I needed to end our relationship and move forward, even if I never saw Miki again. Goche couldn't grasp how I could fall for someone I had just met, and truthfully, neither could I. It was a poignant moment filled with sadness. We hugged, kissed goodbye, and parted ways. It was the most extraordinary day, one that stayed with me forever.

The pain in my legs jolted me awake, returning me to reality. Sweat drenched my face, trickling down my body. The umbrella provided some relief, but exhaustion weighed heavily on me, exacerbated by the bulky backpack on my shoulders. Lost in my thoughts, I hadn't noticed my surroundings, consumed instead by memories of the past. I didn't attempt to halt this mental journey; perhaps I had avoided these memories for too long.

Peter waited for me. We could hardly talk. We closed our umbrellas and proceeded together through Carrion de las Condes. Too weary to appreciate the scenery, I hesitated to admit my fatigue to Peter. He bore the effects of our recent bout with COVID-19 earlier in the year, often fatigued but never complaining. His resilience and positive demeanour were a constant inspiration.

What a positive person, I mused, admiring Peter.

Despite the kilometres ahead, I knew this journey was my choice alone. I resigned myself to silence, focusing on reaching Santiago de Compostela. With these thoughts, we entered a building and ascended to the second floor. A man greeted us in Spanish, inspecting our passports and signing our credentials.

Though his English was limited, he used Google Translate to communicate effectively. I struggled to catch my breath in the oppressive heat. His words translated: "We won't ask you to clean the bathroom like some places do. You're pilgrims. We understand you're tired and want you to rest."

Relieved, I barely managed to rise from my chair and followed Peter into our room. I collapsed onto the bed and finally relaxed my body and mind. The absurd thought crossed my mind: *Now all we need is a bucket and mop.* I chuckled softly, grateful for the reprieve from the arduous day's journey. We both managed to laugh despite everything.

Chapter 15

Unstoppable Transformation

"The line between love and delusion is perilously thin."

On July 24th, we set off early in the morning, destined for Ledigos, where we had booked our accommodation. The journey ahead spanned approximately twenty-eight kilometres, though we anticipated walking a bit further, as was often the case.

At five-thirty a.m, darkness still enveloped the town as we embarked, equipped with head torches illuminating our path through the quiet pre-dawn hours. It was a serene start; few other pilgrims were visible at such an early hour. I remarked to Peter how I couldn't fathom traversing Spain in darkness alone, grateful for his company.

We discussed our itinerary as we walked, aiming to reach Santiago de Compostela by August 11th. Our upcoming stop in Leon, where we secured two-night accommodation, provided a brief respite. Despite having already walked for twenty-two days, concerns about the lingering pain in my legs surfaced intermittently.

Our conversation turned to Apostle James or 'Apostol Jacub' in Orthodox Christian tradition. The feast day honouring him was approaching. Peter recounted the legend with a storyteller's flair—how Blessed Mary purportedly dispatched James to Spain to spread Christianity and how he eventually met his martyrdom upon his return to Palestine, his body later transported by his disciples to Galicia. The discovery of his relics in the ninth century, marked by a miraculous light seen by a monk, validated the apostle's presence and led to the construction of the Santiago de Compostela Cathedral.

Stories and myths abound, such as the tale of a man dreaming of seeing St James adorned with shells. The scallop shell forever links with the Camino pilgrimage routes converging at the cathedral, a testament to the varied paths taken by pilgrims united at their journey's end.

I noticed that in the early mornings, Peter and I enjoyed walking together and talking. But after a few kilometres, we naturally focused on ourselves, settling into our own pace and drifting into our thoughts. That's the rhythm of the Camino. It's no surprise that many people choose to walk the Camino alone. Still, I couldn't imagine doing it by myself. Walking together while giving each other space feels like the perfect balance.

Somehow, I stopped worrying about the long walks. I felt at ease with Peter by my side and my thoughts as my companion.

The lights filtering through the trees signalled the approach of other pilgrims, gradually filling the path. Peter maintained his steady pace ahead while I trailed behind. I soon became lost in my thoughts about Miki and our brief encounter, just like the day before. Reflecting on that moment, I often wondered if I would have acted differently had I known the emotional turbulence that relationship would bring into my life.

Miki's presence lingered long after we parted ways—a haunting spirit that overshadowed my emotions for years. Love, betrayal, loneliness, pain and grief unfolded in ways I never anticipated, engulfing me like an uncontrollable natural disaster. The aftermath left me speechless and unable to articulate my feelings.

My thoughts lead me to my marriage. Meeting my ex-husband brought a semblance of happiness, a chance to turn a new page and bury Miki's memory. Yet, his occasional mentions of Miki, especially during conflicts, resurrected his spirit within me. During my marriage, these moments were particularly painful, as I felt unfairly accused of lingering affections for someone I struggled to forget. Unable to confide in anyone, I silently endured years of inner turmoil, believing my emotions were incomprehensible to others.

I realised that the line between love and delusion is perilously thin. For years, I suffered in silence, grappling with feelings that seemed beyond comprehension and control.

The day after meeting Miki, I felt utterly transformed. The girl who had often felt unhappy and lonely was now radiant. My eyes sparkled joyfully in the mirror, and I couldn't stop smiling. I felt beautiful inside and out. *What has this boy done to me?* I wondered. *How had he managed to bring out the best in me so effortlessly?*

Thoughts of never seeing him again saddened me, yet I clung to his promise to send me the photo, maybe even write a letter. How he looked at me and spoke melted my heart, and I dared to believe in love at first sight.

Reflecting on Goche, I felt a pang of sadness for him. What if he loved me as deeply as I loved Miki? I prayed he would find someone who could reciprocate his feelings. He was a kind and decent boy, but our connection never went beyond friendship in my heart.

I worried a bit about my appearance in the photo. I had been underdressed at the wedding and hadn't worn any makeup. I didn't have many pictures of myself—mostly school photos or group shots from excursions. I had never considered myself attractive or drawn to handsome or wealthy boys. My insecurity was constant, a reminder of who I was and where I came from. Yet, in Miki's presence, I had felt surprisingly confident. I wondered if someone like him might be single.

Back then, our home didn't have a phone, and I was sure Miki didn't either; otherwise, he would have given me his number. He mentioned his upcoming exams and his return to Skopje by the end of June. How I wished we could live in the same city! Every day, I anxiously awaited the postman, disappointed each time he passed without leaving the anticipated letter. Finally, after three long weeks, it arrived—a letter containing two identical photos.

My hands trembled as I held them, my heart threatening to leap from my chest. I was ecstatic. We both looked stunning in the photos— Miki's dark, almost black hair, fair complexion, large eyes and dark eyebrows strikingly resembled mine. Miki had his arm around my shoulders, holding me gently close. He towered over me by twenty to thirty centimetres, and we both wore gentle, content smiles.

We looked remarkably alike, almost like brother and sister. Gazing at my bewildered yet joyful expression, I couldn't recall ever seeing myself so happy. Miki's note mentioned the photographer had given him four photos, keeping two for himself.

As I kissed the images and whispered to them, "I will wait for you forever, Miki. I would gladly give my life for you," I knew deep down that this feeling and connection was profound and enduring.

I began reading the letter, pouring over its words repeatedly until I could recite them from memory. Miki described me as brave, honest, strong, and beautiful—the girl he had always hoped for.

He acknowledged that if I did not end things with my boyfriend and wished to forget about us, I should discard the photos and the letter without hesitation. His words resonated with love in every line, expressing that he saw something uniquely special in me, though he couldn't define it. He included his address in Prilep, inviting me to write back if I decided to correspond with him.

With wings, I would have flown to him immediately. He signed the letter as Mitridat, which initially puzzled me since I thought he hadn't shared his real name. Later, he explained that he used this pseudonym because he aspired to become a writer and intended to write under that name.

Eagerly, I penned my response and sent it off, anxiously awaiting Miki's reply or, ideally, his arrival. As the summer days passed by without any word from him, I found little interest in anything else. I cherished solitude in my room, gazing at our photos, rereading his letter, and daydreaming about him. Despite my sadness and the possibility of never seeing him again, I immersed myself in novels where love stories unfolded, learning more about the intense emotions that mirrored my own.

One afternoon, my mother called to tell me someone was waiting to see me outside the gate. As I stepped out, Miki stood dressed in light cream pants and a matching T-shirt. His smile lit up when he saw me, and I ran into his arms without hesitation. We embraced and kissed until I noticed my mother observing us surprisedly.

I introduced Miki to my parents and grandparents, though I sensed a disapproving look on my father's face. I had hoped he would be pleased. Miki was polite, educated, and undeniably handsome, which was everything I had thought I wanted at the time. I loved him with all my heart, but my father's reaction worried me. His judgment had often proven right.

That evening, we went out together. Walking through Bitola's bustling main street, the Korzo, I felt a happiness I had never experienced in the city before. I wanted to introduce Miki to everyone I knew, and my smile seemed permanent. Miki mentioned he would stay at his aunt's place that night and return the next morning. The hours we spent together were a blur; his presence alone filled me with contentment. Before he left, I eagerly asked when I could see him again. He promised to return the next day before leaving.

I couldn't sleep that night, eagerly awaiting his arrival the next morning. But he didn't come. I even went to the bus stop when he was supposed to depart, only to find him absent. Later, he explained he had gone to the beach with his aunt and her family that day. Thus began our relationship, marked by his sporadic visits and my unwavering love, always finding excuses for his absences.

At least he didn't forget me and came to see me, I reassured myself, undervaluing my worth.

The following day, my grandfather teased me about what would happen if Miki didn't marry me now that he had already met my family. I jokingly replied that if he didn't, someone else would. My grandfather chuckled and shook his head, reflecting on how different things were back then.

Over the next two years, Miki and I saw each other sporadically, exchanging occasional telegrams instead of letters. Sometimes, he would call my neighbours from public phones, and they would gladly inform me whenever he called. During my first visit to Miki's home, towards the end of that first summer, he introduced me to his parents, who were kind but left me shy and uncomfortable. Yet, seeing how happy Miki was to have me there made everything worthwhile. I remember him carrying me in his arms for over a hundred meters as he walked me to my uncle's house one evening.

I could love him forever, I thought.

* * *

In September, as I entered my third year of high school, my primary focus shifted to my studies. Despite the sadness of knowing I wouldn't see Miki for months, he constantly occupied my thoughts and heart. I planned to excel in school, achieve excellent results by the end of my final year, and enrol at the university in Skopje. But two years seemed like an eternity, and I couldn't shake the feeling that Miki wasn't alone. The thought caused me intense pain, but I had to face the reality.

Our meetings remained sporadic, often just a few hours at a time. Each moment with Miki felt extraordinary, as if distance didn't exist between us. We could discuss anything, and his happiness to see me was palpable. I didn't ask for more; I believed and felt we were in a relationship. People who saw our photos often commented that we looked like siblings, a remark I took as a compliment. His presence brought me happiness, motivation and a newfound confidence. I made more friends at school, and thoughts of Miki filled me with contentment and fulfilment.

I didn't hear from Miki during the second semester of my third year. I couldn't stop thinking about him, wondering if he had met someone else. I didn't believe he was waiting for me, but I hoped he hadn't entered a serious relationship. The idea of him possibly planning a future with someone else in Prilep or Skopje caused a knot in my stomach and pain in my heart.

"Please, God, don't let this happen," I prayed silently. I hesitated to write to him, feeling that our relationship existed only in my mind, not in reality. Perhaps I was too obsessed with him. I longed for someone to confide in, someone to whom I could pour out my heart. Despite having sisters and friends, none were close enough for me to share my deepest feelings.

Yet, my commitment to improving my school performance was unwavering. I excelled in almost every subject. As the school year drew close, an opportunity arose—an excursion across Yugoslavia organised by the school. Knowing my family couldn't afford it, I didn't bother asking my parents or grandmother for money. But unexpectedly, a classmate, Ana, who was involved in the student council and knew my situation, shared surprising news.

"I'll tell you some good news," Ana said one day. "You're going on the excursion. The school is covering your fees because you're the student who's shown the most improvement this year, and your behaviour is exemplary."

I looked at Ana, stunned. I didn't want anyone to know about my financial struggles or to receive special treatment.

"Ana, I don't want to go if the school has to pay for me. I can't accept this," I replied, my voice tinged with frustration and disappointment.

Ana looked taken aback. "Don't be silly. I'd be thrilled if the school paid for me," she laughed. "You deserve this recognition. If not you, they'd pick someone else. Come on, be happy. Stop thinking about that boy. Come on the excursion and enjoy yourself."

Although Ana was an only child, pampered and accustomed to getting what she wanted, I wasn't sure she understood my feelings or the gravity of my situation.

I left school that day, contemplating how to approach my father. He was a proud man who wouldn't take well to the school paying for my excursion. I rehearsed how to present Ana's news as an award rather than assistance. I didn't even consider telling my mother. It wouldn't make a difference. Anyway, she would refer me to my father.

Once again, I simmered with frustration over my family's dysfunctionality. Every autumn, they purchased kilograms of grapes to make barrel wine and rakija (brandy) despite none of us having a drinking problem. They enjoyed social drinking with guests, often feeling some came solely for the free alcohol. Meanwhile, my father tirelessly helped others construct houses or with various tasks, rarely receiving proper payment. He seemed destined to help without reaping financial benefits that could have eased our situation significantly.

Another concern was my grandmother. I had to ensure she wasn't present when I spoke to my father. She was close to my aunt, my father's eldest sister, who lived nearby and significantly influenced our lives through my grandmother. My aunt's four children, older and seemingly perfect in my parents' eyes, often set a high standard against which my siblings and I felt compared. I frequently thought we were not enough for our parents, and my mother's disdain for my aunt was mutual. I shared her sentiments to some extent; my aunt's disapproval of the excursion could easily sway my grandmother, complicating matters further. It felt like our home was constantly embroiled in chaos, akin to a bustling main road.

Finally, I presented the situation when my father returned home from work. Initially, he needed time to think, but eventually, he consented. I was relieved he approved before my grandmother intervened. Learning to navigate around her without involving her became essential, even though it meant I wasn't her favourite granddaughter. Nevertheless, I trusted my father implicitly; once he made a promise, he stood firm, impervious even to his mother's influence. His steadfastness and reliability made him our rock, though I couldn't shake the anxiety that sometimes gnawed at me, fearing something might befall him.

The excursion took place toward the end of the year, offering an enriching experience. Over nearly three weeks, we journeyed through major Yugoslavian cities. At that time, Macedonia was one of Yugoslavia's republics. We visited numerous cities and landmarks across the country. It was 1980, shortly after the death of Josip Broz Tito, the only president I could recall. Though I never saw Tito in person, I remember visiting his memorial in Belgrade, known as *The House of the Flowers*, where mourners gathered in long queues to pay respects. Many wept and expressed fear for the country's uncertain future, a suspicion that proved prescient as Yugoslavia eventually disintegrated a decade later, prompting many to leave—including myself.

I fondly remember the places we visited in Slovenia: Bled, Postojna Jama, and Ljubljana, the vibrant capital. These locations stood out to me because I bought a postcard from there and sent it to Miki. Croatia also left a strong impression on me with its stunning Adriatic Sea and picturesque tourist spots. It was my first time experiencing the sea, and we stayed overnight in Dubrovnik, Croatia's famed historical and tourist hub. Despite the beauty around me, thoughts of Miki occupied my mind incessantly, preventing me from fully enjoying the excursion. I daydreamed about returning to these places with him by my side one day.

I felt immensely grateful for the opportunity to join the excursion as a final high school trip. Reflecting on that time, I still cringe at not expressing proper gratitude to the school for this extraordinary gift. Back then, I lacked guidance on showing appreciation at home and school. Moving to Australia later in life highlighted these gaps in my understanding of gratitude and its significance.

Upon returning from the excursion, I set my sights on preparing for Year Four, my final year of high school. My goal was clear: to excel academically and secure admission to the University St Kiril and Methodij in Skopje, where I aimed to pursue a Bachelor of Pedagogy. This course was a new offering in Skopje, previously only available in Belgrade, and I was determined not to miss out on this opportunity. I kept my plans close to my chest, especially at home, where I didn't want my aunt or grandmother to influence my father against my aspirations.

Regarding Miki, uncertainty clouded my thoughts. If he didn't reach out to me, I resolved not to chase after him, no matter how much I loved him. I decided to focus on my studies and wait until I secured a place at university. If he remained available, we could explore a future together. If he had found someone else, I would accept it and move on, focusing on my educational goals, which seemed the best path forward for me at that time.

During that summer, I met Miki a few times. He visited me, and I travelled to his town to spend time together. The moments spent with him reaffirmed my deep affection, and when he attended the weddings of his relatives in Bitola, he invited me along, granting us more time together. I shared my plans with him, expressing my dedication to studying in Skopje. Miki listened attentively and believed in my abilities.

I mustered the courage to ask him about his life and whether he was involved with anyone else. Miki revealed he wasn't in a serious relationship but didn't explicitly deny seeing other girls. Though relieved he wasn't committed elsewhere, the thought of him dating others unsettled me deeply. I counted on him being available for at least another year while he completed his five-year studies, possibly extending to a sixth year for outstanding exams. I envisioned our relationship becoming serious once I moved to Skopje. Being with Miki made me feel euphoric, like floating above the clouds. His presence alone profoundly impacted me, making me feel loved and valued in ways I struggled to explain. He often spoke of successful relationships where partners could talk endlessly, asserting that we were one of those couples. Looking back, I realise this dependency on him for validation nurtured a deep-seated insecurity within me, a feeling of incompleteness that only he could assuage.

I was in my final year of high school when I decided to surprise him at the start of winter. I convinced my sister to join me, and we headed straight to Prilep, their 'Korzo', where young people gathered to socialise. Every city in Macedonia had its own 'Korzo'.

It was just before New Year, bitterly cold winter weather, but I was certain he had returned from Skopje and would be pleased to see me again. And indeed, we found him there. However, he wasn't alone. There was a girl beside him as they walked together. When he spotted us, he stopped, looking surprised. He greeted us and briefly conversed, asking when we had arrived and how long we would stay. I replied that we had just arrived and would leave early the next morning.

That night, we stayed with our relatives, and I spent most of the time crying with a heavy heart. I felt foolish and naive. How could I have believed that Miki was waiting for me? How could he have looked at me and treated me like he had feelings for me? I had always made excuses for him—his lack of a car, his studies in Skopje. Seeing him with another girl shattered my dreams but didn't diminish my love and feelings for him.

Despite my efforts to convince myself that this encounter marked the end of my so-called relationship with Miki, a voice inside me insisted otherwise. In that fleeting moment we met, I saw a spark in his eyes. I went to bed that night with lingering questions: *Who was he? And why did he hold such sway over me?*

Chapter 16

The Night in Ledigos

"Don't give up, don't take anything personally, and don't take no for an answer. You never know what you're going to learn along the way."

Sophia Amoruso

We arrived in Ledigos around three o'clock. Ledigos is a small village. Most of the pilgrims we knew stayed in the next town a few more kilometres away. However, we had already booked our accommodation. The weather was pleasant, and our room looked charming with a bowl of fruit left for us. We shared the bathroom and toilet with guests from two other rooms, which wasn't an issue. After settling in, we washed our clothes in the laundry outside the main building and relaxed in our room.

The albergue seemed quite full. Later, we went downstairs, where tables and chairs outside the bar were occupied by locals dressed in their best attire, likely due to the upcoming festive day, the Feast of St James, on July 25th. We had a drink there before ordering our dinner early. We chose paella with rice and vegetables and decided to sleep early since the next day's walk would cover twenty-six to nearly thirty kilometres. If we knew we couldn't get much sleep that night, we might have waited to dine with other pilgrims.

While sitting in the bar, we noticed groups of nicely dressed people heading to or coming from somewhere. The atmosphere felt quite festive. Peter and I lingered over our drinks, enjoying the moment and staying longer than planned.

We started talking about traditions. Peter didn't have much to share; aside from Easter and Christmas, his family didn't celebrate many special occasions. I reflected on how festive days seem more significant in smaller places, where most people know each other and the sense of community is stronger.

I shared childhood memories with Peter, reminiscing how much I loved celebrations, especially when we lived in the village and the whole community came together. I told him I still follow some Macedonian traditions and express my gratitude for his support in keeping them alive. We celebrate our patron saint, St Klement, and always host guests on that day. It's a tradition that helps me retain a cherished piece of my heritage.

After dinner, we returned to our room, ready to rest. Around nine o'clock, loud music began playing. At first, we thought it was coming from the restaurant where we were staying, but soon we realized it was from a neighbouring bar. The music was so loud that sleeping seemed impossible. I couldn't help but wonder if this was a regular occurrence or just part of a festive event. As the hours dragged on, my hope of the music stopping and getting some sleep faded.

We both lay quietly in bed, allowing our bodies to at least relax.

My thoughts drifted back to my last year of high school. My focus was entirely on my studies. I hadn't heard from Miki, nor did I expect to. I tried to convince myself that our meetings had a purpose, but we had only seen each other a few times. We did not write letters to each other. From time to time, we would write a telegram. And that was all.

I was certain other girls admired him. Perhaps he was even in love with the girl I saw him with. And who was I? Just nobody. He had given me so much confidence, and I was grateful. It felt like all my faith stemmed from him. I couldn't shake him from my mind.

I tried to immerse myself in schoolwork. By the end of the year, we faced final exams.

The students who achieved excellent results didn't sit for the finals. Many parents used their connections to help their children. In Macedonia, teachers were under immense pressure at the time. My parents didn't even attend the parent-teacher interviews during high school. We lacked connections, and I had no interest in anything I didn't earn. I took pride in every result, regardless of how high or low. I always believed I gave my best effort.

The most challenging part came after finishing high school. I aimed to study in Skopje at the university of my choice. Teaching wasn't my initial interest; I preferred involvement in curriculum and student well-being. Pedagogy suited me perfectly. However, achieving my dream required my father's approval. I knew I had to tread carefully, navigating around my eighty-year-old grandmother, who still influenced my father alongside my aunt. I waited for the right moment to approach him alone.

As usual, after finishing his work, my father was in the other room making brooms, and that's where I found him alone. I felt for him; he rarely had any time to relax. I sat down beside him and brought up the important topic. I explained that the course I wanted to pursue was at the university in Skopje, highlighting the effort I'd put in over the last two years. He listened attentively, acknowledging my dedication, but shared his concerns about our financial limitations.

"Dad, I haven't asked for anything all my life. I've worn hand-me-downs and never complained. It is crucial for my future," I pleaded.

"I understand," he sighed. "But there are courses here, like law or teaching."

"Dad, I'm not sure about the law. There's a two-year diploma in primary education here, but I want a degree for better opportunities, and this course is at the university in Skopje," I persisted.

He looked at me sadly. "If you go to Skopje, you'll struggle. My earnings barely cover our bills. We depend on these brooms. Your grandfather's health is failing; if he can't go to market, we'll stop making them. I don't know where to find the money to support you."

Desperate, I leapt from my chair. "Dad, I'll find a job. There's a student employment agency. Skopje's a big city; there must be work for students."

He was almost ready to refuse outright. Tears streamed down my face as I begged, "Please don't say no, Dad. Please. I respect you so much. I wouldn't do this without your blessing. I'll make it work. You'll never regret letting me try."

Anger and sadness mingled on his face, his voice flat as he struggled with his decision.

"Do whatever you want!" he said sharply. It was a phrase my dad used when he couldn't bring himself to say 'no'.

"Thank you, Dad. I promise I won't forget this, and I won't ask you for anything else," I said. That was the last time I sought my father's permission and I kept my word. I've never forgotten that day; the memory still tears my eyes. From that moment on, he treated me as an adult, and I cherished that newfound independence deeply.

The next day, my father returned from work with a colleague I hadn't met. He asked me to make coffee for them, and the man asked me about my plans after high school. Before I could respond, my father interjected, mentioning my desire to study Pedagogy in Skopje. The unfamiliar man began discussing how many students wasted their parents' money by failing to complete their studies in the capital.

I tuned out the negative comments, focusing instead on my father's voice from the kitchen. What he said next resonated deeply with me and stayed with me forever.

"If she goes, I know she will finish. Our challenge is the money," my father affirmed.

I wanted to embrace him and express the meaning of his words to me. His belief in my determination guided me through university and shaped my approach to life.

My sister and I travelled to Skopje the following week, and I submitted my university application. I learned that the course accepted seventy full-time and ten part-time students, which made me anxious. Despite having high grades and meeting all prerequisites, there was no certainty of acceptance. I eagerly awaited the results of my application, counting down the days until they were released.

When the day finally arrived, I asked a friend who went to work in Skopje to check the results for me. I was impatient and sought immediate confirmation instead of waiting for the letter. Unfortunately, the news was disheartening—he couldn't find my name on the list, meaning I wasn't accepted.

I was stunned and deeply disappointed. I had been so confident in my acceptance. Walking into the room where my parents and grandparents were watching TV, I announced the news with a heavy heart. To my surprise, my father seemed almost pleased.

"I told you so. We don't have connections. It's all about who you know," my dad remarked. His rationale didn't sway me. All I wanted was to be alone, to mourn not only the shattered dream of university but also the loss of Miki. His presence had changed me, even if he was no longer in my life.

The next day, I returned to Skopje to collect my application and apply for the University of Law in Bitola in the second round. It was mid-July, scorching hot, and the campus was almost empty. Most exams had concluded by June's end, and students were on holiday. I searched for the lists posted at the university entrance, hoping to find some consolation.

I finally found a list of Pedagogy students for the academic year 1981/1982. I scanned each name anxiously until I found mine, listed at number fifty-one: Gordana Murgovska. I couldn't believe it. The person I had asked to check hadn't come through, or perhaps he hadn't seen my name. None of it mattered now; I got a place at the university.

I must have stood there staring at my name for a while, unable to comprehend the moment fully. Eventually, I located the student services office and informed the lady at the counter about my discovery. She congratulated me warmly and confirmed that if my name was on the list, I was officially a student at the University Kiril and Metodij in Skopje. She provided details for enrolment, and I could hardly contain my joy.

Leaving the university, I felt like I was floating. The pressure and uncertainty that had weighed on me only moments before had evaporated completely. I was proud of myself and couldn't stop smiling. As I walked away, the next item on my agenda was to find Miki. Whatever his role in my life, I knew a significant part of my happiness at that moment was because of him. I hadn't seen Miki or been in touch since I saw him with another girl. I knew I needed to see him at that moment, so I did.

The police vehicle arrived at the pub around three o'clock, getting a brief pause to the blaring music and offering us a fleeting chance to sleep, snapping me back to reality. I couldn't believe such loud music had been allowed to play almost all night. We knew the next day would be challenging—a long walk awaited us after a restless night. My bones and muscles ached, but we managed to steal barely an hour of sleep, desperately trying to rest despite the circumstances.

Chapter 17

A Plea for the Future

"Walking is a rhythm of life."

It was July 25th. By four-thirty a.m., we were up, tending to our feet and blisters, grateful for the hiking wool that eased much of the discomfort. We felt exhausted, mostly because we had barely slept, but it was important to start early. A hot and long day awaited us, with our next stop in Bercianos—a twenty=six kilometre hike ahead.

Peter's organisational skills and attention to detail impressed me as he smiled through our sleepless night, assuring us that the upcoming albergue stay would be better. Booking hadn't allowed private rooms so it would be our first shared accommodation experience. Hoping for a restful night, we set out early, leaving Albergue LaMorena at five-thirty. We quickly discovered the source of the previous night's music—a nearby bar.

Navigating the morning haze, we eventually found the Camino sign—a yellow star and shell—and aimed to cover most of our distance before noon. As we descended through the fields, discomfort set in; my left knee began to ache, a consequence of the previous sleepless night's toll on my body. Normally, pains from the day before would subside overnight, but today was different.

Throughout my Camino journey, I reflected more on my past than the present beauty around me. While I appreciated the sunrise and the westward path, my heart and soul were opening up, allowing memories and past events to flow freely. The Camino offered me a sanctuary to unpack and understand these memories without fear or anger. It was liberating, except for thoughts of Miki, which I had avoided until now.

The grief over Miki had haunted me for years, an intense pain even though he was still alive. Until these days, I couldn't understand the intensity of strong grief for someone alive. Separating from him had left me feeling incomplete, every thought of him piercing through me, evoking tears and deep anguish. It felt as though every cell in my body was affected by his absence. I found solace in the fact that people around me respected my need not to hear his name mentioned.

My thoughts drifted again to the day I was accepted at university. That day, after I left university, I took the bus that stopped in Prilep on its way to Bitola. I hoped to see Miki but was unsure if he would be alone. I went to my uncle's house and, with my cousins, went to Korzo that evening, hoping to see him there. And I did, surrounded by a few of his friends. When he saw me that evening, he was visibly surprised. Despite my last encounter with him with another girl, there was a deep connection between us that I couldn't ignore. It seemed he felt it, too, evident in the genuine smile on his face as he hugged and kissed me, as though we had been apart for mere days rather than months.

"I'm so happy to see you," he whispered, holding my hand as we walked. I mentioned I would be staying at my uncle's place that night and shouldn't be out too late. We wandered and found a quiet spot. The closeness I felt with him was overwhelming; I felt elated, like I could leap with happiness and excitement. With university ahead and Miki by my side, I believed nothing could come between us now. At nineteen, it felt like the perfect age for a serious relationship. It felt like the time we hadn't seen each other did not exist. It felt like we saw each other the previous day, not several months ago, without any contact.

We paused, and he hugged me, his eyes locking with mine. "I need to tell you something," he said, his smile fading into seriousness.

My heart sank. *He's going to tell me he loves the girl I saw him with*, I quickly thought and felt sharp pain through my body.

"I'm going to be a father," he announced.

I was shocked. "I didn't know you were married. When did you get married?" I asked softly, barely audible over the rush of emotions.

"No, I'm not married, and I'm not planning to marry anytime soon. I couldn't marry anyone because of the child," he explained.

"I don't understand. Is it the girl I saw you with?" – I asked, expecting him to say 'Yes'.

"No, it's someone else," he clarified. Miki explained that he had known this girl since high school. They were the same age and had sporadically seen each other but were never in a committed relationship. She had found a job after high school, and their interactions had been casual.

"She has the same name as you," he added quietly.

My mind recalled his reaction upon hearing my name two years ago. We both fell silent, unsure of what to say next. My thoughts drifted to the girl and the overwhelming shame an illegitimate child would bring upon her and her family in Macedonia. It seemed like an unimaginable burden.

"Miki, I think you should marry her," I finally said.

He looked at me earnestly.

"I love you deeply, but the right thing is to marry her and spare her and your child from the shame and complications. You know how it is in Macedonia. Can you imagine what she's going through? If this were me, I'd rather die than disgrace my family, no matter the personal cost." I spoke rapidly, pouring out my thoughts.

"It's not that simple, Gordana. I don't believe in forced marriage. I'm not ready to accept this child either, not now. She's an adult, she's working, and she made her decision to keep the child. We agreed she would have an abortion, but I had an important exam and couldn't go with her that day. She didn't go either." His reluctance to discuss the matter further was palpable.

How an exam could be more important than addressing this situation? I thought, finding it difficult to comprehend.

"Maybe she thought you wanted the child to be born. If I were in her place, I would probably think the same," I remarked.

"I didn't know what I wanted, but I'm not ready to have a child," Miki replied firmly, his tone resolute and decisive.

"I have to go, Miki. It's almost ten o'clock," I hurriedly interjected. "I told my relatives I would be there by nine." As we walked, our conversation focused mainly on me and my upcoming studies. We agreed to travel to Skopje together, as he needed to enrol for his final year. Upon reaching my uncle's house, I noticed the lights were off, and the gate was locked, suggesting they assumed I had caught the last bus and gone home. Seeing a light on the other side of the house, I pondered what to do next. Miki then offered to let me stay at his place.

"Don't worry. My parents have met you, and you can sleep in a separate room," he reassured me.

"No way. You're too dangerous. I'm not sure I want to go to Skopje now and be so close to you," I joked, though Miki smiled warmly.

After kissing him goodbye, I climbed over the gate, where my cousin Slobodanka awaited me. She remarked that she knew I would come back.

That night, as I lay in bed, unable to sleep, I reflected on the whirlwind of information from that day. I tried to read between the lines of my conversation with Miki. He might have preferred the child to be born, but I wondered why he couldn't take more responsibility. I empathised with the girl; she must have loved him deeply to find herself in such a difficult situation. Why hadn't Miki ended things earlier if he didn't intend to have a serious relationship? He mentioned they had discussed stopping seeing each other on the night she became pregnant. It felt like I was stepping into a tangled web, and I was right.

My phone rang, interrupting my thoughts. It was my younger daughter, Madeline, from Melbourne who was calling. I was thrilled to hear from her, especially while walking through fields and hills in the middle of nowhere. Madeline sounded excited.

"Mum, guess what? We bought the house we talked about before. Logan and I are so happy—it's ours now!" Madeline exclaimed.

I congratulated Madeline and Logan wholeheartedly. "I'm so proud of both of you, my beautiful girl," I told her. Then I remembered the date. "Today is the feast of St James, 25th July. Maybe he helped you out. St James is the patron of Spain, and his relics are in the cathedral of Santiago de Compostela, where we're heading."

"Wow, Mum, you're right. It does feel like we got some help," Madeline laughed joyfully from the other side. I put her on speakerphone, knowing Peter would want to congratulate them, too. After exchanging goodbyes, my thoughts drifted to my daughters, who mean the world to me. I cherished how they had embraced Peter and our relationship.

Madeline, my younger daughter, is twenty-five. She completed her master's degree in counselling and works as a counsellor at one of the TAFE colleges in Melbourne. She and her partner, Logan, had been trying to buy a house in Melbourne, where the prices had skyrocketed. I was relieved they found one they loved and could afford. My older daughter, Christina, twenty-seven, finished her master's in science and biotechnology. She and her fiancé, Jack, bought a house together a few years ago, and their wedding is next year—a day I eagerly anticipate. Our bond is strong, and while we're close, we also respect each other's independence as adults. They have a wonderful relationship with their father, which fills me with gratitude.

Walking alongside Peter, I reflected on how blessed and privileged I felt. A decade ago, I had walked through hell, remembering my mother and grandmother, who shaped me—accepting life's challenges with calmness and sometimes a touch of passive-aggression. Now, with Peter, it felt different. I admired him from a distance as he maintained his steady pace while I struggled, feeling more like I was crawling than walking. Each rest stop brought relief, yet the pain in my knee grew more intense with every step.

I went back to my thoughts. The next day, I returned home excited about my university acceptance but found tension instead of happiness and support. When my father returned from work, he asked where I had been the previous night, his face a mask of anger.

"Dad, I found out I got into uni. The person who checked for me gave me the wrong info. It doesn't matter now. I stopped in Prilep to see Uncle Milan's family. They were kind enough to ask me to stay the night and sent their regards," I explained, hoping to diffuse his anger.

My father seemed unsurprised. "I figured you couldn't wait to see him, I mean, your Uncle Milan," he said briefly and sarcastically. We understood who *him* was, though my father avoided saying Miki's name.

The following week, he barely spoke to me, acting like I didn't exist. During dinners, conversations carefully avoided any mention of my plans to study in Skopje. It hurt deeply. Miki had shown more interest and happiness about my future studies than my own family did, and that realisation stung. Perhaps that was why I cherished him; he made me feel valued and supported in a way my family didn't. I had hardly seen him the previous two years, but he was constantly on my mind and reacted like we were never apart, visibly happy that I would go to study in Skopje.

One day that week, I heard heated voices behind our gate as I approached home. Living on a main street meant our conversations could be overheard by anyone passing by. I recognised the voice of my Aunt Ljubica, my father's elder sister. She was speaking loudly, almost shouting, making it clear she was upset.

"You're keeping secrets from me! Why didn't I hear about this sooner? I'm not surprised by her, but him, my brother." Certainly, *her* was my mother. "Is he out of his mind, sending her off to Skopje when there are schools here? Complaining about money, yet he's sending her away. They're taking advantage of you! You're a fool if you go to market again," my aunt exclaimed angrily.

I was stunned when my normally quiet grandfather interrupted her. His voice filled with rare anger. "Enough! I am not your mother to tell me what to do. You have no authority to teach your brother how to raise his children. Go home and tend to your own family," my grandfather almost yelled.

I approached the gate, making my presence known. My aunt and grandfather turned to look at me, their expressions a mix of surprise and discomfort.

"Hi, what's going on?" I interjected, pretending I hadn't overheard anything.

My aunt's expression softened slightly. "Oh, nothing. I was leaving," she replied curtly before walking away.

I turned to my grandfather, grateful for his intervention, and hugged him tightly, kissing his forehead. "Grandpa, you're the best grandpa in the world. I love you so much," I said, feeling affection for him. His gentle smile in response warmed my heart, reinforcing why my mother held him in such high regard—his protective stance against her overbearing sister-in-law.

Later that day, I waited for my mother to return from work. Reflecting on her life and struggles, I understood her more deeply. She worked tirelessly as a seasonal labourer for a large farming company, silently bearing the burdens placed upon her. Guilt crept into my thoughts as I considered our financial situation. I resolved to find part-time work through a student employment agency in Skopje, determined not to burden my parents further.

When my mother finally settled, I sat beside her, seeking her approval and support.

"Mum, are you happy for me? Are you glad that I'll be continuing my studies at university?" I asked earnestly.

Her gaze softened as she looked at me, her beauty and gentleness shining through.

"I'm very pleased. I always wanted at least one of my children to pursue education. I'm glad you take after your father, not like me—blind and foolish," she replied softly, her words laced with self-deprecation.

"Mum, don't call yourself foolish. Your craftsmanship is exceptional, worthy of any museum," I reassured her. Her traditional dresses, meticulously crafted despite her lack of formal education, were a testament to her talent.

"And you're so beautiful, Mum. Grandma still can't believe none of us inherited your looks," I added genuinely.

A small smile tugged at her lips. "I needed a brain, not beauty. I feel like I belong to a different era. In my world, if you're not literate, you're blind."

I hugged her tightly, showering her with affection.

She hesitated, then continued, "That boy you love ... I don't know what to say. He's handsome and well-mannered. I'm sure other girls notice that, too. In Skopje, take care of yourself," she advised quietly, her concern evident.

"Don't worry, Mum. Everything will be fine," I reassured her, though uncertainty gnawed at me. I knew her worries stemmed from a place of love and caution. Unable to express joy or approval openly, she shied away from responsibility and felt deeply guilty if things went wrong. I was listening to her and thinking how much I wished I could share the news I had heard from Miki the last time I saw him. I wished I could be close to my mother and tell her everything. I couldn't. I did not feel close to her and did not trust her opinion. I was glad that at least she was happy for me.

Retreating to my room, shared with my siblings, I felt a mix of excitement and anxiety. Achieving my goal of university acceptance meant I would soon live independently in a bustling city for the next four to five years. Sonja, a classmate I hardly knew, had asked to share a room in Skopje, and I accepted without hesitation. Besides Miki, I didn't know anyone in Skopje.

At nineteen, I felt mature enough to fend for myself. I promised to excel in my studies, secure a part-time job promptly, and take full responsibility for my life.

I was at a loss regarding Miki. Thinking about him caused a deep ache in my heart. Over the past two years, I had seen him several times, but the news he had shared with me was staggering. I struggled to comprehend how he could acknowledge paternity yet evade responsibility. The idea of separating from him before our relationship even began was agonising. Confusion clouded my thoughts, and I longed to confide in someone, but I didn't feel I had anyone close enough to open up to truly.

We passed a few villages before approaching Sahagun, and I eagerly anticipated finding a place to rest. Fatigue and leg pain were setting in, a reminder of the long journey ahead with over thirteen kilometres to Bercianos. First, we stopped at the nearest cafe for lunch and a well-deserved break. It was a pivotal moment as we were halfway to Santiago de Compostela. Peter suggested obtaining a halfway certificate, which initially didn't excite me much. However, I reasoned that it was a tangible acknowledgment of our journey and the effort we had put in so far.

To achieve this, the first step was locating the pilgrim office to obtain the certificate. This involved following GPS directions, but we initially mistook the location. Here, the Spaniards pleasantly surprised us once again. A helpful woman appeared on a nearby building's balcony and directed us to the correct place just a few steps away.

Once directed correctly, the next step involved climbing the stairs to reach the entrance of the pilgrim office. It was essential to remain polite and thankful to those who had assisted us along the way, acknowledging their kindness.

I could hardly climb the stairs. I was unsure if I felt that way because we did not have a proper rest the previous night or if something was wrong with me.

Upon entering the office, we answered a few questions from the lady at the counter. This step ensured that we met the requirements for receiving the halfway certificate, which was issued in Latin, adding a traditional touch to our accomplishment.

After receiving the certificate, despite feeling physically drained, the final step was to gather the strength to continue silently. While challenging, I understood that perseverance was key. Reminding myself of the voluntary nature of our pilgrimage helped me maintain motivation, encouraging me to press on despite the fatigue.

We had more than ten kilometers to walk to Bercianos. Despite my efforts to stay positive, I noticed the walk was becoming increasingly difficult. After each stop, it was harder to get moving again, and the persistent pain in my legs made every step a challenge. I didn't say anything to Peter, determined to convince myself that everything would be all right.

My thoughts transported me back as if the events had occurred just yesterday, not over forty years ago. I vividly recalled the day of enrolment, brimming with excitement. It was my first time travelling to Skopje with Miki. The bus journey paused in Prilep, and to my delight, Miki boarded the same bus. We talked a lot. After two hours, we arrived in Skopje. Filled with anticipation under the sweltering August sun, I couldn't think of anything else apart from the two of us. The way he looked at me melted my heart.

Initially, we headed to the medical campus to enrol Miki, then hurried across the university grounds to submit my applications. The campus of the faculty of philosophy was on the other side. We ended up walking nearly four to five kilometres. When we finally arrived, we discovered we were too late—student services had already closed for the day. A sign on the window announced that enrolment would resume the following day. The bustling scene of students crowding to enrol only heightened my anxiety. The enrolment window was open for just two hours a day, and even now, I struggle to comprehend how services operated in Macedonia at that time.

I started to panic, unsure what to do next, especially since I had already purchased a return ticket. Miki took charge and phoned his uncle, his father's brother residing in Skopje. Promptly, his uncle arrived and assured me he would handle my enrolment the next day. I felt deeply embarrassed, having missed the crucial task I had set out to complete that day.

His uncle noticed my birthplace while reviewing my application. He mentioned being a godfather and close friend to someone born in Puturus. I was too preoccupied with enrolment to inquire about this connection. Later, I discovered that his friend was none other than my uncle—a first cousin of my father's who served in the military. The coincidence struck me as remarkable, adding a surprising twist to an otherwise stressful day.

My exhaustion and the pain in my legs snapped me back to the present. It was late afternoon, and we had stopped at almost every spot where I could find a place to sit. In the distance, a cluster of houses appeared, but the walk seemed endless. By the end, my legs felt like lead.

"Peter, let's stop in the first place with accommodation. It doesn't matter that we have a booking. I can't walk anymore," I pleaded, nearly in tears.

I realised something was off. Maybe it was the lack of sleep from the previous night, leaving my body without a chance to recover. I didn't know what was wrong, but I knew something was wrong.

"I feel like I've reached my limit," I told Peter, my voice trembling. He looked just as tired, the day's heat and the dry, dusty roads taking their toll on us.

"No problem, my darling. Let's see if we can find something," Peter replied, his voice reassuring.

Finally, we reached a large building that turned out to be an albergue. The gate, which looked locked, was a letdown. The hostel was closed.

With no choice, we continued walking to the next one. We were approaching another hostel when Peter's face lit up. "This is the albergue we booked," he said. We walked in, relieved to see our Camino friends from Michigan, Kevin and Joan, resting at the outdoor bar. They hadn't found a private room, so they planned to stay like us in the same hostel in Bercianos.

After registering and stamping our credentials, we headed to the first floor and found bunk beds near the showers and toilets. The area was clean, the beds draped in curtains for privacy, but it was far less comfortable than a private room. I remembered telling Peter how much I admired the pilgrims who stayed in the hostels throughout their journey. It wasn't the best solution, but we were happy to lay down and relax after the long journey.

Later, we joined Kevin and Joan at the bar for a chat and dinner. It was the last time we saw them. That's how the Camino works—you meet people, share deep conversations, and everyone heads their way the next day. The chances of seeing them again are slim. They became our Facebook friends, and we keep in touch, exchanging messages and following each other's paths.

I skipped the shower that night and went to bed in the clothes I had worn all day. I felt like a true pilgrim. The good thing was that our Camino gear was top-notch, from underwear and socks to T-shirts and tops made from Merino wool—it made a big difference. We didn't unpack our backpacks. The lights were off by ten, and the Albergue fell silent as pilgrims settled into bed. I tried to sleep despite the cramped space.

By six in the morning, pilgrims were stirring. Peter and I left around seven, realising we were the last to depart. It felt late; we couldn't stick to our usual routine. Typically, we wake up around four-thirty, ready by five-thirty. We unpacked our bags every night, repacked them in the morning, and tended to our feet, covering red spots and blisters with hiking wool and tape. But in the hostel, space was limited, and we were careful not to disturb the others. We had a long walk ahead, over twenty-eight kilometres.

Chapter 18

Unbreakable Bonds

"True friendship lasted forever."

It was the 26th of July when we left the hostel, heading towards Mansilla de las Mulas. After two consecutive nights of interrupted sleep, exhaustion weighed heavily on us. Peter admitted he couldn't relax fully, especially not on the top bunk bed. Despite our efforts to stay positive, our fatigue was undeniable. Along the route to Mansilla de las Mulas, there were three villages where we could stop, each spaced roughly ten kilometres apart.

I let Peter walk ahead of me as I retreated into my thoughts, revisiting a chapter of my past that had left deep footprints on my life.

I was eager to begin university. Sonja, with whom I planned to share a room, told me her boyfriend found us a place in a suburb called Kozle. I had no idea where Kozle was or how far it was from the university, but I was grateful to have accommodation sorted. By the end of September, I had moved to Skopje, although my memories of those initial days were few. Lectures officially began in October, and I arrived a day early.

I only recall the new, large house at the forest's edge. Our room was on the ground floor, while a couple and their two teenage children occupied the first floor. There were three or four other rooms on our floor, likely housing other students who kept to themselves. At the end of the corridor was a shared bathroom. Our accommodation was at the last bus stop, about fifteen stops from the university. Sonja and I commuted together during the first few days, but soon we followed our schedules.

Miki mentioned he would come to Skopje in mid-October when exam season began. Thinking about him left me feeling deeply unsettled. Deep down, I knew something about the relationship didn't feel right. Yet, my heart seemed entirely disconnected from my mind. I felt compelled to let things unfold naturally and allow the love I was experiencing to take its course. I realised I didn't know much about him. Over the past two years, we had seen each other only a handful of times. While we shared a strong connection, the relationship had yet to begin.

My thoughts turned to university life. The university environment was vastly different from high school—busy, with students rushing in all directions. I worried about getting lost in the crowd. I searched for the Faculty of Philosophy building, where my classes in pedagogy, psychology, sociology, and related subjects were held. I didn't know anyone there. Some students seemed familiar with each other, having come from the same cities and schools. Feeling shy, I hesitated to strike up conversations.

On the second day, a lecture ended around noon, leaving me a two-hour gap before the next. I went outside and sat on a cement bench near the entrance. It was a beautiful, sunny day. Across from me, on a similar bench, sat a tall, blond girl in a white dress. She appeared engrossed in papers and books. I thought she might be in the same boat as me—new and friendless. I decided to take the initiative.

I sat next to her and introduced myself. She looked up, smiled warmly, and introduced herself as Tatjana shortened Tanja. We quickly discovered that we were both studying pedagogy and were in our first year. Despite not noticing her in previous classes, we started a conversation that flowed easily until the next lecture began. Tanja hailed from Pestani, a picturesque tourist spot by Ohrid Lake. Although I hadn't visited Pestani, I had been to Ohrid on an excursion and knew of its popularity as Macedonia's top tourist destination.

Tanja, one year older than me, shared her journey when we first met. She had completed high school and specialised in nursing in Skopje, where she lived with another family for four years. Originally aspiring to study medicine and become a doctor, she had taken a gap year after not being accepted into medical school before deciding to pursue pedagogy. Tanja was refreshingly easy to talk to—open, confident, and fun. Meeting her marked the beginning of a friendship that would last a lifetime, one that couldn't be replaced by anyone or anything.

From the moment we met, we were inseparable. We attended classes and lectures regularly, always sitting beside each other. Tanja's confidence and sociability were striking—she effortlessly engaged with everyone, including lecturers and professors. She asked questions, led discussions, cracked jokes, and had everyone in stitches. By the end of the first week, Tanja and I were known as a pair around campus. After lectures, we often wandered around Bit-Basar, Skopje's old shopping centre, sometimes stopping for coffee. I confided in Tanja about Miki, and she eagerly looked forward to meeting him.

Tanja also shared stories from her past, including her high school boyfriend, who ended their relationship during an excursion when he developed feelings for another girl, her classmate. Reflecting on it, Tanja wasn't bitter; she found humour in the situation, noting how the boy eventually married the other girl. She joked about her reputation for being unique and knowledgeable yet intimidating to boys who struggled to approach her romantically. She preferred authenticity over pretence, valuing her independence and strong opinions.

I admired Tanja's independence and her unapologetic embrace of who she was. In the conservative atmosphere of 1980s Macedonia, where societal norms favoured quiet, compliant girls like my mother, Tanja stood out with her intelligence, capability, and independence. She had a knack for starting conversations with laughter and ending them positively. Being around her taught me a lot, and I saw her as a role model for embodying positive energy and authenticity.

During her time in Skopje, Tanja lived in the suburb called Airport with a family, having also lived with another family during high school. She valued her independence and didn't want to live under anyone else's 'supervision', as she put it. Despite her qualifications as a nurse, she was on a waiting list for a job and planned to study part time and live alone once she found employment.

Having Tanja as a friend at university enriched my experience profoundly. I looked forward to lectures for the academic content and the joy of being with Tanja. Our friendship also introduced me to students from all over Macedonia, expanding my circle of friends. In a class of seventy students, the majority were girls—teaching, at the time, was seen as a more suitable profession for women than men.

The following week, Miki visited, and I introduced him to Tanja. Instantly, they hit it off, becoming fast friends, which made me incredibly happy. Finally, I had my boyfriend, whom I had yearned to be with for so long, and now I had also found a friend unlike any I'd known before, all while studying at the university of my dreams. Though the money I received from home wasn't much, it was enough to get by, and I didn't mind because I was so content—I couldn't have asked for more.

Yet, despite this newfound happiness, something felt off. The baby, Miki wasn't ready to accept, had been born at the start of September 1981, and since then, Miki had changed. Although he did not speak about his son, he seemed worried, and I started to feel uneasy, as if my happiness was somehow built upon someone else's unhappiness. Despite loving him deeply at that point in my life and not wanting to leave him, I began noticing aspects of Miki's behaviour that troubled me. Almost everything seemed to happen on his terms—we saw each other when it suited him, and he never explained or apologised for being late or unable to come. I was determined to focus on my studies and didn't want anything or anyone to hinder my progress.

I came back to the present and noticed we had walked nearly eight kilometres, reaching a small village called El Burgo Ranero, where I saw Peter waiting for me.

He smiled and asked, "How's the pain in your legs?"

"I'm not sure," I replied. "It feels better while I'm walking, but as soon as I stop, it's worse to start again. I'll see how I feel after this break."

"Take your time," Peter said reassuringly. "There's no need to rush. At least we have our accommodation booked." I could see he was already feeling the strain of the day.

With fifteen days ahead of us to reach Santiago de Compostela, a wave of negative thoughts began to creep in. I couldn't help but feel that the past two sleepless nights had drained us. We'd fallen out of our routine, and our bodies hadn't had the chance to recover. I kept these thoughts to myself as we sank gratefully into chairs at a nearby bar.

We hoped the coffee and breakfast would revive us. As usual, I handled ordering the food while Peter checked the route and directions, ensuring we hadn't missed anything.

"I'm looking forward to getting to León and having a two-night rest," I said to Peter, trying to sound optimistic. Deep down, I hoped the break would ease the pain in my left leg, which was becoming increasingly pronounced.

"We just have one more day to León," I added, unable to hide the concern in my voice. The many kilometres still ahead weighed heavily on me, and I couldn't help but worry about how I would manage the next day. Peter recommended that I see the doctor in Leon. I assured him that the rest at Leon would help.

Chapter 19

A Stranger in the Dark

"Apprehension about what lies ahead."

After an hour's break, we left the bar and El Burgo Raneroand. I tried to resume walking as usual, but something felt off. The pain in my leg had intensified, and I couldn't pinpoint where it was coming from, but each step felt like a struggle. After about ten to fifteen minutes of walking, the pain eased a bit, and I started to feel better. The next village was more than ten kilometres away, and I focused on each step, trying to keep my mind on the journey ahead.

As we walked, I noticed that the pilgrims we had met earlier were already ahead of us. Along the way, we started encountering new faces—pilgrims who had begun their journey from Burgos and even Logroño. I preferred to walk alone, allowing my thoughts to become my sole companion again.

It was early November 1981, a Friday afternoon, and I was in my second month in Skopje. I had a lecture from two p.m. to four p.m. and planned to visit Miki afterwards. The walk to his place took about twenty minutes, and despite the cold weather, I decided to walk to the student accommodation where he lived instead waiting for the bus. I didn't particularly appreciate returning to my place by myself, especially when it was dark, and the electricity was restricted from six p.m. to nine p.m., with the streetlights turned off. I lived in Kozle, a suburb on the outskirts of the city, nestled at the edge of a forest. It was at least ten bus stops away from the student accommodation, and the area still felt unfamiliar and a little unsettling, especially when walking alone after dark. But I was rarely alone. Miki would often walk me home, or I'd make sure to return before nightfall.

When I arrived on the seventh floor where Miki lived, I found a note taped to his door. He had gone back to his hometown, Prilep, for the weekend with some friends who happened to have an extra seat in their car. Frustrated and disappointed by the lack of communication in those pre-mobile phone days, I hurried to the nearby bus stop. It was crowded, as expected on a Friday night, with people rushing home or heading out for the evening.

I felt exhausted, lonely, and upset. Weekends were the hardest. I didn't enjoy spending them alone. My roommate usually spent most of her weekends with her boyfriend, who lived nearby. I often wished Tanja had been my roommate instead. She lived on the opposite side of the city from me and had decided to stay with her host family for the first semester. While waiting at the bus stop buried in thoughts, I noticed a man staring at me—an average figure in a long leather jacket and beret, looking between forty and fifty years old. His gaze unnerved me, but I tried to ignore him. Boarding the bus, which was packed, I moved towards the back, relieved to be inside as the darkness outside grew.

The bus reached the final stop, and only a few passengers remained. As it came to a halt, I noticed the same man lingering near the front, his gaze fixed directly on me. Fear swept over me as he slowly exited the bus, his eyes never leaving mine.

Stepping off the bus, I was paralysed with uncertainty. There were no streetlights, just the dim bus lights casting eerie shadows. The man's presence unsettled me further as he walked in the same direction I needed to go—towards my home, with houses on the right and a dark forest on the left. Unsure if he was following or waiting, panic set in. I began walking slowly, trembling with fear and anxiety.

Suddenly, a young man running to catch the bus caught my eye. Desperate, I stopped him and explained my situation. He was kind and understanding, agreeing to walk with me. Upon hearing my answer, he asked where I lived and reassured me that he knew the house's owner. Together, we approached the house, where I saw lights on inside—a sign someone was home, comforting me. We couldn't see the stranger. It looked like he disappeared into the darkness.

Gratefully, I thanked the young man and insisted he return to catch his bus. He offered to walk me to the door, but I assured him I would be safe now. The house was less than two hundred metres away. Reluctantly, he ran back towards the bus stop while I hurried, relieved to be home and away from the unsettling encounter.

I don't know how many steps I took when I heard the man's voice so close behind me. "Stop! Stop!" he whispered urgently, twice. There were no footsteps, just his chilling voice—deep and loud in its whisper. Instantly, fear gripped me, and I began running faster than I ever had before. It was a sprint fuelled by pure terror. At first, I thought I lost my voice, but then the voice echoed again, and I screamed out in fear, a primal cry that shocked even me. It sounded like the scream of a wild animal—a sound I never imagined could come from me.

I ran as if I were flying, pushing myself until I reached the house's safety and collapsed on the stairs. Loza and Zivko, our landlords, rushed out upon hearing my cries.

"Gordana, what happened? Please, tell us," they both asked simultaneously, concern etched on their faces.

I was still in shock, trying to explain that someone had been following me, pointing into the darkness, tears streaming down my face. I repeated myself through sobs, barely able to articulate the terror I had just experienced.

Kindly, Loza tried to soothe me while Zivko searched for the mysterious man. Later, I learned that the young man who had offered to help me heard my screams and returned to find Zivko, who mistook him for the pursuer in his protective fury. Thankfully, the boy convinced Zivko of his intentions to assist me. That night, they called the police and described the man. Zivko and his friends combed the area but found no trace of him.

I never encountered that man again, but the fear lingered long after that terrifying night. I had never been particularly fond of horror movies, but I couldn't recall watching any afterwards. The experience left an indelible mark, shaping my feelings of safety and security for years.
On Monday, after my lecture, I hurried to see Miki, feeling uneasy about returning alone to my place after Friday's frightening encounter. My

thoughts of what if that man lived nearby and followed me, petrified me. I knocked on Miki's door, relieved to hear his voice inside. When he opened the door, I was shocked to find another girl sitting on his bed, visibly upset and wiping tears from her eyes. Miki introduced me to her, but the atmosphere felt tense and uncomfortable. Something was happening between them, and the girl looked devastated.

She stood up abruptly and announced she would leave. I briefly mentioned the incident from Friday, and Miki offered to accompany her to where she lived, but she declined. Once she left, I asked Miki about the girl. He explained they used to date but were no longer together, and she was upset over their breakup. He seemed unhappy, too.

"Miki, please tell me if you still have feelings for her and want to reconcile. Our relationship is different, but if you want to be with her, please don't hesitate," I said, though inwardly, I prayed he would choose to stay with me.

"No," Miki replied firmly. "Our relationship ended a long time ago. We had our share of disagreements and fights." He looked weary as he spoke.

"You seem so sad and tired. Are you okay?" I asked, concerned.

Miki sighed and paused before continuing, "Something happened over the weekend. They showed up."

"Who showed up?" I asked eagerly, wanting to understand.

"She came with her parents, uncle, and aunt. She had the baby with her. They came to our door, but I didn't invite them in. We talked at the door," Miki explained, avoiding eye contact.

I listened in disbelief, feeling deep sympathy for the girl and the baby, who deserved love, not to be shuttled from one doorstep to another.

"What did you do? How did you feel?" I asked softly, trying to grasp the situation.

"I told her we would see each other in court," Miki replied sombrely.

I was at a loss for words, my mind racing with questions about why this had happened and whether Miki was certain the baby was his. But I kept my thoughts to myself, sensing his worry and turmoil.

"You can't imagine how much I wish I could trade places with her at that moment, Goca," he said softly, using his affectionate nickname for me. "If it were you instead of her, everything would be so different, so much easier."

"I wouldn't want to be in her position," I replied, my tone firm. "I don't want anyone to marry me just because of a child."

"I wouldn't marry you just because of the child," Miki assured me, meeting my gaze earnestly.

"That night we met, she sent her sister to fetch me. Sometimes, I feel like I was set up. It was Christmas, and I had a few drinks. I'm not blaming her, though; she's a very honest person. But that's what happened. We also discussed how we wouldn't see each other again," he talked slowly.

I sat quietly, absorbing his words. Deep in myself, I believed that was the reason the baby was being born. It brought back memories of my birth and the drama that surrounded it.

The weather was warm, and I tried to savour every step of our journey. However, I began noticing something concerning. Each time we stopped to rest, getting back on my feet became increasingly difficult. My left knee felt strained, a discomfort I initially brushed off as typical after days of walking. Ivona from Slovenia, a fellow pilgrim, shared her experience of needing a five-day break due to walking difficulties, and others spoke of shin splints halting their progress. I prayed I wouldn't face the same fate. With accommodations booked and no alternative apparent, continuing to Santiago de Compostela with Peter seemed my only path forward.

Our destination for the night was Mansilla de las Mulas, a town we approached after a brief stop a few kilometres away. Despite an hour's rest, my attempts to resume walking were thwarted by excruciating knee pain. I tried to rally myself, knowing the next day's walk to Leon was shorter, and we had planned a two-night stay there. Peter gently urged me to see a doctor, but I stubbornly declined, convinced that two nights' rest in Leon would help.

Upon arriving in Mansilla, we settled into a lovely apartment in the town centre. We ventured out to find a pharmacy for essentials, stocked up on groceries from a local supermarket, and treated ourselves to a simple yet comforting dinner with a bottle of Vino Tinto. The shower brought some relief, yet the night was restless, the pain in my legs seeping through my entire body, leaving me deeply anxious.

The prospect of continuing the journey for another fifteen days, including crossing high mountains and traversing Maseta before reaching

Galicia, weighed heavily on my mind. The decision to book two nights in Astorga ahead of our arrival there from Leon brought a glimmer of relief. I looked forward to exploring Leon, though it felt like an elusive dream at that moment. Peter showed me images of the 'Romantico' apartment in Leon, its striking black and red decor resembling an art studio, ideally located near the cathedral. Despite the lack of reviews, it intrigued us both.

Chapter 20
Unravelling Truths

"With the right effort and commitment, anything is achievable."

On the morning of July 27th, we woke early and departed from Mansilla, heading toward our next destination: León. It was a relatively short walk, around eighteen to nineteen kilometres, with a few villages where we could take breaks. Peter and I couldn't contain our excitement at the thought of staying two nights in León, giving us a much-needed opportunity to rest and recharge.

We relished the peacefulness of the dark, quiet town as we began our walk. Despite the constant pain in my knee, I convinced myself that walking continuously without stopping would keep my muscles warm and manageable. Peter took a few photos of the surroundings, but I had nearly stopped taking pictures, focusing instead on relying heavily on my hiking poles and pushing forward. I refused to feel sorry for my situation, constantly reminding myself of my commitment to this journey.

These reflections remind me of the guiding principle of my life: *"You can achieve anything if you know where you're going and commit with the right effort."*

Embracing resilience over self-pity became my mantra—a mindset forged during my student years in Skopje. Growing up, my mother often leaned toward a victim mentality, but living independently in Skopje taught me to face challenges head-on. As an immigrant in Australia, I learned to prioritize gratitude and resilience, focusing on my blessings and marvelling at the almost miraculous events that have shaped my life.

I always felt a sense of guidance and support from deep within, providing peace and encouragement to pursue my goals. This inner strength reassured me that despite the pain in my knee, I would complete my journey to Santiago de Compostela on foot. While living in Skopje, I had ample time to listen to this inner voice, which often protected and guided me, especially in my relationship with Miki.

While Peter walked ahead at his own pace, my thoughts drifted back to Miki, the person I always believed had come into my life for a reason. Despite my deep love for him, I struggled to imagine a future for us beyond our time in Skopje. My inner voice was unrelenting, and though the idea of a future without him brought me to tears and filled me with fear, I couldn't ignore its clarity. Miki and I shared everything and talked about almost everything—except our future. One day, to my surprise, he brought it up.

We were sitting in his room, both unusually quiet.

"I've noticed you avoid talking about us and our future," he said.

His words caught me off guard, but I couldn't hold back. "I can't see us together in my vision, Miki. I don't trust you. You belong to too many others, and I can't imagine having a husband I don't trust," I admitted, my honesty cutting through the silence.

"What if that part changes? Would you see us together then?" he asked, his voice tinged with hope but shadowed by uncertainty.

Even in that moment, I couldn't see a future for us, no matter the promises or changes.

"Why are you with me if you can't see us together in the future?" he asked, frustration creeping into his tone.

"Because I love you. I love being with you. I can't explain it, but I can't imagine myself with anyone else. I have these overwhelming feelings for you and feel like I could do anything for you. But I can't see us together in the future," I said, trembling.

"But you don't do *everything*," Miki replied sharply, and I knew what he meant.

From the beginning of our relationship, I made it clear that I wasn't ready for an intimate relationship, and he accepted that. He never forced me into anything or did anything without my consent, for which I was grateful. I was aware of his affairs with other girls but felt I had no right to be jealous or angry.

I couldn't fully understand him either. I always believed that intimacy was necessary for a loving and trusting relationship. We had been together for almost a year in Skopje, and I couldn't trust or rely on him for anything. I didn't believe that advancing our relationship would change Miki's behaviour towards other girls, and I was right. But it did change mine.

I wasn't particularly eager to share him with anyone else, but otherwise, Miki was a gentleman. He never spoke ill of or judged any girl, often saying that we are all different and that some people don't link sex and love. Miki didn't diminish the girl who had his child either. He never blamed her for what happened, but he didn't support her either, leaving her to go through it alone.

When I told Miki he belonged to many others, I wasn't just thinking about other girls. I also thought about his parents but never mentioned it to him. He was an only child, and his parents were preoccupied with him. They bought an old house next to theirs and planned for him to build on it.

He had a very traditional view about being close to his parents. He reminded me of my father, who always put his parents before my mum and us children.

I noticed Miki was very close to his parents. When I imagined marrying him, I saw myself in my mother—seen but not heard, without a voice, silent and following decisions made for me. I wanted my future husband to talk to me, make decisions together, appreciate my opinion, and ask me where we would live and how to raise our children.

I saw the dysfunction in my family and didn't want to repeat it. My mother often said, "I told your father, but he doesn't listen to me." She probably tried harder when she was young and eventually gave up, becoming completely dependent and unable to protect herself or us. I was determined not to end up like her. I was happy to have freedom and felt no one expected anything from me. I could decide who to marry and where to live without my parents interfering. Miki didn't have that luxury. He didn't see anything wrong with living next door to his parents and continuing to make decisions with them, even after marriage.

Reflecting on our conversation, I asked him if he would like us to stay in Skopje after finishing university. He looked at me and said, "You know it's impossible."

"Why? Why is it impossible? We can find professional jobs and buy an apartment. We can spend weekends with your parents. They're still young. When they get older, they can come to live close to us. Besides, two of your uncles live in Skopje," I argued.

Miki looked at me and said, "Who do you have in Skopje?"

"I have Tanja. And she's more than family."

"I can't leave my parents, and it's better to be first in the village than last in the city." That was our last conversation about our future together. I believed he knew how I felt, but we never discussed that part again.

I spotted Peter in the distance, waiting for me while scrolling on his phone.

"We're close to a spot where we can have breakfast," he said as I approached. "There's another village not far from here. Do you want to stop here, or should we walk further?"

"Let's stop here," I replied, grateful for the chance to rest.

"How are you feeling, my love?" he asked, concern evident in his eyes.

"It's better when I'm walking," I admitted. "I'm looking forward to getting to León. I want to stay in bed and get some proper rest."

"I think you should see a doctor in León," he said gently. "I've noticed you're not walking with ease."

"Don't worry, my love," I reassured him. "A good rest will do the trick."

Hoping to ease his concern, I changed the subject, and we started talking about the apartment, 'Romantico', where we'd booked our stay. Peter was surprised by the limited information—no detailed Google reviews and only one photo online.

"I'm sure it'll be fine," I said, trying to reassure him.

We saw the bar in the distance and headed towards the bar. We enjoyed the morning sun, the coffee and the rest. I was surprised at how little Peter and I talked about the Camino. I think the walk absorbed most of our energy, and we used to rest in quiet.

I told Peter we were lucky that our apartment was close to the cathedral. We did not plan to walk around Leon. We did not have enough energy. However, I would like to see the cathedral. It is a main attraction in Leon, and a short walking distance from the apartment we had booked. Also, I was happy to see Mary. She said she would stay one night in Leon, and her accommodation was close to the cathedral.

We were about to leave the bar when reality hit me hard—I could barely move my left leg. I started walking slowly, struggling with each step. Peter urged me to see a doctor in Leon, but I ignored his advice. Looking back, I deeply regretted not listening to him.

We continued walking together, each lost in our thoughts. My mind wandered to Tanja. I never stopped thanking God for the privilege of meeting someone like her. My life in Skopje would have been vastly different without her. She was my rock.

At the start of the second semester, Tanja and I became roommates, moving to a place near the city centre. We shared an apartment with a woman and her young daughter in a popular neighbourhood called Idadia. It was close enough to the university that we rarely needed public transport, choosing instead to walk. Miki lived in student accommodation just ten minutes away and usually went home on weekends.

I didn't miss home much and spent my weekends studying and socializing with Tanja and a few friends we'd met at university. I only returned to Bitola for Christmas, winter break, Easter, and the summer holidays. Tanja was similar, visiting her family just a few times a year. I enjoyed her company immensely. We studied, talked and often spent weekends either visiting mutual university friends or hosting them at our place. Miki spent most weekends at home. Being in the final stages of his long studies, he no longer had regular lectures, only practical sessions and exams. We saw each other during the week.

Studying together with Tanja proved to be incredibly helpful. We managed to pass most of our exams in June and left a few for the September session.

When I returned to visit my family, I felt their excitement to see me, and I was overjoyed to reunite with everyone. I especially loved spending time with my niece, Elizabeth, fourteen years younger than me, and my other nephews. I cherished the moments I spent with them. Those days remain some of my fondest memories. Elizabeth and I share a special bond.

She's also a teacher, lives with her family in Melbourne, and remains one of my closest friends to this day.

Much of my summer was dedicated to studying for my upcoming exams, but I also had the pleasure of visiting Pestani, Tanja's hometown and meeting her wonderful family. I met her parents, siblings, and some cousins. Her older sister and brother were married, and her father, who worked in Germany, was home for the summer. My time spent in Pestani will forever hold a special place in my heart. They were incredibly welcoming and made me feel like part of their family.

They lived in a beautiful three-story house that stood at the edge of town, near the shores of Lake Ohrid, about ten kilometres from the city of Ohrid. This region is Macedonia's most famous tourist destination, often called the 'Jerusalem of the Balkan Peninsula' for its abundance of churches in and around Ohrid. I had never experienced a proper summer holiday before, as Ohrid and its surroundings were expensive, making this visit even more memorable.

I was grateful and privileged to spend time with Tanja and her family, enjoying the beautiful atmosphere, not just that summer but many summers. The area was filled with tourists, the restaurants and hotels were bustling, and music played everywhere. The lake looked stunning at night. Our friend and colleague, Nela from Skopje, who studied with us, also visited.

Tanja's brother took Nela and me on his boat one evening for a ride around the lake. We returned around midnight, and seeing the sky full of stars from the small boat was amazing. I remember Trajce, Tanja's brother, catching a fish that escaped. He laughed and said that every fish that gets away always seems the biggest, which saddens the fisherman.

I also visited Miki during the summer break, and he tried to come to see me. His aunt, his father's sister, lived in a suburb near Bitola, where he stayed during his visits. Miki didn't have a car, and it was common for many young men not to have driving licenses or vehicles. One day, he cycled over forty kilometres to see me, saying it was to show how much he loved me.

I avoided asking him about his time in Prilep because I didn't want to confront the truth. Miki deliberately refrained from mentioning his adventures, knowing it would upset me, but that didn't mean they didn't happen. Each time we parted after a visit, I felt a deep sadness and a sense of misery, uncertain about who might be waiting for him when he returned. I knew our relationship wasn't right, but I couldn't find a way out.

Miki and I came from very different upbringings. As an only child and the eldest grandson and nephew, Miki was adored and treated like a king by his immediate and extended family. He made decisions alongside his parents, whose approval seemed to matter deeply to him. His father, an accountant, strongly influenced him, while his mother, a housewife, was closely involved in his life. They were polite and respectful towards me, but I always felt out of place around them. I was shy, often overthought everything I said, and worried about making the wrong impression.

We never ate meals with his parents; Miki and I always dined alone. He said it would spare me from feeling even more uncomfortable in their presence. I remember once commenting that I liked a particular cheese we were eating.

The next time I visited, I was surprised to find that same cheese on the table. Miki explained that his parents had bought it because they knew I liked it. I was touched; it showed they respected and cared for me. Yet, deep inside, I felt a quiet sadness. In my future vision, I couldn't see myself as their daughter-in-law. I imagined myself in their household, fading into the background, much like my mother. I pictured myself trying to please everyone, shy and reserved, always putting others' happiness ahead of mine. No matter how much I loved Miki, it was a life I couldn't embrace.

It made me realise how lost I was. I didn't want to leave Miki—just the thought of it made me feel sick—but thinking about a future with him made me uncertain. I was confused and didn't know what I wanted. I couldn't make decisions or discuss it openly. Deep in myself, I felt very uneasy, but on the surface, I pretended everything was fine.

Somehow, I came back to reality. I noticed that we were approaching the outskirts of a big city. I could feel the pain from my leg going through my body.

Peter asked if I'd like to stop for a rest, and I quickly agreed. We found a spot near a cluster of residential buildings and paused there. While we were standing, a little girl emerged, holding a plastic bag full of rubbish. She approached us and began speaking rapidly in Spanish, gesturing toward me with the bag.

I wished I could understand her or respond in Spanish, but the words eluded me. Peter was equally puzzled. After trying to decipher her request, it dawned on me—she needed help throwing the bag into the bin, which was too high for her to reach. I took the bag from her hands and tossed it in.

Her face lit up with a big smile, and she seemed thrilled that I understood her. We managed to communicate with gestures and smiles, bridging the language barrier. When I told her I was from Australia, her eyes widened with excitement, and she began listing Australian animals in English—kangaroo, koala and a few others.

She proudly told me her name, and when I asked her age, she held up eight fingers with a cheeky grin. Her enthusiasm was infectious, and it warmed my heart to see her practising the English words she'd likely learned in school. It was a simple, joyful interaction that brought a welcome brightness to our journey.

We said goodbye to the little girl and continued walking, each of us lost in our thoughts. I felt safe and content on this journey, with Peter by my side and my thoughts as quiet companions.

It was 1982. The summer passed, and towards the end of August, I returned to Skopje to prepare for my final exams in the September session of my first year at university. Completing my first year at university successfully and starting fresh in my second year was a moment of pride and excitement.

However, shortly after I left home, my grandfather had a stroke and was bedridden. We couldn't afford any equipment to help my grandfather or ease the burden on my family, especially my grandmother, who was his primary caregiver. It significantly strained my family, and my situation also changed. The money I received from home was halved, and I could no longer afford to share a room and pay the bills. Tanja and I relocated to a more affordable house in the same suburb, but even that felt overwhelming for me. Although Tanja kindly offered to cover half my rent, I couldn't accept her paying for me. In the end, I moved into student accommodation. It wasn't perfect, but it was the best option available to me at the time.

Towards the end of September, I moved to a student village in Aftokomanda, close to the university. The room had five beds, and to my surprise, one of my roommates was a student I knew from high school. I was happy to see someone that I already knew. We weren't close friends, but I happily shared the room with her.

However, from the moment I moved in, I felt out of place. The only spot available for studying was the crowded library, and my room was constantly filled with other students and their guests. I experienced a side of student life that simply didn't suit me. I felt lonely, unhappy, and deeply unsettled.

One day, Miki came to see me. Compared to my barracks-like dormitory, his student accommodation felt like a hotel with just one roommate. One of my roommates was an attractive girl with long blond hair and beautiful blue eyes, resembling a model. She was a year older than me and studied Pedagogy, like me, though I hadn't met her at the university. She mentioned she rarely attended lectures and still had exams from the first year. Her boyfriend, a nice-looking boy, was smitten with her.

When Miki arrived, I introduced them. Before this, the girl (whose name I can't recall) hardly noticed me, but as soon as Miki walked in, she was all charming and beautiful, sitting opposite him and engaging in lively conversation. I didn't feel jealous; I was too preoccupied with my unpleasant situation and worried about how it might affect my studies. They talked and laughed, enjoying each other's company. When Miki left, I went outside to say goodbye and returned to my room.

Soon after I walked back into the room, she asked me how I had found Miki, and if I realised I had such a handsome boyfriend. Instead of answering, I commented that her boyfriend was also nice looking. She then started talking about observing Miki's hands, smile, mouth, and teeth, describing how perfectly shaped he was. She went on and on. I stopped listening and thought about how I felt the first time I saw Miki. I hadn't considered or analysed his appearance since that initial moment. My thoughts were interrupted by her question.

Finally, she asked if I would mind her spending one night with him, adding, "I hope you wouldn't mind." At first, I thought she was joking. When I saw she was serious, I replied, "I would!" and then tried to ignore and avoid her for the rest of my time in the student accommodation.

That night, I couldn't sleep. I felt sorry for her boyfriend and for myself. I never saw Miki as just a 'person for one night.' To me, he was much more than that. I wondered if Miki had affairs with girls like her. Do people who are attractive use the 'gift" and think they can do whatever they want? Did her boyfriend know who she was? He probably did, just as I learned about Miki's affairs, yet I continued as if nothing happened. It was why I couldn't envision a future with him. Perhaps there was something more, but this was the main reason. I was angrier with myself than ever before. I knew I had to leave Miki but didn't know how. I would miss his soul, his company, how he looked at me and my attachment to him. I felt he was a part of me. I liked something about him that went beyond his appearance. I silently cried under the blanket, feeling the tears coming straight from my heart. I never told Miki what she had said about him. I knew that if he found out, that 'night' would happen, and it would be even more painful. However, it didn't stop me continuing to see him.

The next day, I found out about a student employment agency. I was confident. I knew I could study and work. The agency was on the other side of the city. After taking the bus and finding the place, I lined up. There was a long queue, mostly male students asking for jobs. I saw hardly any girls in the line. At that time, studying and working weren't very popular in Macedonia—you worked or studied. After waiting half an hour and finally reaching the small window, I wondered if any jobs were available. The man at the counter first asked for my identification, the student card, or the index, as we called it in Macedonia.

"Unfortunately, we do not have anything for female students," he told me, asking the next person to step forward.

I left the office disappointed. The next day, I went back. He asked what type of job I was interested in, and I requested a part-time position that would allow me to study and work. He said there was nothing available now. Every day after lectures, I visited the office and left feeling dejected. By Friday, I was too tired and unmotivated to continue my search. I was losing hope of finding a job, convinced the answer would always be the same. Yet, I decided to try again, knowing that jobs came and went quickly. I had to be there when a job opened up. Despite my efforts, I felt unsuccessful.

I missed Tanja. Living on the other side of the city, we saw each other at university and spent time together, but returning to my noisy room made it hard to relax. I couldn't study in the library. I wasn't sure if I missed Miki. I felt I shouldn't be his security guard. If he couldn't protect himself, he could be with whoever he wanted, but I disliked being part of his life.

With these thoughts, I lined up again, and when my turn came, the employment agent looked at me with sympathy and asked me to wait. After the queue of students had dispersed, he called me back and told me there was a position for a cleaner—three days per week, around nine hours. The job involved cleaning offices in central Skopje, about twenty minutes from where I used to share the room with Tanja. *I can move back and use my earnings to pay the rent*, I thought. I accepted the offer and was elated. I thanked him, and he informed me I needed to go to the office on Monday. If they accepted me, I could start working. I was overwhelmed with positive emotions.

I went straight to see Tanja, and we were both very happy. During the weekend, I moved back. My nearly two weeks in student accommodation were enough to see how some students experienced university life. While I was there, some joked that if parents lost their children, they would find them in that student accommodation. It sounded funny but was somewhat true. I thanked God many times for meeting Tanja. To this day, I don't know if I've thanked her enough. She was my true friend, saviour and one of the most beautiful souls I've ever met.

The following Monday, I had an interview and started the job. Being able to support myself financially was a huge relief. At that time in Macedonia, there were few jobs for young people, especially students. I felt lucky.

Peter and I continued walking, reaching the edge of Leon, which was almost four kilometres from the apartment we had booked. I pushed myself but didn't want to bother Peter, who was trying his best to walk, manage GPS, and wait for me. However, I couldn't hide the pain anymore. By then, I was sure I had done some damage to my knee or leg, but I didn't know the extent. We saw a taxi coming from the opposite direction. Peter raised his hand, and the cab made a U-turn to pick us up. In a few minutes, we were in the central part of Leon. The driver told us that the street where our apartment, Romantico, was located was not accessible by car, so he dropped us off on the nearest street. Spending ten minutes in the car made it difficult for me to move, and I could hardly get out of the vehicle.

The taxi driver looked surprised and smiled when he found the apartment's name. Seeing two pilgrims, with me barely moving, he was probably wondering what we were doing at Romantico. We started moving towards the apartment, but the PIN didn't work. Fortunately, the owner saw us on the camera and provided another PIN to get in. I crawled up the stairs, relieved to be there finally. However, we couldn't hide our surprise and disappointment when we entered the apartment.

"Peter, why did you book this place? It looks like it was an apartment for filming porno movies." We both burst out laughing, finally understanding the taxi driver's smile. The bedroom was decorated in red and black, with mirrors everywhere, including on the ceiling and above the bed. Around the bed were various accessories, ready to be used if needed. The sheets were black, and the pillows were red.

"Darling, I don't like staying here. Who knows what has happened in this apartment and on this bed?" I said, feeling uneasy.

"What are your suggestions?" Peter asked. "You know, I couldn't find much information about this place," he added.

The lounge area and the bathroom looked normal, and the apartment was perfectly clean. We were too tired to care much about the appearance of the bedroom. I had no energy left, so I took off my backpack and lay on the bed.

Peter suggested I see a doctor. I couldn't walk without my hiking poles, even to the bathroom. I knew what the doctor would recommend and tried to avoid it as long as possible. I tried to convince myself and Peter that after two nights' rest in Leon, I could continue walking. We still had more than three hundred kilometres to go. Deep down, I was very worried. I didn't want to separate from Peter and reach Santiago de Compostela by bus. I loved walking, but the pain in my left leg suggested I was nearing the end of my journey.

Later that evening, we went out to see Leon at night. I was so grateful for my hiking poles, which I had never used before starting the Camino. I hadn't realised how much they could alleviate the strain on my body.

The apartment was in a popular part of the city, so we didn't have to walk far to reach the cathedral and restaurants. The cathedral looked stunning, especially with the lights illuminating it. Despite being almost eleven-thirty p.m. the city was bustling with people, and the restaurants were open late. It reminded me of Bitola, where I grew up in Macedonia. The night life was vibrant, and I enjoyed being in this beautiful place with Peter.

"One day, we'll return to this city," Peter said.

Maybe we would—who could say? For now, I just wanted to savour the moment. I felt happy and content, walking beside Peter, soaking in the warmth of a beautiful night in León.

The next day, the 28th of July, we stayed in the room most of the time. I tried to ignore the accessories around the bed and relax as much as possible. For dinner, we went to an Italian restaurant. The food was nice. After dinner, we met Mary, our Camino friend, and visited the cathedral. Most of the cathedrals we had seen were similar, but I was always impressed by their architecture and grandeur. We took many photos and enjoyed spending time with Mary. I felt uncomfortable walking with the hiking poles, but I had no other option. Deep down, I was very worried. I was curious to see if I could walk the next day. We would arrive in Astorga in two days and spend two nights there. I hoped the two nights' rest would help me continue the walk.

Chapter 21

Reflections and Realities

"Letting go of the past and seeking the future."

After two nights in Leon, we left the apartment 'Romantico' early in the morning. It was 29th July. Our next stop was the Hostel Alto Paramo in Villadango del Paramo. We walked to the cathedral and started our Camino Walk from there, following the yellow arrows. We encountered people who seemed drunk, leaving bars and restaurants early in the morning. Some of them tried to engage in conversation. We focused on our walk, following the Camino signs and trying to exit the city. It took us almost two hours.

That morning, we enjoyed a late breakfast in one of the villages along the way. We discussed the place we had booked for the night as we ate. It seemed to be in the middle of nowhere, but I didn't mind. I only cared about reaching it and knowing we'd have one less day of walking ahead.

We started walking again after our rest, which was tough for me. I tried to hide my struggles from Peter, not wanting to burden him with my worries about the pain. I told him I would walk slowly and might need frequent breaks that day, encouraging him to keep his own pace and not to worry about me.

I didn't share that my hope of recovering with the extra night in León was fading. The pain in my knee was worsening, and deep down, I knew it wouldn't improve easily.

Walking slowly, my thoughts returned to the time we started Camino. It was our twenty-second day walking. I had enjoyed walking from village to village over the past few days, marking off the kilometres as we progressed. I knew we had two more days of walking through the Meseta before reaching Galicia. On the map, Galicia appears so different from the vast flatlands of Meseta. Would you be able to climb the hills and the mountains? My thoughts did not give me the answer. I felt a high level of uncertainty. I would have been much happier if I hadn't been in pain and could walk without my hiking poles. "I am not going to give up! I will stay with Peter and get to Santiago de Compostela." I felt my voice talking over my pain.

Though I appreciated the Meseta's surroundings and the simplicity of its landscape, I couldn't say how much of it I truly noticed. It felt like I had been walking through my inner self rather than the physical terrain. What was it about this journey that stirred up my past, making me dig through old memories? Even I couldn't fully explain it.

Yet, in a way, I felt I was sorting through my life, organising my memories and viewing everything from a distance. The heaviness I had carried at the start of the journey seemed to have gradually dissipated, leaving a sense of clarity in its place. I liked to go back and be with my thoughts.

My thoughts took me to my second year at university. I enjoyed this year. I had settled in, and the cleaning job helped me overcome financial challenges. The house where Tanja and I lived was shared with another girl named Carmen, who studied piano at the university. Initially, Carmen shared the room with her boyfriend, and we didn't interact much beyond saying "Zdravo." After her boyfriend joined the army, she spent more time with Tanja and me. Carmen, who was from Nish, Serbia, was an excellent cook. Sometimes, we cooked and had meals together. Tanja's relative, Zdravko, and his girlfriend, Jasmina, visited us almost every weekend, and Miki, who was in his final year and often in Skopje, joined us whenever he could. That year, I felt we had a proper relationship.

I decided to stay with Miki for as long as he remained in Skopje. My love for him deepened despite my ongoing concerns about his behaviour. During my second year of university, we spent even more time together, but his attitude toward other girls remained unchanged. I knew I would leave him one day when the time was right.

I stopped questioning him about his infidelity, knowing it wouldn't lead anywhere. Occasionally, we spoke about his child, which left me conflicted. I couldn't believe he and the child's mother had never discussed the child's future. He admitted he wasn't ready to embrace fatherhood then but might be some day.

Once, he mentioned that if something ever happened to the mother, he would step up to take care of the child and asked if I would be okay with that. I told him I saw nothing wrong with caring for the child of someone I loved, but deep down, I knew the situation was complicated and unfair. My doubts were confirmed when the mother took him to court to establish paternity, bringing the messiness of it all into stark focus.

The sharp pain in my leg jolted me back to reality. I realised I was moving at a very slow pace. Some pilgrims stopped briefly, greeted me and asked if I was okay before continuing. I wasn't fine, but I preferred to be alone with my thoughts.

I thought about Peter, walking slower than usual, frequently turning back to check on me. Deep down, I felt I was confronting something profound that had lingered within me for far too long and was now demanding my attention.

I thought about the girls from my era. In the seventies and early eighties almost every bride was visibly pregnant at her wedding. Rarely was there a wedding without a pregnant bride. Many of these brides' smiles disappeared after the wedding, leading to frequent divorces or unhappy marriages. Many girls who married due to pregnancy found themselves in difficult situations, often unemployed and completely dependent on their husbands and in-laws.

We received no sexual education or protection. At home, most of us were taught to keep our virginity until the wedding day; that was the extent of our education on the topic. For boys, it was different. They were allowed multiple girlfriends and usually chose the one their parents favoured most. No one talked about STDs or pregnancy prevention. If a girl visited a gynaecologist, she was assumed to be pregnant and seeking an abortion, which would quickly become gossip, especially in small towns.

In small towns, privacy was a luxury few could afford. Rumours spread like wildfire, and medical professionals were not always ethically responsible. Gossip often originated from nurses and doctors.

I remember a university colleague sharing her experience of visiting a gynaecologist to discuss contraception before taking her relationship to the next level. The male doctor questioned her marital status and why she was seeking contraception if she wasn't married, leaving her feeling embarrassed and regretful for even going.

Another incident involved a nurse gossiping about a seventeen-year-old girl who came in with her mother, seeking an abortion. The doctor laughed and rudely asked who the father was, to which the girl angrily responded that it was none of his business. The nurse was appalled at the girl's perceived disrespect. Stories like these deterred many girls from seeking advice or help. It's no wonder that many parents encouraged their daughters to marry young rather than pursue higher education.

Boys and girls were equally confused and struggled to form healthy relationships. Like many girls of that time, I was raised to be obedient and accept things as they were. Assertiveness in girls was not encouraged; it was often suppressed. Finding someone to love you and, more importantly, having his mother love you, was considered fortunate. My grandmother frequently reminded me that loving him back was a bonus. By twenty-five, most girls were expected to be married. Otherwise, finding a partner became increasingly difficult.

My thoughts turned again to Miki. Reflecting on my relationship with Miki, I focused on our shared moments. I had no clear vision of the future. I concentrated on my studies and cherished the time we spent together. Miki was more than just a boyfriend; he was a friend. I wished something would change to give our relationship a different direction. We shared chemistry, connection and communication, which Miki often cited as the foundation of a successful relationship. However, to some degree, I disagreed. I didn't trust him and doubted he would ever be faithful. I didn't share his views on family or the Macedonian tradition that children needed to stay close to their parents and look after the parents even when the parents did not need any help. Still, I never felt comfortable expressing my opinion.

I felt relieved that, as a girl, I didn't bear that responsibility. Even if I had been born a boy, I wouldn't have followed such an outdated custom. Parents should care for themselves and allow their children to live their lives. While I respected my parents, I wouldn't prioritise them over my children and partner, unlike what my parents did. I never explicitly told Miki this, but he knew my thoughts well. I often reminded my parents that my brother was not solely responsible for them; we were all responsible when needed. To this day, I follow this principle and do as much as possible for my mother.

I saw Peter waiting for me. He looked exhausted, yet a smile lingered on his face. I walked up to him and hugged him tightly.

"I love you, Peter. I love your smile. It feels like it neutralises my pain," I said softly.

"Honey, I love you, too. But you needed to see a doctor in León. It would be best if you listened to me sometimes. I can see you're struggling to walk," he replied, his concern evident.

I nodded, silently agreeing with him, but didn't say anything. Instead, I changed the subject and asked what he'd been thinking about while walking.

Peter smiled. "Nothing. I try not to think; if thoughts come, I just let them go. We've got two more kilometres to the next village. Let's take a longer rest there."

I agreed and let Peter walk ahead of me, reflecting on how blessed I was to have him in my life. His presence had given me the courage to delve deep within myself and revisit memories, especially those tied to my relationship with Miki. During my marriage, I had buried these memories, believing that even thinking about them could stir up more trouble. With Peter, everything felt different. I could truly be myself—free to think, speak and feel openly and honestly in a way I never had before.

My thoughts drifted back to early May 1983, when Miki passed his final exam. I was overjoyed for him, yet I couldn't ignore the ache in my heart; this was the beginning of the end for us. It was a beautiful midday, warm and sunny, with spring in full bloom. We went to a restaurant and sat outside, alternating between quiet conversation and long, comfortable silence. Words weren't always necessary; we understood each other without them.

I looked at him, thinking, *How much I'll miss this handsome, unfaithful man who gazes at me like I'm his whole world while quietly breaking my heart.* He had a way of lifting me to the skies, only to let me crash back down. His face was tinged with sadness, and I couldn't help but wonder what thoughts were running through his mind.

I remembered the last time we visited the cinema to see an old classic: *Gone with the Wind*. Afterwards, he told me I reminded him of Scarlett. The comment stung. I wanted to be like Melanie, the devoted and loving woman her husband adored. I said nothing then, but later, I told Tanja about it.

True to form, she knew how to lighten the mood. *"Goca, take it as a compliment,"* she said. *"The movie was about Scarlett, not the other character!"* We both laughed.

Miki's voice interrupted my thoughts. *"What are you thinking?"* he asked, holding my hand.

"Nothing," I replied, forcing a smile. *"I'm very happy for you."*

He looked straight into my eyes like he did the day we met. *"You don't need to worry about anything, Goca. You're a very strong person."*

I felt my composure cracking. If he kept trying to prepare me for the inevitable, I knew I'd start crying. *"Please,"* I said softly, *"don't say anything about me. Today is your day. Let's just celebrate."* I smiled, even as tears threatened to spill.

In that moment, I wanted to tell him everything—how much he meant to me and the profound role he had played in my life. But I held back. I wanted to say he was more than just a boyfriend; he was my entire world. Meeting him had changed me in ways I couldn't fully explain. I chose my career and moved to Skopje because of him. Without him, my life would have taken a completely different path.

He gave me confidence and made me intellectually stronger, yet emotionally, I felt weak—like a part of me was slowly dying. I often felt alone in our relationship, much like I did within my own family. Almost everything seemed to happen on his terms. Even when we were together, I still felt a deep sense of loneliness. But I didn't know any better, nor did I know how to continue without him. I had grown used to his coming and going pattern, though I knew it was nearing its end.

Instead of saying everything on my mind, I said, *"I love you so much. I don't know how to live with you, and I don't know how to live without you."*

Miki never promised to change or acknowledged his behaviour as selfish or hurtful. That's why his response surprised me. *"You are the last person I ever wanted to hurt,"* he said quietly. *"And I know I did."*

I looked at him, reflecting on how much he reminded me of my father regarding promises. He would honour a promise if he made one, but he rarely, if ever, made promises. He knew I didn't share his traditional views on family or a husband's role, which, in his mind, seemed to include infidelity.

What I wanted was clear: a trustworthy husband, someone who would share everything with me and keep others out of our relationship. I had no desire to live as a woman dictated to, or worse, one who had to share her husband's attention with others. He admired my independence and respected me as much as he could, but he never made promises.

What he wanted was equally clear: a wife who wouldn't question him, someone obedient who fit neatly into his family's expectations.

Despite our differences, we shared a connection that was hard to define. We loved spending time together, talking, walking and laughing. That part of us never changed from the day we met to the day we parted.

Sitting opposite him, I recalled a winter night in Skopje. The weather was mild, and it was snowing. Everything was covered in snow and looked beautiful. We walked by the Vardar River, crossed the Stone Bridge and ended up at the central square. It was around eleven p.m., and few people were around. We stopped. Miki looked at me, lifted me and twirled me around a few times. He set me down, looked into my eyes, and said, "You are so beautiful. Your face is whiter than the snow, and your black hair is covered with snowflakes. I wish I had a camera to take a photo of you. You would love it." He hugged me tightly, and I felt so happy I could die from the sheer joy and fulfilment.

At that moment, I looked at him and said, "I am the happiest person in the world. No one could be happier than me right now." I clung to him, trying to savour the moment despite the sadness creeping in. I had realised long ago that sometimes love isn't enough for marriage. I tried to be realistic about our relationship.

* * *

I realised I had been daydreaming, lost in thought. The sharp pain in my knee snapped me back to reality. I stopped and sat on a log beside the dusty path, trying to catch my breath. I was amazed those thoughts of romantic moments with Miki from the past no longer stirred any emotions within me. Deep down, I felt nothing for him anymore. Those painful emotions had faded long ago—who knows when? Only the fear had lingered, keeping me trapped. But now, for the first time, I felt free.

Feeling unburdened, I was drawn to revisiting that winter day with a fresh perspective. I felt free and curious, eager to observe those moments from a new angle. I remembered how we continued talking about his future. Miki spoke about his upcoming compulsory military service, which he planned to complete before starting his career as a dentist. He envisioned opening a private practice with his future wife to assist him. His parents expected him to marry after the army and build a house next to theirs.

As I listened, I couldn't help but reflect on how his plans already included his future wife, even though she was only an idea for now. Gently, I shared my aspirations, explaining that I intended to finish university and focus on building a career. Our dreams did not align, no matter how strong our feelings for each other were.

We stayed at the restaurant for hours, savouring our time together. Deep down, I knew it would be painful when he left, but I also understood that I had to let him go.

During those few hours, so many memories flashed before me. I remember the day when we were sitting in his room, singing. He sang beautifully, and I loved listening to him. The song was about a brother and sister, an old Macedonian tune. After he finished singing, I asked him how he became an only child when most families had several children. He explained that his mother had a miscarriage, losing a baby girl several years after he was born.

I listened and said, "I wish I could have been that girl. I wish I were your sister."

Miki stopped and looked at me seriously. "Why did you say that? It's not okay to think of us like that."

I clarified, "If we were siblings, I would love you as my brother and be together forever. We would be the best brother and sister. Besides, many people think we look like siblings." I started laughing.

Miki laughed, too. "I'm sorry, but I prefer you as my girlfriend."

My thoughts were interrupted by Miki's voice. "Tell me, what are you thinking about?"

"I'm thinking about us and our past," I said, smiling. I saw the time and realised it was close to his departure. "We need to move. You don't have much time. Your bus leaves in less than an hour."

That afternoon, Miki left, happy to start a new chapter of his life. I went to the bus station and said goodbye. I didn't plan to see him or see him as little as possible that summer, preparing to end the relationship. I knew this wasn't the end, but in my heart, it was the beginning of the end.

That summer, I tried to stay strong, but there were many moments when I found myself crying and missing him deeply. Without phones at home, reaching out felt complicated, and I avoided contacting him altogether. It was my third year at university, with one more year and a few additional months to complete my exams after the lectures ended.

Tanja had started a job as a nurse at a childcare centre while continuing her studies part-time. She stayed in Skopje over the summer and found a new apartment for us. I was relieved—excited even—at the thought of starting the year in a fresh space, free from the memories of Miki and me. The apartment was in a central part of Skopje, a convenient and lively location.

I returned to Skopje at the end of August and quickly grew to love the new place. We shared it with two other girls from Bitola, which made the atmosphere feel familiar and comforting. I was also glad I hadn't shared my new address with Miki. It seemed better, healthier even, to let us drift apart naturally.

The weather was scorching. Peter had found shade under one of the few trees along the path and was scrolling through his phone. I stopped briefly to rest, and then we continued walking together. Before long, we reached the village where we had planned to take a break. Finding a bar didn't take much effort—most bars on the Camino were conveniently located right along the route. Peter asked me what I wanted for lunch and then went inside the bar to place our order. It was a change from our usual routine. Typically, I handled the food orders while Peter focused on checking the route and arranging accommodations. I leaned heavily on my hiking poles, and every step felt like a struggle.

"Darling," I began, "while we were walking, I found myself thinking about Miki, my ex-boyfriend. I was surprised by how many memories came flooding back. Those memories made me so emotional in the past, but now, they're just thoughts." I smiled at Peter. "Tell me about some of your romantic days when you were young."

"Pumpkin, you think too much," Peter said with a chuckle. "Of course, I have memories. I remember buying my first car and taking a girl to the outdoor cinema. She almost raped me!" he added, laughing heartily.

I couldn't help but laugh along. Looking at Peter—tall, blond, with piercing blue eyes, regularly compared to his maternal German grandfather—it wasn't hard to imagine how attractive he must have been in his youth. Even in his sixties, he was stunning.

"What do you mean by 'she almost raped you'?" I asked, intrigued. I vaguely remember him mentioning this before, but I wanted to hear more.

"Well," Peter continued with a grin, "as a young man, I believed that if I slept with a girl, I'd have to marry her. I was only eighteen, far too young to think about marriage. But she wanted to have sex with me—right there in the back seat of my car. I barely escaped!" He laughed again. "Sweety, Australian girls were different back then, baby boomers. They liked to have sex."

"Don't worry," I replied playfully. "Girls in Macedonia weren't exactly naive. They wanted to have sex, too, but usually waited until after marriage to 'pay the price'."

We spent the rest of our time at the bar laughing and reminiscing about our younger selves. It was a lovely moment, sharing stories and imagining what we were like in those carefree days of youth.

After almost an hour's rest, we left the bar. I could hardly move, completely relying on the hiking poles to relieve the pain that was spreading throughout my body.

The walk to Villadangos del Páramo felt endless. We had booked a private room at Hostel Alto Páramo, situated along the route but far from any villages or towns. I pushed myself to keep moving, each step feeling heavier than the last.

Peter, as always, waited patiently for me, but this time, I caught a glimpse of restlessness on his face. From a distance, I heard his voice calling out.

"Come on! Just a bit further. We're almost there," he encouraged.

I wanted to explain to him that I had reached my limit—probably even surpassed it—but the words wouldn't come. The area felt remote, the accommodations catering almost exclusively to pilgrims.

After passing several other lodgings, we finally arrived at the hostel.

The woman who ran the hostel was very polite and guided us to our room via an outdoor staircase. But I could barely move, let alone climb the stairs. Clinging to the railing, I inched my way up, my body protesting with every step. I couldn't even fathom, let alone explain, how I had managed to make it to this place on my own two feet.

She looked at me with sympathy, probably wondering who was forcing me through this suffering. I crawled into the room and collapsed on the bed, crying. I couldn't even make it to the bathroom; my left leg was immobile. I wondered how I had managed to walk that day. The lady kindly provided an ice pack, which helped a bit. I decided to see a doctor the next day as we had booked two nights in Astorga.

I lay on the bed, unable to move, certain that the damage was done. But I had no idea just how severe the injury to my left leg might be. The pain was excruciating, radiating through my body like flashes of light.

Equally exhausted, Peter tried to encourage me to shower and have dinner, but I couldn't even sit up. Even lying still on the bed offered no relief from the relentless pain.

This is the end of my Camino Walk, I thought. *I probably won't even be able to get on a bus. I might need an ambulance to take me to the hospital tomorrow. Why didn't I address this sooner? My optimism failed me this time—it only made things worse.*

I kept these thoughts to myself, not wanting to burden Peter, who lay quietly beside me, his worry and concern clear. He suggested we take either a bus or a taxi the next day, depending on how I felt. The bus seemed like a convenient option since the stop was right in front of the hostel, and the station in Astorga was close to our hotel.

That night was long. I couldn't sleep, feeling the pain spread from my leg throughout my body. I was glad Peter could sleep; it must have been hard to support and wait for me during most of our walk, even though he never showed it. He was taking care of both himself and me. I tried to keep quiet and let him sleep. I wished I had listened to him and seen a doctor in León.

"I love you, Peter, my beautiful soul," I whispered. If I could predict the future, I wouldn't worry so much about the past. I once thought love could only happen once, but how little did I know about love and life.

While I lay in bed, unable to move or sleep, my thoughts went, and I could now see my relationship with Miki from a different perspective. Why had I been avoiding this painful part of my past for so long? Perhaps I was scared to touch that old wound. Clearing these emotions felt like cleaning out an old wardrobe. The powerful emotions that once dominated my life were gone, and I felt lighter for facing them.

Our relationship ended more than five years after we first met. Miki managed to fulfil his army duties in Skopje, claiming he had done everything possible to be stationed close to me. However, his habits with other girls didn't change, not even during his time as a soldier.

One Sunday morning, I decided to surprise him. Soldiers could leave for the day if someone visited and signed them out or for the night if it were a wife or girlfriend. I arrived at the office, and the soldier on duty asked for the name of the person I was visiting and my identification. I gave him Miki's name and my ID. He looked at the photo and asked if I was his sister.

"No," I said. "I'm his girlfriend."

He looked at the photo again. "You look like his sister," he remarked.

The soldier turned his head away and said, "He already had a visitor and is out for the day." It felt like a hard slap. I didn't ask who had taken him out; I just thanked the soldier and left. Deep down, I knew he was with another girl. That was the end of our relationship in my heart.

The next Saturday evening, he rang the bell. I quickly dressed, and we went out. Neither of us said much, especially about the previous Sunday. At the restaurant, I chose a corner table for privacy. We ordered our usual drinks: beer for him and Coca-Cola for me. I couldn't hold back any longer.

"Miki, I came out tonight to tell you this is our last evening together. After today, I want nothing more to do with you. You can have as many girlfriends as you want; it's not my business anymore. I've made my decision, and I won't change it. I'm glad you're returning home after the army, and the chances of seeing you again will be zero. The soldier at the reception asked if I was your sister. At that moment, I wished I were your sister to avoid all the humiliation you've put me through."

"I prefer you as my girlfriend, not my sister," he replied.

"No, you don't," I protested, raising my voice. "If you wanted me as your girlfriend, you'd spend time with me, not with someone else. I've had enough. You've met many girls, but I must be the craziest for tolerating your behaviour for so long."

"You're not stupid or crazy," he said, listening quietly.

I expected an apology or some sign of remorse, but there was none. I continued to pour out everything I had held inside, mainly about his double life.

"I'm disgusted. Anyone can do what you're doing, but most people have respect for themselves and their partners. They don't chase after every skirt they see. You don't respect yourself or me."

"I respect myself, and I respect you. I respect and care about you," he said slowly and clearly.

"I know." I replied sarcastically. "You showed me last Sunday and many other times." On the surface, he was childish regarding girls and felt he always had to say 'yes'. But deep down, he was a gentle and caring person. Still, I had made my decision.

"If you respect me, then please respect my decision. We need to end this. I've suffered enough, and I refuse to suffer any longer. If my only choices are to die for you or to stay with you and endure humiliation, I'd rather choose death. Saying this out loud gives me the strength I need to survive."

Miki remained silent, listening without interruption.

We left the restaurant and walked back to my place. We stopped and looked at each other.

"Miki, you haven't said anything," I said.

"I didn't know what to say. You were right," he replied.

"Please, don't ask for me anymore. It'll be hard for me. I'm sure many other girls would be happy with you. Stay away from me," I said.

He hugged and kissed me. "I'll try, but I can't promise," he said quietly. I left, promising to be strong and prepared to live without him.

After two months, he came to my door, and our relationship continued, but it was never the same. He tried many times to repair what was broken, but my heart couldn't be fixed. After finishing his army duties, he went home. Two weeks later, he returned and told me he had enrolled to study part-time journalism, something he had always liked. I felt he wanted to continue coming to Skopje and keep our relationship going, but I knew he wasn't alone in Prilep.

The following week, I made my decision. I went to Miki's hometown and clearly stated that I wanted to end our relationship. I begged him not to come and ask for me anymore. He wasn't surprised but looked sad. He promised to respect my wish. His mother cooked lunch for us, but I couldn't eat anything. Before leaving, I asked Miki if he loved me. He said that was a question I had to answer myself. I told him I didn't know why I wondered when everything was over. I left, and he followed me. I said goodbye to his parents, who were outside. I didn't hug him or say anything. It was too painful. I wasn't eager to change my mind. I left, and it was forever.

I went to the bus stop. I was so close to Bitola, my hometown. However, I couldn't imagine going home and let my parents or anyone from my family see me like that. It felt like a part of me was gone.

The bus for Skopje was already there. I sat in the back seat and let my tears flow. Outside, a storm raged, mirroring the turmoil inside me. I cried the whole way to Skopje, more than two hours.

I remembered a dream I had shortly after starting my studies in Skopje. In the dream, I needed to cross a large pond to reach Miki on the other side. I knew snakes were in the pond, but I wasn't scared. I walked through the water, trying to get him. It was just the two of us in the middle of nowhere. A big black snake appeared before me when I was only a few steps away. Miki was so close but did nothing, standing still and watching. I decided to go back. I wasn't angry, just sad, wondering why he didn't help me. I woke up feeling very sad that night. Somehow, I knew we wouldn't be together. He listened when I told him about the dream and said, "Don't worry. It's just a dream." Our relationship ended very similar to the dream.

I felt exhausted and broken when I arrived in Skopje, grieving for what was lost. This time, I knew it was truly over. I knew my decision was right and never regretted it, but my heart and mind were disconnected. My heart was bleeding and screaming, while my brain knew it was the right thing to do. After more than five years, something significant to me had ended. My feelings for him had been strong from the moment I first saw him until the end, but I couldn't let emotions lead me anymore. I had lost myself in that relationship, caring more for him than myself, and he had taken it for granted.

I will never share my future boyfriend or husband with anyone. If I don't meet an honest and faithful person, I am ready to be alone, I thought.

When I reached the apartment, Tanja was home. She didn't know what had happened but looked at me with sadness and empathy. I told her briefly about my trip and decision, then went to bed. I couldn't sleep. The pain in my heart was so sharp; the pain lasted almost three years. I couldn't believe that grieving for someone still alive could be so intense.

The pain in my legs remaind constant, unyielding. The penadol tablets offered no relif. I desperately tried to push the thoughts away and get even a little sleep, but I lay quietly in bed as my worries spiralled out of control.

What would happen to our walk now? After so many days of effort, I felt like I had failed myself and Peter. He had done so much for this journey: the preparation, the hope, and the way he had cared for nearly everything. And now, because of my foolishness, it felt like all of it had been for nothing.

If only I had seen a doctor in León—perhaps things could have been different. But beneath my regret lay a deeper fear: what if the doctor told me I couldn't walk? The thought sent my worries into overdrive.

Tears rolled down my face as I lay there, praying silently, hoping for some semblance of a solution or strength to face what lay ahead.

I wasn't alone—Peter was by my side—but my thoughts continued their unstoppable journey, pulling me back to where I had left off. I didn't try to resist them but let them flow freely.

My relationship with Miki ended in November 1984. With a year and a half left at university, I threw myself into my studies. I also took on a full-time job as a cleaner in a large building housing the offices of an international bank, working from two to ten p.m. My mornings were reserved for attending lectures.

I avoided mentioning Miki, always teetering on the edge of tears. I was silently grateful that no one around me brought up his name. Determined to suppress my emotions and bury the pain, I managed to do so for years. Shortly after our relationship ended, I tore up all our photos—it was too painful to see them. I thought I had destroyed every trace, unaware that one image had somehow survived, hidden away like a quiet testament to my feelings for him. That photo resurfaced when I least expected it, guiding me toward a new chapter in my life.

I graduated at the start of 1986, and was immensely pleased with my achievement. The topic I chose for my final exam required extensive research, which was later published in an educational magazine. At the end of May, I was invited to present my research at the annual conference the Faculty of Pedagogy and Psychology organised. My accomplishments filled me with pride.

After graduation, I returned to Bitola. It was a sunny May morning, and I prepared to submit my application for the student's summer camp. I had worked the previous summer, and this opportunity seemed perfect. The office was on the other side of the city, and I decided to walk instead of taking the bus, relishing the chance to stroll through the town.

Walking down Shirok Sokak, the main street in Bitola, around ten a.m., I found myself surrounded by the usual morning bustle. Suddenly, I spotted Miki on the opposite side, walking towards me. I froze, hardly believing my eyes. I had heard he got married a few months after our relationship ended, but that was all I knew about him. Our eyes met briefly. He wasn't alone, but the crowd obscured whoever was with him. We didn't greet each other; instead, we kept walking in opposite directions, occasionally glancing back. My body trembled. I couldn't deny the overwhelming effect seeing him had on me, a stark reminder of the deep influence he once held over my life.

I continued walking, lost in thought. I wondered if he was with his wife. Despite the distance and time, I felt we still held special places in each other's hearts. Our relationship might not have worked for marriage, but we had a unique bond. We were both strong-willed and unable to compromise on our values and beliefs.

After submitting my documents and having a brief interview,

I returned, convinced Miki had left the street. Shirok Sokak could be walked from start to finish in five to ten minutes, so it seemed unlikely I would run into him again. However, as I walked, still deep in thought, he suddenly appeared before me, emerging from a shoe shop. This time, I saw his mother with him.

We both smiled and stopped to greet each other. His mother hugged and kissed me warmly, more affectionately than I remembered. We started talking like old friends who hadn't seen each other in a long time. Miki shared that he was working as a dentist and had married. I congratulated him sincerely. He spoke about his job, the house he was building, the car he bought, and his plans to open a private practice soon. When I asked if they had a child, he proudly said they had a son named Oglen, a name he chose.

"I'm happy for you," I said genuinely. "All your dreams come true."

His face changed, and he looked straight into my eyes. I couldn't handle the situation and quickly put on sunglasses to hide my tears. I didn't want him to see me cry. He asked his mother to go into the shop, assuring her he would join her later. She left reluctantly.

We started walking together, and Miki wanted to know how I was doing. He congratulated me on graduating, but I didn't have much to share. Other than my degree, I felt I had nothing else. I was still grieving our lost relationship. He noticed my weight loss and commented on it.

"Probably I worried too much," I said, forcing a laugh to lighten the mood.

He stopped walking and didn't laugh. "Take care of yourself," he said gently, his face filled with sadness.

His mother returned quickly, clearly uncomfortable with her married son walking alone with his ex-girlfriend. "Come on, we need to buy a few more things," she said.

I apologised for interrupting their plans. His mother and I hugged, and Miki and I shook hands. We said our goodbyes and went our separate ways. As I walked towards home, I saw him glance back at me. I felt a mix of sadness and happiness. I believed there was a reason we saw each other amidst the crowded street – to have a proper farewell. And that was the last time I talked to Miki.

I saw Miki for the last time a few years after our relationship ended at the train station in Skopje. By then, I was already married and teaching at a primary school in Bitola while my now ex-husband worked in Skopje. While rushing to catch a train one weekend, I spotted Miki walking towards me on the crowded platform. Despite the surprise on his face, I kept walking briskly, not intending to stop. He greeted me with a simple "Hello," to which I nodded and continued, relieved that the old feelings towards Miki no longer stirred within me at that moment. It marked the final encounter with him.

Yet, Miki's spirit lingered in my marriage for many years, especially during its most challenging moments. My ex-husband often accused me of never fully letting go of my past with Miki, questioning if I still held feelings for him. I couldn't help but wonder if Greg, too, felt the echo of Miki's spirit around me as strongly as I did. Our marriage lacked open communication, and I often thought that sharing more about my past might have helped me heal sooner. But that chance never came.

I never truly understood the depth of my emotions, the pain, grief and strong attachment I carried for Miki. Over time, I've learned to accept the imperfections and complexities of our relationship. I no longer try to make sense of what may be beyond understanding. Instead, I've embraced it for what it was. Perhaps everything faded long ago, but I wasn't ready to confront the buried feelings and memories until recently.

Now, I'm grateful to have revisited my past, allowing myself to release it and feel a newfound freedom within my soul. In the end, there was nothing left to hold onto.

Being away for more than four years and not keeping in touch with my old friends, I felt lonely in Bitola. All my friends were either in relationships or married, and I felt like an outsider in the city where I had grown up. That summer, I worked at a student summer camp, which was a good experience because I met new people.

After I returned from the camp, my neighbour Suzana, who was the same age as me and worked in an office, mentioned that some of her single colleagues were interested in meeting me. One of her friends had met me at camp and spoken about me, which sparked their curiosity. I hadn't been on a date since my relationship with Miki ended. While a few boys had tried to talk to me and ask me out, I wasn't ready to move on. I told Suzana I'd think about it and let her know.

A few days later, she gently reminded me about her co-worker and encouraged me to meet him, mentioning that he was a bit older than me and a genuinely nice person. I agreed, and we arranged to meet a week or two later. We had dinner together and chatted about a variety of topics. He walked me home afterward, asking me to share more about myself and offering kind compliments along the way. He seemed genuinely surprised that someone like me was still single.

When I mentioned I had been in a relationship but was no longer with that person, he asked me to share more. I tried to explain, but something unexpected happened. Instead of speaking, I broke down in uncontrollable tears.

It was dark, so I couldn't see his face, but I heard him softly say, "Oh my God. How could anyone hurt you so much? I haven't experienced this in my life. What did he do to you? He didn't know what he lost." He then fell silent, listening to my sobs.

Finally, I stopped crying and spoke. "No one hurt me. I hurt myself. There's no one to blame. I'm sorry. I'm so sorry. I must go. I can walk by myself." I felt so embarrassed.

As I left, he said, "I would like to see you again."

I didn't want to see him again, but it was a wake-up call. At that moment, I realised I needed to start working on myself and stop living in the past.

I was lucky to get a one-year contract teaching Prep in September 1986, at the start of the school year. It helped me a lot. I was the youngest teacher at the school and developed a very good relationship with the staff. I enjoyed teaching young kids and my mental health improved. I made new friends and stayed in contact with my friend Tanja, her boyfriend, and later her husband, Jovan. Towards the end of 1987, my contract ended. The teacher I replaced returned from the army and no teaching positions were available.

I started to feel lonely and anxious. I wanted to meet someone suitable for me but was disappointed by the young men I encountered. Many pretended to be single and available, reminding me of Miki. It seemed normal in Macedonia at that time for girls to wait at home for unfaithful boys. Deep inside, I believed something was wrong with society and parenting. I felt that many of us, boys and girls, were confused and didn't know how to form proper relationships. Boys with more than one girlfriend were more popular, but few knew what they wanted in a relationship. Some boys asked me out, but many were already in relationships. I had nothing in common with them.

Chapter 22

Miracles and Hope

"A blessing beyond words."

I glanced at the clock; it was three o'clock on the 30th of July. I realised I hadn't slept at all. The pain, worries, and endless thoughts had kept me awake. I made sure to move quietly, careful not to wake Peter, who usually got up around four or four-thirty a.m.. Who knew what the day ahead would bring?

Astorga wasn't far, just about thirty minutes by bus. I felt relieved knowing we had already booked two nights there. I promised myself I would make an online appointment with a doctor and ask for the strongest painkiller available.

"I'm not giving up. We have twelve more days to walk. It seems impossible, but I'll try to make it happen," I vowed silently. With that promise, I let my mind drift to a different time—a new chapter of my life—hoping it would distract me from the pain and uncertainty.

Towards the end of October 1987, I was introduced to Greg by a mutual friend. Our first meeting was brief; he was in a hurry, and we didn't talk much. He was tall, at first I thought almost too tall, quiet, and serious. I learned that he worked as a lecturer at the University in Skopje. Coincidentally, he had the same name and height as a boy I had met in high school—Greg, or Goche, as his friends called him. It felt like a strange echo from the past.

Although we were briefly introduced, we didn't have a proper conversation until nearly two months later when we went out for dinner with our mutual friend Zoran and a few others.

Looking at him that evening, I thought about how different we were. *I don't like distant relationships anymore, and I'm not fond of someone so quiet. But there's something about him that intrigues me.*

Despite my initial reservations, I could feel that I might love him. During dinner, a deep voice inside me whispered, *I will marry this person, and not long after, I did.*

Through the conversation that evening, I found out that Greg rented an apartment in Skopje, just a few buildings away from my friend, Tanja. At the end of the dinner, we left. Greg accompanied me and asked me to see him again. I accepted, and it made me very happy.

Soon after we began seeing each other, Greg invited me to Skopje to spend more time together and get to know each other better. Since I wasn't working then, I was happy to visit. Tanja, ever supportive, offered me a place to stay.

Not long after I visited Greg in Skopje, I told him about my past relationship with Miki. I kept the details brief, thinking we'd have plenty of time in the future to share more about our histories. I noticed early on that Greg was a very private person. He didn't share much about his past, aside from mentioning the family struggles they faced after his father passed away.

Things between Greg and me moved quickly. I believed it was meant to be. He expressed his desire for us to live together, and before long, we introduced each other to our families. A few months later, we started planning our wedding. His family—his mother and sisters, who were both married and settled with their families—lived in Bitola. I felt proud to be with Greg, who was admired for his achievements and known for his intelligence and wisdom. I couldn't have been happier.

However, there were subtle signs of trouble. He had an unshakable sadness, a tendency to withdraw from people, and a preference for solitude that worried me. He often waited for me to make decisions. During my stays in Bitola, I noticed how delicately his family treated him, almost like a fragile flower. All their attention seemed directed toward supporting his academic and professional success.

The wedding was set for August, 1988 and everything seemed to spiral out of control once the invitations went out. Looking back, it felt like I was sleepwalking, letting life take the lead instead of actively choosing my path.

One moment that stood out happened just before the wedding. Greg and I had returned to Bitola, and the plan was for me to stay with his mother to prepare while he went back to Skopje for a few days. He had forgotten the key to his apartment, so I called Tanja for help. Regardless, as she wasn't in Skopje then, she told me where to find a spare key. That evening, Greg stayed at her apartment and came across an old album of hers, which contained one photo of Miki and me.

The next day, he called me, his voice heavy with anger and disappointment.

"You'll never love me the way you loved him. I have proof. I don't think we should marry," he said.

I was stunned. After that conversation, I wasn't sure I wanted to marry him. I felt lost—scared, alone, and afraid of bringing shame to my family. With no one to turn to for support, I decided to let *life take charge*.

From that moment, I began to lose sight of who I was. It was just the beginning of my turbulent life; the rest became history.

Our marriage lasted for thirty years on paper. I have no regrets; it was something I believed was meant to be. We have two wonderful daughters, whom we deeply love and who love us in return. I couldn't ask for anything more.

After we separated, I noticed something peculiar; Miki's spirit also seemed to depart. I no longer felt his presence around me. Did his spirit linger because Greg mentioned his name, to protect me or to cause trouble? Who can say? During our time together in Skopje, I knew Miki cared for me as much as he could and tried to shield me from harm as best he could. Yet, our relationship was often confusing and messy, reminiscent of my tumultuous childhood.

After thirty years I felt that two significant people in my life left, creating space for my self-discovery without any interference.

Peter interrupted my thoughts. He woke up and asked how I was feeling. I told him about my sleepless night but tried to reassure him that things would improve once I spoke to the doctor. With some effort, I managed to book an online appointment for noon.

I attempted to stand, but without my hiking poles, it was impossible. Slowly, we made our way to the hostel bar for breakfast. We decided to take a bus, conveniently stopping in front of the hostel. I was so grateful I could manage the short walk to the bus stop. In less than thirty minutes, we arrived in Astorga on that quiet Sunday morning, around ten-thirty a.m. Peter stayed close by, offering support at every step.

"Peter, having you here means everything to me. You missed your walk today, and yet you're still amazing," I said gratefully. He hugged me and kissed my forehead.

"Don't worry, my dear. We're in this together, through thick and thin," Peter said with a reassuring smile.

We sat at an outdoor café across from the hotel, passing the time until we could check-in.

We entered the lobby of Hotel Gaudi just as the doctor from Portugal called. While other guests waited to check in, I focused on the consultation. The doctor diagnosed me with knee overuse, leading to tendonitis, and emphasised that rest was critical to avoid further damage.

"You must avoid walking for at least four days to allow your knee to recover. Continuing to move could worsen the inflammation," he explained.

I requested painkillers, which he agreed to prescribe, though he reminded me they would only alleviate the pain, not address the underlying issue.

While I managed the medical details, Peter efficiently checked us into our hotel room. The digital prescriptions arrived by one-thirty p.m. We noted that most pharmacies in Astorga closed by two p.m. on Sundays. He rushed to the nearest pharmacy, only to find it already closed. I was so disappointed. I had believed that taking painkillers as soon as possible would ease the pain and help me sleep.

I lay in bed, striving to rest as much as possible. While respecting the doctor's orders, I was hoping against hope for a miraculous recovery. My determination to reach Santiago de Compostela on foot remained steadfast despite crossing O'Cebreiro, the mountain's highest point.

I have to walk. I must make it to Santiago de Compostela, I thought firmly, even as the pain persisted. The doctor's words echoed in my mind, advising caution with the strong painkillers prescribed.

With two nights and a day of rest ahead, I steeled myself against the discomfort, focusing on the journey ahead while trying to ignore the severity of my knee injury.

Our hotel on the lively main street offered a front-row view of the Roman historical festival. We watched people parading in period costumes from the window, capturing photos and videos. Despite the vibrant atmosphere, my spirits were dampened by my condition and the uncertainty of my recovery. I clung to hope that the medication and two nights of rest in Astorga would bring some relief.

Many pilgrims faced similar challenges, often walking alone. I felt fortunate to have Peter's unwavering support and didn't want to hinder his journey. We had pre-booked accommodations in Santiago de Compostela, and Peter suggested I take the bus while he continued on foot. I hesitated; I wanted to walk alongside him.

I lay on the bed, letting my thoughts drift back thirty years, reflecting on my marriage and the struggles we faced. One of the greatest challenges was our inability to conceive. In my mind, I could almost hear the voice of Dr David Wood, the renowned Australian gynecologist who pioneered IVF and played a key role in the birth of the first IVF baby.

Greg and I moved to Australia in October 1992, four years into our marriage, filled with hope and dreams of starting a family. Despite our efforts, conceiving naturally remained out of reach. Medical tests back in Macedonia had shown no issues, and we held on tightly to hope.

Our first two years in Australia were particularly challenging as we adjusted to a new life in a foreign country. We both enrolled in full-time English courses, though Greg's English was more advanced than mine. He progressed quickly, moving to a higher level of study and eventually securing a job as a computer programmer, which eased our financial burdens and gave us a sense of stability.

We eagerly awaited our appointment with Dr Wood, a professor at Monash University in Melbourne. When our turn came, I couldn't contain my impatience. Both of us sat anxiously as Dr Wood reviewed our case.

"After six years without conceiving, natural pregnancy is unlikely. IVF is your best or only option," Dr Wood stated matter-of-factly, shattering my hopes for a natural conception. I had hoped for a simpler solution, perhaps medication, but his words were final.

Despite this, I clung to hope. Each month brought disappointment with my menstrual cycle, but I never lost hope. For years, I meticulously tracked my temperature and ovulation, holding onto the belief that one day we would have children.

"Why do we need IVF if our tests show no issues?" I asked, hoping for a different answer.

Dr Wood, likely accustomed to such questions, replied, "Around ten per cent of couples face unexplained infertility despite normal test results."

Trusting Dr Wood, we proceeded with the necessary pre-IVF examinations at his hospital, though the costs were daunting. Eventually, we joined the Royal Women's Hospital waiting list for IVF. The year that followed was filled with tears and disappointments as we endured four unsuccessful IVF attempts. After the last session, the doctor advised me to pause for two to three years due to exhaustion and the development of an ovarian cyst, which would need removal in two months.

That day, after my final IVF session, I went to the hospital alone. It marked the end of my hope to become a mother. I was devastated, knowing the treatment hadn't worked and that I couldn't try again for another three years. Sitting outside the hospital, I let my tears flow freely. I lost track of time as people passed by; their curious glances went unnoticed. It felt like the death of a lifelong dream I had cherished since childhood. When I finally returned home, my hope returned to me. I rebuilt it, repeating that we could still have a baby somehow.

I began using the bath daily, finding solace in warm, salted water. Too drained for work or study, I turned to knitting and crocheting—skills I had learned long ago. I continued monitoring my body temperature, staying positive, and focusing entirely on my well-being.

Two months later, on Monday morning, on the way to the hospital for my cyst removal appointment, I had a car accident that prevented me from reaching the hospital that day. Though shaken, I was physically unharmed except for the car's damage. I called the hospital to explain the situation, and they kindly rescheduled my appointment for the next Monday.

When I finally made it, I mentioned to the doctor that my period hadn't arrived that week, likely due to the accident-induced stress. Consequently, the cyst removal was postponed while I gave blood for testing.

The next day, I anxiously called for my test results. To my disbelief, I learned I was pregnant. I asked the nurse to double-check, ensuring it was indeed my test. She laughed warmly, congratulating me—the same nurse who had supported me through my IVF sessions. At that moment, I couldn't imagine anyone happier than me. Excitedly, I called Greg at work, who initially questioned if the hospital had verified the results properly. But soon, we both shared in overwhelming joy.

Both of our daughters were conceived naturally, and miraculously, my cyst dissolved during the pregnancy. Dr Wood, a respected specialist, had been definitive in his assessment, but life had other plans. I believed in miracles then, just as I do now, trusting that somehow, against all odds, I would find my way forward.

The next morning, July 31st, I woke up early, disturbed by the pain that had kept me awake during the night. However, I still managed to get some sleep. Our hotel was located on Astorga's bustling main street, where activity persisted until the early hours. Despite the vibrant surroundings, I knew I wouldn't get to explore the historic town as planned.

Maybe we can visit Astorga another time, I thought, waiting for the pharmacy to open so Peter could pick up my medication. By ten a.m. he returned with the tablets, and I eagerly read the instructions before taking one of each. I researched online to confirm the dosage—one tablet every eight hours for one, and one or two per day for the other. I began with the tablets, hoping that by Monday's end, I would feel some relief.

In the afternoon, we visited the post office near our hotel to arrange for half of my backpack to be transported daily to our next planned accommodation. We opted for this service to lighten my load. Peter decided to continue to carry his heavy pack bag. I was glad I managed to walk to the post office, relying on my hiking poles.

On the way to the hotel, we bought another bag and packed the remaining belongings, ready to leave in the hotel lobby the following morning before departing Astorga.

* * *

It was 1st August. Around five-thirty a.m. we left the hotel and started walking and looking for the Camino signs. Though still not feeling well, I was grateful that the painkillers were starting to take effect, allowing me to walk. The difference was noticeable with my backpack reduced to essentials—two litres of water and a few necessities. The daily cost of seven Euros for the baggage transfer was a small price for the relief it brought.

While the painkillers provided relief as prescribed, they didn't solve the underlying issue. I leaned heavily on my right leg and hiking poles as we navigated the early morning darkness, relying on the occasional torchlight to find the Camino signs amid the buildings. Dogs barked in protest as we passed, and at one point, a helpful local guided us back on track, pointing us in the right direction with kindness and patience.

Our destination for the day was the village of Foncebadón, where we had booked a room at BNB La Posada del Druida. Despite my injury, we arrived without incident, thanks to the regular medication intake that kept me going. Without those pills, continuing the pilgrimage would have been impossible.

I walked slowly, my determination fixed solely on reaching Santiago de Compostela on foot, regardless of the hours it took each day. Some pilgrims paused to check on my well-being, but I remained focused, knowing Peter was nearby should I need assistance. Rest breaks were crucial, often taking an hour before I could continue, feeling somewhat better.

In the past ten days or so, the thoughts that once surrounded me seemed to have dissipated. Perhaps the intensity of the pain from my knee overshadowed them, or maybe I finally let everything out. It felt like I had walked into a closet and cleared out old clothes stored there for years. Those clothes had served their purpose, whether beautiful or worn out, and now it was time for them to go. That's how I viewed my thoughts—released and free.

I wondered why I hadn't made time for this sooner. Now, I felt liberated. Everything had been laid bare, and I could observe those thoughts as an outsider. Perhaps they would return, but not to consume me. They would come and go, and I welcomed them with gratitude.

I am thankful for everything in my life: my upbringing in a loving family who did their best, the experiences of love, my marriage, my beautiful children, having Peter in my life, and all that has transpired. I believe each event has a purpose and has shaped me into who I am today.

Chapter 23

Overcoming Challenges

"Every step brings you closer to your destination."

We had just two days left to reach O'Cebreiro, and I knew it would be one of the most challenging parts of our journey. Climbing to the highest point and reaching the Cruce de Ferro seemed daunting. I couldn't dwell on thoughts too much, but this stretch of the Camino demanded attention. Looking at the map, the terrain appeared rugged, similar to the Pyrenees where we had climbed before. At least then, I had no physical issues to worry about.

The following day, 2nd August, we stayed in Ponferrada at the Hostel San Miguel, where we had a private room. We picked up the key from the restaurant across from the hostel and ate in our room. Exhausted from the day's walk, we washed our clothes as usual and retired early.

The next leg of our journey was another long walk. We had booked accommodation at the old monastery, St Nicolas el Real, now serving as a guesthouse in the heart of Villafranca del Bierzo. We had plans to dine with Mary at a renowned restaurant that evening, known for its excellent food. However, we arrived late, nearing six p.m. Unfortunately, the painkillers didn't provide much relief that day. After checking in at reception, we headed straight to our room. The surroundings buzzed with tourists and pilgrims, but I felt too unwell to explore. Regrettably, we had to cancel our dinner plans with Mary.

As hunger set in later that evening, we realised it was after eight p.m., and all nearby options for food were closing up. Even the bar and restaurant at our pensione were shut. We decided to try a restaurant next door with concern growing about my strength and the days of walking ahead. Peter was attentive and supportive, despite my worries, always asking how I felt. Although I didn't want to burden him, I appreciated his care deeply. He bore the physical challenges of the walk alongside me while ensuring I rested as much as possible.

We settled into the restaurant's outdoor area, which was bustling and cool. The traditional three-course dinner typical along the Camino was delicious, providing much-needed sustenance. Afterwards, we returned to our room, focusing solely on rest and sleep, skipping laundry that night. The next day, we awaited a thirty-kilometre trek and the climb to the mountain's highest peak. Peter had meticulously planned our accommodations, including our stay in O'Cebreiro, and we were determined to stick to our schedule despite the challenges ahead.

On the morning of August 4th, we departed from Villafranca del Bierzo. As we passed through several villages, we found nothing open for breakfast. Despite not feeling hungry, I knew I had to eat something due to my medication. That day, I followed the doctor's recommendations rather than relying on internet advice. I took the prescribed number of tablets on an empty stomach. After nearly fourteen kilometres of walking, we finally reached a small town where we bought some essentials from the pharmacy—bandages and gauze—to manage the blisters on our feet. Surprisingly, the blisters didn't trouble me much. We diligently covered them each morning before starting our walk, and by day's end, they were under control.

As we passed by an albergue on the opposite side of the road, a man around our age emerged and approached us. He introduced himself as a fellow pilgrim who had noticed us over the past few days. I remembered him as he spoke fluent English and had stopped to check on my well-being several times. He explained that he couldn't continue his journey due to knee problems, similar like mine and was waiting for his son to join him so they could drive to Santiago de Compostela together. He mentioned he was a Spaniard who had previously walked parts of the Camino Frances with his sons.

Just as Peter and I were preparing to move on, the man looked at me and said something unexpected: "If I had another life and were born again, I would come to Australia and marry a woman like you. I've been watching you and don't know how you keep walking. You're a very brave woman."

I smiled and replied modestly, "The painkillers have been a big help."

Before long, he wished us 'Buen Camino', and we continued.

I glanced at Peter, curious about his reaction to the man's statement. Many men might feel uncomfortable or insecure, but Peter remained unfazed.

"Darling," I teased, "if he's looking for women like me to marry, Macedonia is closer and full of them."

We laughed, and Peter replied, "Come on, my pumpkin, let's stay focused on our walk. We have to cross the mountain and reach O'Cebreiro by tonight. Don't worry about him."

I often found myself amazed at having met someone like Peter, who understood the true essence of a relationship and never took it for granted. Using all these affectionate names made me feel youthful. After all, we're never too old to feel, express, receive and give love.

We decided to take a break and rest at a lovely restaurant towards the edge of town. The weather was warm, so we sat outside. Our routine on the Camino typically involved stopping at every village or town to get our credentials stamped, use the facilities and grab a bite to eat or a coffee.

While public toilets were sparse along the route, I didn't view it as a major issue. Every place serving food—a bar, restaurant, or cafe—had facilities. Of course, pilgrims were expected to purchase rather than use the restroom, but this arrangement posed no problem for us.

In each of these places, there was also a stamp available. We needed at least one stamp daily, though sometimes we collected more. From Sarria to Santiago de Compostela, we required two daily stamps to receive a Compostela Certificate at the end of our journey. We were expected to walk this section, around one hundred kilometres without assistance, such as taking a bus or taxi, even for short distances. We had just two days left to Sarria.

We were prepared to depart when we encountered our Camino companion, Mary. We spent some time catching up with her before continuing our journey together. She planned to stay overnight at the foothills of the mountain, cautioning us about the challenge of walking to O'Cebreiro in one day. It was the last time we saw Mary, but our connection with her continued.

O'Cebreiro sits at an altitude of thirteen hundred metres, nestled in the O Courel mountain range. It was nearing two p.m. when I watched Peter begin to ascend the narrow trail, cutting through the trees and forest. I hesitated, unsure how I would manage. In the preceding days, I had favoured my right leg to ease my left knee strain.

My hiking poles became indispensable as I started my climbing. Few pilgrims were around, and those who passed me seemed to move like commuters on a freeway, contrasting sharply with my slower pace. The dense woods and steep, narrow path presented a formidable challenge.

As I struggled, thoughts filled my mind. *My dear God, what have I done to deserve this suffering?* Yet, I knew self-pity and negative thoughts would only hinder me. Climbing what felt like an endless, vertical path through the woods, something shifted. The pain in my knee seemed to vanish, and I felt strangely light. It was as if I were flying through the mountain, observing myself from the outside. I felt detached from my usual self, climbing almost without pausing. I couldn't comprehend the unusual sensations but was reluctant to interrupt them.

Eventually, I reached Peter at the summit, where he awaited me. We embraced, silently looking down. Any fleeting euphoria quickly dissipated, replaced by exhaustion. I felt my body acutely again, sensing it might fall apart. The knee pain returned, a stark reminder of my physical limits.

"How was it for you, honey? That was a tough climb. How are you feeling?" Peter asked, concern evident in his voice.

"I don't know. I'd love to find somewhere to sit and catch my breath," I managed, struggling for air. How had I climbed? What was happening to me? Words failed me, and I could not even articulate to myself the experience I had just undergone. Sometimes, words can't capture the profound shifts within and around us.

"The app shows there's an albergue about two kilometres ahead. Let's head there and get something to eat," Peter suggested, already setting off.

I followed, though two kilometres felt like an eternity through the undulating terrain. My body began to relax into the motion, and I felt detached, as if moving an empty vessel. I was numb to pain and worry, accepting whatever came next with a calm resignation. Whatever energy remained was just enough to keep my body moving forward.

We glimpsed rooftops through the trees, signalling our approach to a place of rest. Among a scattering of houses along the street, there was a tap with running water. I sat down and splashed my face, drained of words and energy, focused solely on enduring. Glancing at Peter, I sensed he shared my fatigue, yet, as always, he assumed the role of leader—managing the GPS, navigating the Camino route, and ensuring my well-being.

In front of one of the houses were chairs and tables, indicating it was likely the albergue we sought. We settled in, and Peter admitted he had overestimated the day's distance—it was nearly twenty-eight kilometres, with challenging ascents through high hills.

The albergue host was surprised when we mentioned our plan to walk to O'Cebreiro. He cautioned us that it was late, and pilgrims typically did not attempt such a trek at this hour. It was nearing four p.m. when our Swiss Camino friends arrived, visibly exhausted like us. They opted to stay at the albergue, where we were resting.

Our meal lacked freshness and flavour; perhaps my exhaustion coloured my perception. I had no appetite, only the desire to finish walking for the day and retreat to our room for sleep. Conversing with fellow pilgrims, we reassured ourselves that the toughest stretches were behind us—once we crossed O'Cebreiro, the path would supposedly become easier.

After an hour's respite, we resumed our journey. Passing the statue marking our entry into Galicia, the landscape transformed dramatically. Unlike the dry Meseta, Galicia greeted us with lush greenery spread across rolling mountain ranges. Despite the warm, sunny weather and picturesque views, our fatigue dampened our ability to appreciate it fully. Along the way, we encountered two young pilgrims who, like us, were heading to O'Cebreiro for the night. However, we had little energy left for conversation or taking photos.

Spotting a few distant houses, I felt relieved, knowing the day's walk would soon conclude. By nearly six-thirty p.m., we reached La Venta Celta. True to routine, we tended to our washing and retired to bed, grateful for another day's progress on the Camino.

Chapter 24

A Heavy Heart

"Love does not begin and end the way we seem to think it does. Love is a battle, love is a war, love is a growing up."

James Baldwin

We woke early the following morning to a dark, cold, rainy day. We decided to head to the restaurant for breakfast, where we found it bustling with pilgrims who had likely arrived early the day before. Most pilgrims typically reach their destinations before two p.m. I knew Peter would have arrived much earlier if I hadn't walked so slowly. Despite my efforts, I struggled to keep pace with Peter and walk faster.

I wasn't in the mood for coffee or any drink and could barely touch the toast before me. Hunger escaped me, which surprised Peter, as food and coffee usually lifted my spirits. Still, I forced myself to eat a piece of toast to help with my medication. Despite it all, we were grateful to have survived the previous day. I focused on staying positive, knowing we had seven days left until Santiago de Compostela, and hoped everything would go smoothly from here.

We dressed in waterproof pants and coats, ensuring our backpacks were covered. The walk ahead was challenging; it seemed the village lay atop a mountain, and we felt enveloped in clouds. It was difficult to discern whether it was darkness or thick fog. However, as we neared the Cruz de Ferro, the weather began to clear.

The Cruz de Ferro stood before us—a monumental iron cross surrounded by thousands of stones left by pilgrims worldwide. It was a place where many tears had been shed. Peter and I hadn't brought stones, I didn't feel burdened by any specific sins. In my heart, I felt the presence of all those dear to me. I don't believe in carrying sins; everyone must confront challenges or seek guidance.

Walking among the stones, I embraced the cross, overcome with emotion. Peter photographed me beside the cross, and I returned the favour. Seeing Peter there, watching the cross, I reflected on how we had seen it so often on TV, yet, in reality, it held a different significance. Observing the stones, I thought about the countless pilgrims over the centuries who had journeyed here, some with clear intentions and others, like me, unsure of their purpose.

Continuing our walk, we found a food truck near the main road, where a few pilgrims were gathered, chatting animatedly around a fireplace. Despite it being summer, it felt like winter. We met Christina, a young woman from Australia who shared her journey after finishing university. Her story impressed me. She had embarked on the Camino seeking direction, much like several other young pilgrims we encountered.

I recall my youth when the Camino wasn't as well-known or accessible. Back then, I lacked the financial means and confidence to travel alone. The past forty years have brought significant changes, and in the last decade, I have travelled extensively, often encouraging my daughters and students to explore the world. Travel, to me, was an eye-opening experience.

We conversed with a French pilgrim who walked different sections of the Camino annually. He had walked to León the previous year and continued his journey this year. The Camino allowed people to walk according to their schedules and preferences, making it convenient for Europeans.

After a pleasant chat with fellow pilgrims that morning, we set off, knowing our interactions would likely end there, as was common on the Camino.

Our next stop was Triacastela, where we had booked a room at Pension Casa Simon. The twenty-two kilometre walk initially seemed manageable, but I felt very unwell towards the end. Aside from the toast at breakfast, I couldn't stomach any food for the rest of the day, opting instead to drink water to stave off dehydration. Peter, noticing my condition, waited patiently, and his concern was evident, despite his fatigue. It was our twenty-eighth day walking, and though I kept my discomfort to myself, I appreciated Peter's unwavering support throughout our journey.

I approached where Peter was waiting, gently placing my backpack on the grass before lying down, overcome with nausea. Initially, I thought it might be food poisoning or gastroenteritis from the previous day's suspect food. It hadn't occurred to me that vomiting and diarrhea could be side effects of the medication I was taking, a realisation that came a couple of days later. Peter looked concerned.

"We're close, just an hour's walk. If you can't manage it, I'll call a taxi," Peter suggested, worry evident in his voice.

After emptying my stomach, I began to feel a bit better.

"I think I can walk," I replied weakly, pushing myself to follow Peter.

We eventually reached Pension Casa Simon. I struggled to sleep that night, spending most of it in the bathroom. Peter, thankfully, didn't experience any symptoms. The next morning, I was too weak to walk and couldn't take my medication due to the vomiting.

"I can't walk today," I admitted to Peter, feeling defeated. "You should go ahead to Sarria. Maybe I'll catch up by taxi later."

Peter hesitated, reluctant to leave me alone.

"No, we'll go together by taxi," he decided firmly.

Leaving Triacastela behind, we arrived in Sarria. I knew using taxis or buses wasn't permitted on the Camino after Sarria. I felt ill, doubting whether I could continue the journey. However, the thought of being separated from Peter spurred me on.

"I have to walk the last one hundred kilometres. I must finish this journey," I repeated to myself, determined to give it another try. I was uncertain how I would manage but unwilling to give up.

Chapter 25

Unyielding Determination

"Angels are defined only by their name."

It was 7th of August. We set off from Sarria early in the morning, trying to maintain a positive outlook despite my ongoing health challenges. As we began walking, I was astounded to see hundreds of pilgrims, who seemed more like tourists, starting their journey from Sarria. The atmosphere was completely different compared to the previous thirty days. Many people were lining up for food, stamps and to use the facilities. Waiting for the bathroom was particularly challenging for me, given my condition, which hadn't improved despite continuing with my medication. We sometimes had to push on to the next village because finding a place to rest was difficult amidst the bustling crowds. It seemed like all of Spain had come out to walk the Camino, with some families even accompanied by young children still in primary school.

I was deeply touched by the hospitality and kindness of ordinary Spaniards along the way. When we finally found a table outside a restaurant, I unwittingly sat on a broken chair. Two girls nearby noticed and immediately brought me a sturdy chair. Their generosity left me grateful and humbled.

When it came time to order food, I requested a roll with avocado, but the server seemed confused and couldn't accommodate my request as it wasn't on the menu. A compassionate voice from the crowd tried to assist in translation, but the response was firm.

"We only serve what's on the menu," the man behind the counter reiterated. Disappointed, I prepared to leave when someone from the restaurant unexpectedly brought me a piece of bread and a bowl of avocado. Their thoughtful gesture warmed my heart and lifted my spirits amidst the day's challenges.

Across from us, a group of young men and women caught my attention. One of the boys resembled Prince William when he was younger. Curiously, I asked him if anyone had ever told him that he looked like Prince William.

"No, who's he?" he replied, prompting his friend to chime in,

"How do you not know? He's from England. His mother was very popular. I forgot her name."

"He's the future king of England," I explained, amused by their innocence. I asked where they were from, and the young man who resembled Prince William mentioned he was from Denmark, immediately reaching for his phone, likely to look up images of the British royal family.

Our next stop was the village of Portomarín at the Vistalegre Hotel-Spa, a twenty-two kilometre trek for the day. As we approached the town, we noticed an alternative path winding through the hills. Unfortunately, we missed the warning sign in Spanish and English indicating it was a hazardous route. In Australia, such a path would likely be closed for safety reasons, but here, we hesitated.

Peter paused, concerned about the danger, suggesting we turn back and find another way. I hesitated to retreat. I favoured continuing downhill with my right leg and hiking poles to avoid unnecessary backtracking. Despite Peter's warnings, I urged him to continue downhill rather than retreat. Reluctantly, he turned back. Nearby, a group of young adults aged between twenty and thirty offered assistance. Peter declined, but I accepted their help, a decision I soon questioned.

Some young men carried my bag while the girls held my umbrella in the sweltering heat. One of the boys, later introducing himself as José, reassured me as we began the precarious descent. Holding my hands firmly, he led me backward down the steep, rocky path. I felt fearful for his safety and regretful for not heeding Peter's advice. Despite my anxieties, José maintained a calm demeanour, smiling and assuring me we would make it through safely.

As we navigated the treacherous terrain, the pain in my knee miraculously disappeared. Grateful, yet anxious, I inquired nervously about our progress.

"How much farther to the main road?" I asked, hoping for reassurance.

"I'm not sure. This is my first time here, too," José smiled.

Approaching a dangerous stretch, I pleaded with José to prioritise his safety and leave me. Yet he insisted on staying by my side, encouraging me to follow his careful footsteps. He was going backwards and holding tight to my hands. I was so worried and prayed for him. The group rallied around us, offering support and camaraderie despite my embarrassment at needing their help.

Finally, we reached safer ground, greeted with applause, hugs, laughter and congratulations for navigating the perilous path together. I introduced myself to José and thanked him profusely. We took photos together, and I asked about their origins.

"We're from different countries. We met at the hostel in Sarria last night," they explained. Their easy camaraderie and mutual support highlighted the essence of the Camino for me: a journey where love and compassion know no boundaries.

I repeatedly expressed my gratitude to José and the others, promising José that I would never forget him. In return, he said he had never encountered such a challenging path and would remember me, too. I refrained from asking if he was an athlete or a physical education teacher; his strength and focus spoke volumes. He embodied a beautiful soul, an angel without a surname or fixed abode—just José.

The group stayed together as we continued our journey. They accompanied me until Peter caught up, walking along the main road. Peter was visibly displeased with my choice to descend the rocks, unable to comprehend how I managed without José's assistance. Crossing the bridge and ascending the stairs into the terraced village of Portomarín, I tackled the climb without complaint. After the earlier ordeal, the stairs seemed manageable.

Portomarín, nestled in the province of Lugo, greeted us with its picturesque charm. The Vistalegre Hotel, where we stayed, was nearby and quite lovely. Despite my desire to explore the town, my exhaustion held me back. We settled for a simple meal from our bags, did our laundry and retired early, feeling drained. With just four days left until Santiago de Compostela, the end of our journey felt within reach.

It was Tuesday, August 8th. We left the hotel early, skipping breakfast since it started too late for our departure. I still couldn't eat much besides bread and water, and Peter was in no mood to wait. Our destination, Rua do Mercado, lay about twenty-five kilometres away, so we set off promptly, aiming to cover most of the distance in the morning. The road was bustling with people, though the crowds would thin over the next few days.

Passing through several villages, we found no place to buy food or drink until we reached a town with a bar. I urgently needed a bathroom, and my condition prompted me to decide to see a doctor. I was certain the medication was causing my troubles; I felt weak and drained of energy. We pushed on, but after a few kilometres, with fifteen more to go to Rua do Mercado, my frequent need for the bathroom became too much to continue. We reluctantly decided to call a taxi, expecting a thirty-minute wait. Peter considered coming with me but ultimately decided to continue on foot to earn his Compostela Certificate. He was right; after walking so far, we both deserved it. I convinced myself to soldier on, to be resilient and keep walking. We cancelled the taxi and pressed forward into the late afternoon, encountering a few pilgrims still on the road, most having already settled into their accommodations.

Along the way, we met a distressed young couple sitting by the roadside, exhausted from their journey starting in Sarria.

The girl was nearly in tears, overwhelmed by the challenge. "This is so difficult. I had no idea," she lamented.

I empathised deeply with their struggle; nothing truly prepares you for the rigours of the Camino. The weather was so hot. We stopped at nearly every bar on the route to Rua do Mercado, finally arriving. I was relieved we hadn't taken the taxi, though it had been a tough day, made bearable by Peter's support. As we passed a restaurant, I spotted my Camino friends, José and the others, waving and smiling at us.

We stayed at Acubillo, a small hotel with a cramped bathroom that night. I promptly scheduled an online appointment with the doctor I had online appointment with before. At nine o'clock, we had a video call. The doctor was astonished that I was still able to walk, confirming that the tablets were indeed causing my symptoms. He advised me to stop taking them immediately. Aware that I still had three more days of walking ahead, I asked for a prescription for alternative medication with fewer side effects. The doctor swiftly emailed me a prescription, and I hoped to find a pharmacy the next day on our way to Arzua to fill it.

Chapter 26

On the Edge of Endurance

"Unconditional love means not expecting anything in return but cherishing the happiness of the person you love."

We were nearing Santiago de Compostela, but the journey remained arduous. From Palas de Rei to Arzua, it stretched nearly thirty kilometres and took more than ten hours. We set out very early that morning, and I decided to forgo painkillers. I was uncertain how I would manage, but Peter reassured me. We planned to rest at every opportunity and find a pharmacy to pick up the necessary medication.

I noticed an immediate difference without the tablets, and my digestive system started normalising. I resolved to continue to Santiago de Compostela without medication, albeit at a slower pace. Peter patiently waited for me, and we took several breaks before arriving around six-thirty p.m. at Casa Abeleira in Arzua.

As we entered the building, a kind and courteous lady greeted us. After checking in and obtaining our stamps, she handed us the key to our room on the second floor. I stared at the daunting marble staircase, realising I couldn't rely on my hiking poles. Despite Peter's help, I found it agonisingly difficult to ascend. Crawling became my only option, my injured pride and dignity taking a painful blow. I felt exposed and vulnerable in that humiliating moment, imagining the lady's sympathetic gaze.

To ease the tension, Peter asked if she had walked the Camino herself.

She admitted she hadn't, prompting me to think, *She's not foolish like me. How many others has she seen crawl up these stairs?* Feeling like a wounded creature desperately clinging to survival, I reached our room and collapsed onto the bed, overwhelmed by tears.

My ego berated me, insisting I couldn't continue and that I was causing irreparable harm to myself. *Go home*, it urged. I drowned in self-pity and negativity, convinced I'd never recover from this ordeal, and questioned why I'd embarked on this journey in the first place.

Peter sat beside me, his expression a mix of empathy and concern. "I didn't realise you were feeling this bad," he said softly.

"Peter, I can't go on. Once I feel better tonight, I'll book a ticket back to Melbourne," I sobbed. "I don't have to finish the Camino," I continued, my voice heavy with despair. "I don't even know why I'm here, enduring all this suffering. Maybe I'll never recover from this walk. I want to go home."

Peter remained silent momentarily before gently responding, "Just two more days. We're almost there."

"I don't care how many days are left," I insisted. "I've reached my limit, or maybe I've gone beyond it."

That evening, I cried until I couldn't cry anymore. Lying on the bed, I lost track of time, but gradually, a glimmer of resolve flickered within me. I got up, washed my clothes in the bathroom and returned to Peter with a renewed determination.

"Forget what I said earlier," I told him with a smile. "I'll continue walking with you and reach Santiago de Compostela on two feet."

Peter hugged me tightly, kissing my forehead. "I love you, my sweetheart. You'll be okay." He helped me tidy up, and we settled into bed together, preparing to face whatever challenges the next day would bring.

The following day's journey was shorter, about twenty kilometres from Arzua to O Pedrouza. Upon arrival, we indulged in a delightful dinner at the restaurant adjacent to our hotel for the night. Both of us were filled with excitement and joy. We savoured our meal and engaged in conversation with the restaurant's proprietors.

During our dinner, we had the pleasure of meeting individuals from Cuba and Colombia who had established businesses, primarily restaurants and had chosen to settle in Spain. Their proficiency in Spanish facilitated their integration into their new homeland.

After dinner, we returned to our hotel room without tending to any washing that night. Instead, we packed our belongings and prepared for the final day of our walk.

"How are you feeling, my love?" Peter asked me.

"Very happy," I replied. "I want to savour every moment of our last day."

"You will," Peter assured me. "It's less than twenty kilometres. We don't need to leave too early."

Chapter 27

Mission Accomplished

It was August 11th. Rising at four-thirty a.m. felt like the norm by now. Both of us were brimming with excitement. After thirty-four days of walking, it was surreal to think we wouldn't have to rise early or cover all those kilometres anymore. We left the hotel and headed to the open bar for breakfast. Normally, we'd have breakfast after five, sometimes ten kilometres, but this last day was different. We planned to arrive leisurely around two or three in the afternoon.

The walk was delightful. We conversed with many pilgrims along the way, most of whom had started in Sarria and were curious about the journey from Saint-Jean-Pied-de-Port. Describing the experience was beyond words for me. I couldn't believe I had traversed that distance, and I was certain each pilgrim would have a unique story to tell.

As we reached a point where we could spot the cathedral in Santiago de Compostela, a statue pointed toward it. We snapped a few photos, and at three p.m., we passed through the tunnel with numerous other pilgrims, completing their journeys and reaching their destination. It was incredibly emotional. The square in front of the cathedral was bustling with people—some lying down, some crying, some taking photos. Many pilgrims queued, waiting to enter the cathedral and pay homage to St James and his relics at the Santiago de Compostela Cathedral.

Peter and I paused and gazed at the cathedral. Tears welled up in my eyes; I was overwhelmed with emotion. We looked at each other and took selfies with the cathedral in the background. Peter hugged and kissed me, and I returned his kiss.

"We made it here. Thank you, my love. I love you. I couldn't have done this without you. I'm so grateful we met," I said, gazing at him.

"I love you, too. I wouldn't have done it without you, either. Meeting you has been everything," he replied.

We lingered in front of the cathedral, observing pilgrims arriving from various Caminos that converged in Santiago de Compostela. Many faces showed weariness but also a profound sense of fulfilment.

A voice within me whispered, *Thank you, my God. Thank you, Santiago, for helping me reach my destination.* I couldn't believe I had walked over four hundred kilometres with hiking poles, almost on one leg. My heart and soul felt wide open. Standing before the magnificent Santiago, who followed Jesus devoutly, was awe-inspiring. Everything seemed incredible and overwhelming. I felt something indescribable, something that words fail to capture. Throughout the journey, the depth of my emotions defied description.

The apartment we stayed in was right next to the cathedral. The following day, we queued up and patiently waited to pay our respects to the revered Saint James. I wasn't sure if taking a photo of the room with his relics was appropriate, but I did so anyway. Inside the cathedral, the statue of St James depicted him as a warrior, pilgrim and saint. I observed pilgrims walking past, some embracing the statue and pausing in reverence. It seemed like most pilgrims shared a similar sense of awe and respect. Standing there, I felt I was in the presence of someone who had personally known Jesus and had profound wisdom thousands of years ago and sought to aid others. Love and light seemed to emanate from every corner of the cathedral.

Walking the Camino was an indescribable experience that profoundly changed me. Words fall short of capturing its impact. I embarked on this journey without fully understanding why, but I found the answers within myself upon returning. This experience has left an enduring imprint on my heart, which will remain forever.

We stayed in Santiago for five days, originally planning only a two-day stay with intentions to continue walking to Finisterre for three more days. However, completing my pilgrimage to Santiago de Compostela, aided by painkillers, hiking poles and Peter's unwavering support and understanding, was a significant achievement. The trek to Finisterre was no longer a priority. Instead, we took a tour on the third day of our stay and reached what was historically considered the world's end. I continued to use my hiking poles throughout, but it didn't bother me. I had achieved my goal of reaching Santiago de Compostela on my own.

Epilogue

"If you have a purpose or goals in life, nothing can stop you ... except yourself."

Michael J. Duckett

Nothing was wrong with my life. Everything seemed to fall into place. So why did I feel this way? Crying, anxious, withdrawn, for no specific reason. These thoughts plagued me before I embarked on the Camino.

There was nothing major to worry about. My difficult marriage had ended without much drama. My daughters were thriving in their careers and personal lives, bringing me immense happiness as a parent. My relationship with Peter was blossoming beautifully right from the start. Often, I would pinch myself in disbelief that I could meet someone so compatible with me later in life. I had been prepared to spend the rest of my life alone, but the universe, or perhaps fate, had other plans for me. I was supposed to enjoy my life, and I genuinely did. Peter and I travelled extensively and enjoyed socialising with friends and family.

Yet, beneath this seemingly perfect exterior, I felt a deep inner turmoil. Emotions and memories, long buried and never fully expressed, haunted me for nearly two years before I embarked on the Camino.

"Why did I feel so vulnerable?" Despite achieving many life goals as a daughter, wife, mother, partner, and teacher, deep within me I felt that it was not enough. I needed to do more and more to prove myself. But to whom? I questioned myself many times.

My life changed drastically after my two beautiful daughters grew up, and I realized I needed to let them find their paths without interference. Having spent over eight years trying to become a mother, I never took parenting for granted. That doesn't mean everything I did as a parent was perfect. I did the best I could with what I knew at the time. I'm endlessly grateful to God for blessing me with them.

My daughters taught me the true meaning of love. From the moment they came into my life, everything changed. They filled me with energy and purpose. With my broken English, I returned to university to complete a Graduate Diploma in Secondary Education when my eldest was just twenty-one months old and my youngest was only three months old. Nothing felt too difficult because I wanted them to be proud of me and to have a mother who would always guide and support them.

The person that I forgot was myself. I often needed to pay more attention to my needs throughout my life. I tended to prioritise others over myself, a trait I likely inherited from my upbringing and family dynamics.

Around the age of forty-five, I began to feel overwhelmed by a sense of emptiness. Giving tirelessly without expecting anything in return drained me to the point where I could not provide any more. It was a time when I realised I could no longer shoulder the burdens or expectations imposed by culture, tradition or family. I needed to find myself and prioritise what was best for me and my children, regardless of others' opinions.

The cracks in my dysfunctional marriage had started to widen irreparably. Despite efforts from both sides to salvage it over many years, my husband and I were fundamentally different people with little in common besides shared responsibilities. Unhappy marriages often cast long shadows over children's lives despite our best intentions for them. It took nearly a decade to formally separate and divorce, a decision that, looking back, was crucial for our well-being. Today, we are both much happier apart than we ever were together.

Reflecting on the final stages of our divorce, I realised the immense emotional and financial investment involved in dissolving a thirty-year marriage.

We initially opted for a single lawyer to facilitate our settlement, but legal counsel urged us to retain separate representation. However, I refused to sever communication with Greg, now my ex-husband, emphasising that despite our parting, he remained the father of my children and a significant part of my life history. Sorting through the legal documents, I discovered the exorbitant costs associated with court appearances and felt betrayed and manipulated by a system meant to support vulnerable individuals navigating divorce.

I pondered the plight of others in similarly vulnerable situations who were misled and exploited by legal professionals. This experience underscored the importance of understanding one's rights and seeking trustworthy counsel during challenging life transitions.

I called Greg and asked him to let me know how much he expected me to pay him, since I stayed on the more valuable property compared to where he lived. Fortunately, we owned two properties and we arranged for me to stay in the house until our daughters became independent. He agreed to a figure and sent it over. We sorted out our financial matters between ourselves. When I later saw the bill from the lawyer for filling out and submitting the forms, I was shocked. It was twice the amount we had initially agreed upon. The bill matched what my ex-husband paid his lawyer. I felt both lawyers had taken advantage of us, although thankfully, they hadn't exacerbated our already sensitive situation.

I share this experience to caution couples navigating divorce and settlements. It's often best to resolve matters directly between yourselves, especially when children are involved. You don't need a legal representative to dictate what's best for you and your family.

During my Camino pilgrimage, I had ample time to reflect and sift through memories I had carried since childhood—memories that no longer had a purpose. It was a profound period of self-reflection. I confronted a myriad of emotions, from sadness and feelings of victimisation to anger. I realised that while I held onto memories of past loves, the intense feelings associated with them had long faded. It was as if I could peer into the empty spaces where those emotions once resided.

Throughout my walk, my thoughts wandered over various aspects of my life: my childhood, family dynamics, and my career as a teacher—each playing a significant role in shaping who I am. I hadn't always had the time and space to process these thoughts. The demanding Camino journey compelled me to delve deep into myself, walking through the corridors of my body and reliving my past experiences.

Many reflections led me to a pivotal decision with my ex-husband—to move to Australia, perhaps one of our best decisions. I arrived in Australia at thirty in 1992, with little command of English. Over the years, I completed several English courses, returned to university, and earned a Graduate Diploma in Secondary Education. This qualification enabled me to teach language and English as an additional language and pursue a career in secondary education. Since 2000, I have taught in Melbourne's northern suburbs for over twenty-four years, a journey that continues today.

My teaching career began in Macedonia, where I initially taught primary school and later started teaching Macedonian at a Saturday school upon arriving in Australia. I briefly worked as a kindergarten teacher before finding my calling in high school. I vividly recall the joy I felt after a successful interview, followed by an offer for an ongoing teaching position. Starting mid-year, during the second semester, presented challenges as students knew more about the school's routines than I did.

As a devoted and passionate educator, I've always strived to support every student who entered my classroom. Over the years, students from my classes have earned three Premier awards, a testament to their achievements and recognition from peers, parents, and colleagues. Yet, like any profession, teaching had its challenges and moments of difficulty, not always as bright and straightforward as one might hope.

The challenging parents I encountered during my teaching career could be counted on one hand. However, the hurtful words, the abusive emails I received and the anxiety and stress they caused me seemed to linger forever. Walking the Camino along the dusty paths of Spain amidst silence and stillness, I felt as though I was walking through my soul. I unearthed memories and emotions that had long been buried, once painful but now merely dusty relics. I confronted actions and words that had wounded me deeply, realising that their weight had dissolved over time.

Reflecting on my childhood during those long, contemplative walks, I began to appreciate the positives that surrounded me then and now. Raised by two hard-working parents and cared for deeply by grandparents whose lives vastly differed, I saw resilience and quiet strength in their example. My mother, especially, allowed us the space to be ourselves and make our own choices and quietly supported us through it all. I am grateful she is still with us, caring for her four children, seven grandchildren, and eight great-grandchildren.

Upon returning from the Camino, I visited my mother, who looked at me with a gaze that spoke volumes. Despite not having seen her for over two months, time had flown by unnoticed.

I longed to share my journey and experiences with her, but words seemed unnecessary. She said, "I love you. I love you very much."

Holding her hand, tears streamed down my face as I replied, "I love you too, my beautiful mum." We didn't need many words; being together silently was enough.

Sitting beside my mother, holding her fragile hand, I remembered a day more than ten years ago. Back then, she seemed much stronger.

We were having coffee when I asked her, "Mum, I know nothing about your life before you married. Did you have a boyfriend before you met Dad?"

I didn't know why I asked, expecting her to say, "No." Instead, she turned her head away and said, "Yes, I did," with a shy look.

I was excited to learn more about something she had never mentioned before.

"I was nineteen, and he was from a village near mine. He was a few years older and asked me several times to marry him, but I couldn't. My brother was older and unmarried; if I married before him, it would shame the family. My mother would never forgive me." Mum spoke as if trying to unburden herself.

"Did you love him?" I asked.

"A lot. But it didn't matter. It was meant to be this way." She smiled.

"Did you tell your mother?" I asked.

"No, I didn't. My mother would never let me marry before my brother. He wanted me to marry him as a 'begalka,' a runaway bride. I couldn't do that."

"If I were in your place, I would have married him," I laughed.

"Your father was a good man, and I had a good life with him. Besides, you wouldn't have been born if I had married him," my mother replied.

This made me laugh. "Big deal if I wasn't born. You know my birth caused trouble." We both laughed together.

Looking at my mum then and now made me wonder if she had ever made a bold decision or taken a risk in her life. How many secrets were hidden in her heart? This made me think of Rose's statement in the movie *Titanic:* "A woman's heart is a deep ocean of secrets." I believe the human heart is deeper than the ocean, and I wish all these oceans were drained so that all secrets could come to the surface and free the heart and soul. They are neither good nor bad; they are part of our journey. What I saw in my mum's life was a struggle; she saw it as a blessing.

Memories of my parents moving to Australia in 1995 flooded my thoughts. Sponsored by my brother, they briefly lived with his family. Then, on September 19, 1996, tragedy struck unexpectedly. My daughter Christina was only four months old when I received the call. Climbing the stairs with her pram, I struggled to answer the ringing phone, only to hear the devastating news that my father had passed away suddenly at two-thirty p.m. The shock was overwhelming. I remembered our last conversation; him calling to listen to my voice, assuring me not to worry about anything. Little did I know it would be our final farewell. A man who rarely visited the doctor, he succumbed to a heart attack, leaving a void that no one else could fill.

In 2006, another tragedy struck when my dear friend Tanja passed away from a heart attack. She was one in a million, and her role in my life was irreplaceable. I'm unsure if I ever fully expressed how much she meant to me and how deeply she impacted my life. She was only 45. Our friendship was timeless, and our shared memories will stay with me for the rest of my life.

Watching my mother quietly, I felt blessed and grateful that we had all moved to Australia and settled in Melbourne, as my father had always hoped. His presence felt palpable, watching over us as we navigated life together. Throughout my Camino journey, I reflected on the importance of family and the people who weave in and out of our lives for reasons beyond our understanding. I realised love manifests itself in countless ways—often unspoken because words could never fully capture its beauty, wonder, and sweetness as love is.

It was Tuesday, June 4th, 2024, just five days before Christina and Jack's wedding. After work, Peter and I headed to Sunbury, a suburb on the outskirts of Melbourne. Peter was recently elected president of the Sunbury Rotary Club, and the president exchange ceremony was scheduled for that evening.

At ten-thirty p.m., my daughter Christina called. When I mentioned I wasn't home, she replied calmly, "Don't worry, Mum. Call me when you can." Despite her composed tone, I sensed an urgency behind her words. Excusing myself, I stepped outside and returned her call.

Christina shared that the hospital had contacted her to inform her that her father had suffered a stroke and had been admitted. The details were sparse, but she mentioned he would likely attend her wedding in a wheelchair. What she didn't yet realise was that her father was fighting for his life at that moment.

She added that her colleagues were throwing her a party the following morning, and she wasn't sure if she could make it to the hospital that night. I thanked her for letting me know, reassured her not to worry, and promised to visit the hospital to get more information about her father's condition.

After explaining the situation to Peter, we left the event and headed straight to the Royal Melbourne Hospital. Sitting in the car, I felt a wave of gratitude for Peter. Without experiencing his kindness firsthand, I might never have believed someone like him could exist.

On the way, Madeline, my younger daughter called, her voice heavy with concern. I reassured her we were on our way to the hospital and promised to call her back once I knew more about her father's condition.

When we arrived, Peter dropped me off at the entrance, and I hurried into the emergency department. I learned that Greg had been brought in earlier that evening by ambulance, unconscious, in a critical condition. The medical team was working to stabilise him. They explained that he had suffered a stroke four days prior but hadn't been discovered until a concerned friend, unable to reach him, found him on the floor of his apartment and called for help. Thankfully, Greg had left the front door of his apartment unlocked.

I entered the emergency room with a sinking heart. His face was swollen, and his eyes remained closed. Softly, I called his name and tried to talk to him. He attempted to open his eyes but didn't seem to recognize me. He struggled to speak and couldn't form words.

A young doctor entered and introduced himself. Due to privacy policies, I wasn't given detailed information since I was his ex-wife. However, the doctor shared that Greg had arrived severely dehydrated and in critical condition. They were still assessing the extent of the damage. He emphasised that he was incredibly lucky to be alive, crediting the friend's timely intervention for saving him. The team was doing everything possible to aid his recovery.

After the doctor left, I stayed with Greg, holding his hand as I spoke softly. "You must fight. You're strong. You can do this. Our daughters need you. They need both of us."

Tears streamed down my face, and to my surprise, I saw tears roll down his cheeks, too. He opened one eye and looked at me, his gaze a mixture of pain and emotion. His right side remained motionless. Slowly, he pulled his hand away and motioned for me to leave the room. Respecting his wishes, I stepped out quietly.

Almost immediately, my phone rang. Madeline let me know she and Logan, her partner, were on their way to the hospital.

Waiting in the corridor, I found myself praying—for my ex-husband, for the father of my children and for the man I had once been so proud to marry. Memories of his accomplishments and the moments we had shared flooded back. Clinging to hope, I silently willed him to find the strength to recover.

As I walked Christina down the aisle on her wedding day, I couldn't help but think how proud her father would have been to be there. Life is unpredictable, a constant reminder to cherish and be grateful for every moment.

Six months have passed since that difficult time, and with a great deal of support, Greg is slowly recovering. In this journey, I've come to a profound realisation: when a couple has children, their bond never truly severs. The children are the threads that keep us connected.

We may not be the family we once were, but we are still a family—a different kind, yet happy in our own way.

Gordana Murgovska

www.ingramcontent.com/pod-product-compliance
Lightning Source LLC
Chambersburg PA
CBHW051425290426
44109CB00016B/1441